D0065961

# CLOSE CALLS

Also edited by Susan Fox Rogers

# CLOSE CALLS

## New Lesbian Fiction

•

*Edited by*
*Susan Fox Rogers*

•

St. Martin's Press ⚏ New York

Library of Congress Cataloging-in-Publication Data

Close calls : new lesbian fiction / edited by Susan Fox Rogers.
    p.   cm.
    ISBN 0-312-14755-4
    1. Lesbians—Fiction.    2. Lesbians' writings, American.
I. Rogers, Susan Fox.
PS648.L47C56   1996
813'.01089206643—dc20                96-25585
                                    CIP

First Edition: November 1996

10  9  8  7  6  5  4  3  2  1

24.95

*For Cat,*
*who tells the best stories,*
*and listens*

# Contents

# *Preface*

## SUSAN FOX ROGERS

When my editor suggested this collection, my first thought was: Another anthology? Do we need even one more? There has been such a frantic outpouring of lesbian collections from both small presses and New York publishers in the past five years (and I know I have contributed to this) that I felt the last thing we needed was another anthology.

Then I sat back and thought about anthologies. Anthologies have always been a part of our culture, have traditionally been put together to reveal and bring together "lost voices" (as in a black women's or Latin American collection) or to offer "the best." This anthology does not do either. Lesbian voices are far from "lost"—they are some of the strongest and most exciting new voices in American fiction and are being published in every imaginable venue. And this collection does not pretend to be the "best of"—this is a selection of twenty-one stories out of many I could have chosen.

The other promise of anthologies is that they are doing something *new*. This anthology does offer this: there are two writers, Emily Fox and Sue Pierce, whose work has never been in print before; Linda Smukler's "Mainstreet," which reads as a prose poem, experiments with the form of the short story, as does JoNelle Toriseva's "Strip Uno," which shifts into poetic form. Style is played with by Gwendolyn Bikis, who writes in the language of a streetwise black girl. And the subjects here are not all familiar: Zélie Pollon touches on one unspoken aspect of lesbian life, and Rebecca Lavine's "Skin Queen" and Ruthann Robson's "Choices" take us into a world that for many will be unfamiliar. Kathryn Kingsbury rewrites a classic fairy tale from a modern lesbian perspective, and Sharon Lim-Hing offers a futuristic vision—with a modern twist.

This is not to say that every piece in the collection is experimental. There are many traditional narratives, many rich and satisfying stories as we know stories. The only thing that will not be found here is a classic coming-out story. These are, without doubt, our most loved narrative. But I wanted stories that were not focused on the process of becoming a lesbian, but rather ones that reached beyond this to look at how we live and love as lesbians in this world. This was partly my own literary desire to read something new in plot. But also, even though we each individually still have to come out, as a culture we are collectively far beyond that. I wanted to see what was in this wide-open field.

For what anthologies offer, it became clear that they are important—for both readers and writers. The enthusiasm for anthologies, and not just within the lesbian and gay community, is perhaps testimony of this. They allow new writers a place to publish for a wide audience and afford readers the opportunity to explore specific ideas or themes (such as writings on the body or on sports) and get to know writers they might not otherwise read.

But within the lesbian and gay community, anthologies really function as our literary magazines, and in them we introduce new writers, experiment with new writing, and celebrate those writers who are more established. The difference is that these books have a longer shelf life than the month or two of a magazine. They will be there for the next generation of lesbian readers and writers (I hope) and so they are more than literary artifacts, they are cultural ones as well.

As such, anthologies are indicators of our cultural lives—that a large fistful of erotica collections have appeared in the past two years says *something*. They reveal what we are fascinated with, but they also serve to bring together fragments of our culture, to create a meeting ground for voices or visions. In this sense, these collections are vital to our growth as a community.

This frenzy of gathering stories and publishing is, I feel, a sign of health: we are coming into our voices, exploring facets of our common lives, creating cultural artifacts. We are, in a sense, re-balancing the scales after years of silence imposed from within and without.

Once I was done exploring these higher literary and cultural reasons for publishing anthologies, I also had to admit my real interest in working on this collection and the others I have published: anthologies are fun. They are fun to edit (except when an author disappears or refuses to send back their copyedited story—ladies, you know who you are). There is also the plea-sure of reading a writer unknown to me, of being surprised by a story, or getting back a revision that is better than hoped for. There is enormous satisfaction in creating a whole out of very disparate parts, to put writers in the company of other writers they might never find themselves next to. Being a part of an an-thology offers writers a sense of a community of literary lesbians. And the readings held at bookstores and community spaces around the country once an anthology is published are won-derful events, ones where we meet intellectually, creatively, and socially.

One more anthology was not too much. One more anthol-ogy was fine, I concluded, and we could certainly have many, many more.

And so it slowly dawned on me that I had been handed a dream project: to read a big pile of lesbian stories and to select those that I thought were good.

I smiled. Then panicked.

What is good? After all, isn't "taste" culturally bound and rather subjective? How should I chose: Style? Content? Theme? Was it important to represent certain political aspects of lesbian life? How PC did this have to be? And, above all, what is a les-bian story? When I twisted out of this literary-existential spin, I decided I would simply watch (or read) and wait: I would see what came to my mailbox and let writers show *me* what lesbian fiction is.

I was open to anything in form, style, or plot. All I required was a character who was lesbian and a story that was written by a woman. This later point has been hotly debated—should men be allowed to write "lesbian" stories—and though I think it's great if they do (please do imagine yourself into our lives), I decided not to include men because I wanted to give more women the opportunity to write and publish. Then I wanted a story that was compelling in some way—idea, form, character, or plot. But mainly I wanted good writing. And what is that? It was what kept me glued to my seat from beginning to end; it was a story I felt I could read five or six times and not tire of.

I read hundreds of wonderful stories, and I offer twenty-one here that have never been published before. There are several funny stories—those by Anna Livia, Sue Pierce, and Rhomylly B. Forbes—that are also at once tender or sad. But I was pleased to be able to read and then offer these gentle jabs at our lives and ways as lesbians—because I love to laugh, but also because in being able to laugh I think we show our strength. There are stories of illness and of loss, violence and sex, children and therapy (though not in the same story)—just a few of the many aspects of lesbian life. I hope that you as readers of this anthology will be surprised and entertained, and that you will join me in supporting and encouraging the writers in this collection so that they will continue to write and to publish.

Selecting stories was incredibly difficult, at times painful, because there were more stories that I wanted to include than I had pages. But one of the unexpectedly hard parts was choosing a title for this literary gathering. I spent hours with my editor musing over what would be right, would set the tone for what lies between these covers. I drove my local country roads, looking for inspiration (No Right Turn at one point seemed just fine). And then I found it nestled here among these stories: "Close Calls," the title of Wickie Stamp's provocative tale. There are many "close calls"—psychological, emotional, and physical—in these stories, but the collection could have just as easily been titled *Mainstreet,* because these are stories of women, of life that is not ordinary or mainstream, but a part of the main, what is becoming (I am forever hopeful) a more free society that has plenty of room for our stories.

Putting together this collection was long and detailed, and I was given all kinds of inspiration and support along the way. So I want to thank all of the writers who submitted and shared their work with me; Keith Kahla, who gave this project to me, believes in lesbian writers and writing, and has energetically championed the book; Sam, for reading and technological support; my sister Becky for her unending support and love; the girls of New Paltz, for long runs that kept me sane; AOL, for making my life easier; Babka and Moose, who were mostly a distraction. And Linda, for everything.

# CLOSE CALLS

# Choices

## RUTHANN ROBSON

*A*nn-Marie is my rent. I am her identity, her adultery, her orgasm. We are each other's Thursday evenings.

She tells her husband she is taking art lessons, to fulfill her long-neglected talents. She tells me this, conversationally, guiltily proud of her deceit. She tells me this, week after month after year. Sometimes we go to museums as if we are art students, and then go to dinner at mediocre midtown restaurants as if we are tourists. Other times we go to galleries, because Ann-Marie wants to see work that is trendy. But our schedule demands we hurry back to my apartment on Riverside Drive; Ann-Marie must leave the city by eleven P.M. And if she does not linger too long after sex, petting my head and practicing her excuses, I sometimes have time to see someone else. But usually I read; sometimes I study.

Ann-Marie is a large woman. She wears size eleven shoes and shops at Tall-Girl. Middle age has not eroded her hesitancy about her height. She hunches, folding her shoulders as if they are flaps that would close the envelope of her body. Her back curves like a question mark; the one which I answer. It is the hook by which I hooked her.

Ann-Marie is a good woman. Balancing generosity and morality. She is not paying for my services, she is helping me out. She is a minister's daughter, a minister's wife. She is a cheerleader's mother, a choir director. She calls herself my lover, or my friend. She calls me Tamara. She pays cash, the first Thursday of every month.

Ann-Marie wants to be an artist, a painter perhaps. Or even a potter. Instead of practicing those techniques, she flexes her long fingers above her head, gripping my pillows as I touch her. Her talents are evident as she arches her back, inverting her interrogatories into declarative moans; her shoulders stretch, unselfconscious, smoothed by my talents. Afterwards, I massage her broad back and watch the clock.

"Tamara," she says when she leaves, hunching into a blazer that seems too small.

"Thursday," I say. And smile at her as she shifts her long, long bones toward the place she calls home.

This Thursday she seems preoccupied. I move to soothe, but also to excite. It is a precarious balance. I suggest a museum, an important one with a new show and Thursday evening hours. She declines, shaking her head.

I swallow to allow me a second to contemplate my reaction. Compassionate or rude? What does she really want, beneath the bent wings of her shoulder blades, kindness or direction? Or some subtle combination?

"Oh," I say, "I should have known." I sound contrite.

"Known what?" Ann-Marie betrays her curiosity, but also her anxiety.

"That show would probably upset you," I say.

"It would not."

"I've heard it's very graphic."

"What does that mean?"

"Graphic, you know, like sexually explicit." I wink at Ann-Marie.

"I know what graphic means. I mean, what do you mean?"

"About what?" I lick my lips, slightly. Ann-Marie's eyes follow the edge of my tongue. She no longer seems so preoccupied.

"About that. About me being upset by some show. What do you mean?"

"Oh, nothing."

"I can't believe you think I'm like that."

"I don't." I say. But now Ann-Marie is riveted on me, or more precisely, on my perception of her. Ann-Marie wants me to value her artistic judgments; sometimes it seems as if she forgets I am not her art teacher.

"I've just heard that this show isn't as spectacular as its hype."

"Probably not," I agree.

She smiles.

"But it does sound fun," I tell her.

"Let's just have dinner."

It is my turn to smile, so I do.

"Some take-home."

I nod. We turn back and walk a few blocks to that most famous and most crowded of Upper West Side delicatessens, a department store of gourmet food. I always meet Ann-Marie here, near the cheeses. She usually has one of the store's distinctive white with orange print bags full of treats to bring home to her husband and child. Nothing that needs to be refrigerated. But this evening she buys a bag for us. "What would you like?" she asks me.

"You choose," I tell her. Her eyes brighten and focus, rewarding my hunch. She wants to take care of me tonight; she wants to nest; she wants to try me out as a different life but not too different from the one waiting in Connecticut. I assume that things are not going well at home. I sense her fear.

I let her unwrap the packages in my kitchen. Roasted chicken, how wonderful! I compliment her. "Do you really like it?" I kiss her neck and take out a bottle of wine from the cupboard. "Just a glass." I kiss her neck again, almost chastely but certainly appreciatively. "I hope you like potato salad," she holds up a plastic container, "it has some of that French mustard in it." I kiss her neck again, murmuring about mustard.

After our kitchen picnic, Ann-Marie commenting several times on the smallness of my apartment, she takes out the final box from her bag. "Russian pastries," she announces.

"Would you like some coffee?" I offer, although I do not want to dilute the effect of her three glasses of Cabernet.

"Coffee?" She turns on me as if I have said something ugly. She softens quickly, not only because she is a woman who always softens quickly, but because she must realize she is being silly. "Oh, I must not have told you. I'm giving up coffee. Have given it up, really. I think it's ruining my life. All that caffeine. You know, it just takes over your life. It's really been my major problem."

I stifle a smile, but she does not notice.

"Did you know I started drinking coffee when I was thirteen years old?" She looks at me for confirmation of this tragedy. "I mean, my parents gave it to me. My own parents! Can you believe that? That parents could be so uncaring. It was my parents who started me on coffee!"

She is nearly shrieking now, so I nod sympathetically. And pour her another glass of wine. And lead her to the windowless bedroom, where I will lick the chicken grease from the side of her mouth, where her lipsticked lips meet.

Tamara browns the lamp and sits next to Ann-Marie on the bed, taking the glass of Cabernet and putting it on the shining white night table within reach. She holds Ann-Marie's hand for a moment before unbuttoning Ann-Marie's crêpe blouse. Ann-Marie sighs, tilting her head back as if to offer her throat, or perhaps her still-encased breasts. Tamara accepts both, starting with simple kisses that accelerate to untoothed sucks with the pace of Ann-Marie's breathing.

Tamara is careful not to make slurping sounds, careful to remove Ann-Marie's blouse and drape it neatly on the white bedroom chair, careful not to snap the elastic as she unfastens the substantial bra, careful to modulate her motions to the blotches of excitement speckling Ann-Marie's chest. Ann-Marie shifts, stands up, slips off her shoes, and removes her skirt and stockings, tossing them toward the crêpe blouse. When the clothes fall to the floor, it is Tamara who folds them neatly, arranging them more sturdily on the chair. Ann-Marie poses on the bed, imitating a Renaissance artist's model. She pats the empty space next to her, as if Tamara is a painter who will color and shape her with admiration, making her real.

Afterwards, Ann-Marie cries. Ann-Marie sobs on Tamara's still-shirted shoulder about her minister husband, the one who will not fuck her. Ann-Marie rages against Tamara's ceiling about her first lover, the woman who did fuck her—oh, did she ever—but then left her for the army. These weepy monologues are as predictable as Ann-Marie's orgasms, only more passionate and less efficient. Ann-Marie says "fuck" as if it were the ultimate release, prolonging its single syllable as long as she can. Tamara delivers the attention required of her by listening for a change in Ann-Marie's weekly narrative—a detail embellished or omitted, an insight gained or erased—but it is always the same, almost exactly.

Always ended by Ann-Marie asking curtly, "The time?" and Tamara announcing it, passing her clothes. The dressing, the bathroom, Ann-Marie gathering her things together, checking the bedroom again. Ann-Marie's polite kiss at the door with her re-lipsticked lips in the same pucker she uses for the elderly parishioners. And if it is the first Thursday of the month, there will be Ann-Marie's envelope of money, a rectangle remaining on the chair where her clothes had been.

When I step out of the shower, steam still circling around the black vinyl curtain, I am no longer Tamara.

I slip into my closet. That long hallway of a closet that separates my apartment from itself, that separates my life. On the other side of the closet is the back bedroom.

It is just past midnight, but the lights of the city flicker off the river and through my three windows, my three glass graces. I look west, out the windows, as if trying to see a future I could choose. But my horizon is interrupted by New Jersey.

In these moments, I am no one. Hovering. Pure. Like an angel. Like the moon or a river on another continent. Like the brightest blue.

My hair is still wet. I could wrap it in another towel, but I don't want to go back through the closet, back out there. I could check my messages from my numerous services, but I don't. I could study, but I have no classes on Fridays, so I don't. I could masturbate, read a book, get dressed and go get an ice cream or a coffee or a slice of pizza, but I don't want to do any of these.

I just look out the long, narrow windows, rehearsing how they came to be my windows. Reciting silently how this boarded-up back bedroom came to be my room, as if examining a bolt of expensive fabric for a hole in my story. Retracing my steps, looking for the missing link whose name is Dominique.

Maybe I was fourteen, maybe a bit younger, maybe older. But definitely not twenty, not yet eighteen. I was still a ward of the state. I was illegal.

"I'm from Australia," I told her.

She laughed, tilting her chin toward the rip in my American jeans. "And I'm from France."

"Paris?" I hoped I could make a sophisticated joke, something about April in New York. But she did not answer me, only posed on the sidewalk as if allowing me to look at her. I did. She had hair that was every color human hair could be and eyes of no color that any human would remember. Her skin was beige, covered in some places by makeup or a sidewalk-colored blouse or tiger-print pants that were tight only if one looked closely. I looked closely. One had to look closely at Dominique because she blended with her surroundings. And I looked closely because I knew enough to be wary of people who seemed malleable. I was one of them. We are smooth-striped snakes waiting in the grass until it is safe to strike at what we want. So, I needed to figure out what it was she wanted with me, so she'd never have the chance to strike. Unless what she wanted was what I wanted. Which meant I needed to figure out what it was that I wanted, or at least what I needed.

I figured she wanted a friend, a daughter, or even a trick.

I knew I needed a place to sleep and a bath.

But she did not want what I thought she wanted; maybe she did not know what she wanted. Except perhaps a cat, a witness to her existence. Maybe she just picked me off the streets because her elegant prewar building prohibited pets. I was something she could comb when she wanted and ignore when she didn't. Camouflage is useless without background, without danger.

And after I got what I needed, some sleep and a bath; and after I got other things I needed, some French bread and Greek cheese which I folded together like a common sandwich; I did not know how to think about what I wanted.

So I watched her, since she seemed to like that. I watched her treat her hair with an artist's paintbrush she dipped into different bottles she kept on an oval tray. She would stretch a strand tight as a canvas, then stare at it in the mirror until she decided where the bit of highlighter or bleach or auburn toner would go. Watched her watch me. Watched her slide the needle under her tongue, pretending I wasn't watching, pretending I didn't notice that even the inside of her mouth was beige, like a faded paper bag.

Valium was plentiful. As were Quaaludes. And beauties, those black whirls of amphetamines. Some of her clients were physicians, she told me, but that didn't explain the cocaine, the heroin. Sometimes I think that what she wanted was for me to save her. To watch her long enough and hard enough that rescue would be the only obvious option.

Instead, I organized her. Her drugs, her clients, her clothes in her long closet that was as narrow as a coffin. I organized her back bedroom that was behind the closet-coffin, which was really a hall, a secret passageway like in a European mystery. I dusted the haircolor bottles and the bottles of tea rose, the only cologne in the apartment. I shined the wooden floors to reflect the light from the trinity of windows that framed Riverside Park. When I looked out the windows, I could see trees, trees that were budding a jaundiced green against the background of the wide, almost-blue Hudson River. I straightened piles of papers: old newspapers, little notebooks with half the pages torn out, calendars that could fit in the palm of a hand, cocktail napkins ripped with ballpoint pen numbers. And then I organized other papers: ones in a bag she pushed toward me. There were rent receipts and yearly leases, bank deposit slips and

checkbook starter kits, bills from Con Ed and Ma Bell, some
Canadian currency, and a hospital bill from an emergency room
stamped PAID.

She told me I did a good job. I waited for her to ask me how
I knew how to do all these things. I was ready to smooth over
the virtual slavery of being a foster child into something more
glamorous. But she didn't ask.

So I asked her. More for something to say, I guess. To fill up
the space where her question about my past would go. I asked
her if her name was really Sarah Tudor, like Con Ed and
Citibank and the Ridgeway Management Company seemed to
think. She laughed a raspy laugh and told me I'd better learn
her rules if I was going to stay with her. "Rule one," she said, "I
don't answer personal questions."

I didn't ask anything else, just thought about the "if" in the
possibility that I might stay with her. Just thought about
whether it was an invitation or not. Just thought until I knew
I couldn't think about it anymore.

Instead, I thought about whether that was really rule number one. And whether it was her rule or my rule. And thought
about scrawled notes I'd seen in her tiny notepads: *Never trade
sex for money with a woman. Plan for 40. Never pity clients. No
chains.* I supposed these were other rules.

Sometimes they appeared next to numbers, like lists. Mostly
they just floated on what remained of torn-out pages. *No whor-
ing for women,* she wrote. Over and over. I wondered whether
it was a litany to lost opportunities. Or whether it was the way
she convinced herself she had limits.

We sat in the back bedroom, which I realized must have
been intended as the living room and dining room of the apartment. Someone had bricked over the entrance between the
kitchen and this room; someone had transformed the hallway
into a closet. She took off her shoes and I took them to the
closet, placing them on the floor in line with the other pairs of
shoes. I rubbed her feet, first the arches and then the heels, first
with my thumbs and then with my whole hands. She sighed,
sipping what I thought was iceless water. The lemon rind re-

fused to float, despite her prompting with a long index finger.

Later on I asked her: "What's rule number two?"

She asked me why I wanted to know.

I told her I didn't know why I wanted to know; I just wanted to know.

She told me that I shouldn't ask a question if I didn't know why I wanted to know the answer; that I shouldn't want anything unless I knew why I wanted it.

I asked her if that was a rule.

She laughed.

She told me I had to find my own rules; she told me I had to make my own choices.

She told me she wasn't my mother.

I didn't ask her what she was. I didn't ask her if rules were choices. Or if choices were rules. I only rubbed her feet some more, with some cream I mixed with tea rose cologne. I took her glass through the closet and into the kitchen, pouring from the bottle of Tanqueray she kept in the freezer, and returning to sit on the bed next to her. I ironed her clothes and washed out her underpants. And I kept all the pills in the right bottles and all the needles clean.

Sometimes it seemed like I was her maid, sometimes her devoted lover. But sometimes her student, her apprentice. Especially when she lectured me; even explained her rules. Rules about never fantasizing about clients; the rule was they should fantasize about her. Only she said "you": "clients should fantasize about you, not vice versa." I tried to pretend that the "you" was a metaphor, not a prediction. Or a rule that I twisted in an attempt not to fantasize about her. That she was a beautiful lady and I was her lady-in-waiting. That she was my lover and I was her beloved. That she was not a junkie, even a junkie-trying-to-get-clean. That she was not a common whore.

She never offered me drugs. They were there; I knew how to ask. And that had always been one of my rules: not asking. Still, I was alone in the apartment often enough, I could have just taken something. Or taken something for the road when she asked me to leave the apartment. Or taken something for the boredom when she told me to stay in the hidden back bedroom because she needed the front one for a client.

Only once, in all those months. It was late in the summer, probably past August. The wafer rested in the palm of her hand, her index finger curled over it like a fern. Wafers and ferns reminded me of Betty, the foster mother who lived in the country and took me to church three times a week. I slipped the methadone under my tongue, letting it melt like Betty had taught me to take communion. Closing my eyes against the holiness.

It was raining in the city, in the park and on the river, and through the trinity of windows into the back bedroom, onto the bed that we had pushed under the unscreened windows to catch the humid breezes. It was raining on my face, next to her face. I licked drops from her face; she tasted pure with the slight burn of tea rose. I stroked her tongue with mine; she seemed swollen and reluctant. I lifted my head away from her, hitting it on the bottom of the casement. She laughed, but this time her laugh seemed easier, lower in tone and longer. I thought of Betty again, how her face set on the other side of the window when she watched me run away; how her stomach rolled up beneath her breasts then rolled back down to her crotch, then back up, like one of those change-color waves encased in a small square of acrylic, on sale for amusement. I had wanted one once, I remembered it even now, remembered the church carnival and not asking Betty about it, it was blue and pink. . . . I stopped thinking about the toy, about Betty. That was my talent: I could control my mind. I could think about this but not that; about that but not this. Even stoned on a junkie's maintenance, I could refuse to think about anything unpleasant.

Dominique moved a pillow under my head. The pillow was wet with rain and I pushed my face into it. She pushed my hair around with her fingers; I thought my hair pushed back. She pushed my flesh with her index finger, along my neck and around my breasts. My skin did not push back, but let her sink into it, let her sink into my bones with a dampness that made them twitch. Still, I didn't push back until I couldn't help myself, until her index finger was on my clitoris and the rest of her hand was inside me. And then it began to rain inside my head, steady and comforting. Outside did not exist.

It wasn't the first time I had ever had sex. Not even a time that still had a number. I was street-smart and a graduate of foster-home sex-education classes where it was best not to count the times with foster siblings, foster parents, and even the government workers. But it was the first time I ever had an orgasm. Not just a sort of sparkly feeling that spread through my cunt, but a feeling of being folded inside out, like swallowing my own skin and surfacing inside someone else. Coming up for air inside her, swimming against a current swollen with rain.

She was laughing.

And I was crying, though I didn't know why. Drops slid down my face onto the damp bed, and finally into the flood of her cunt, followed by my tongue. I felt a little shy, but soon I hit a stride we both seemed to share. I convinced myself I knew the exact moment when she shifted into her own pleasure, not an easy accomplishment given her profession, or so I flattered myself. And I convinced myself that I knew the exact moment when her orgasm rippled through her hips as I fingered her bones and my tongue dove deeper, although there were a few times I thought this was happening.

She pulled my wet face to her shoulder. I started crying again. I really didn't know why I was crying, but knew enough to be grateful in my knowledge that she wouldn't ask. I guessed it was just the orgasm; now I knew what all the fuss was about. Why everyone else had always seemed to want it so much. Although if I'd known that was going to be my last orgasm as well as my first, I would have been able to tag a reason to my tears.

The next day, Dominique was dead.

I sat in her chair, looking out the middle window and not-thinking. Waiting for her. Waiting for her to come back to me, back from her "date." But I didn't think it was a client; I thought it was a connection. Which was why I wasn't thinking. Wasn't fantasizing any longer that her methadone maintenance was working. Just watching. Watching the people on the sidewalk, coming out of the park as if summer would never end. And then watching her, staggering out of the park holding her hand against her mouth. Her hand remained there when she tumbled on the curb; it did not break her fall. It only moved when she was otherwise motionless, stretched across the sidewalk, and her index finger pointed back toward the park. Someone stepped over her, a few people gathered.

Waves swept over me, from the inside coming out, but not demanding like nausea. I recognized it as inertia, the wave that would pull me close, pull me under whenever Betty had started slapping me in the face on the way home from church; whenever any foster parent veered toward violence. The wave that rocked me back and forth, trapped in the acrylic enclosure of my life. I watched the paramedics and the police. I watched them strap her to the stretcher with her face covered, no tubes dangling from her nose, her arms, her body. It was as if she sloughed off her life, like it was no longer useful. I looked down five stories and watched them drive her away. I noticed a leaf that was starting to turn red. I noticed the dark spot on the sand-colored sidewalk.

I waited for her to come back. Thinking it might be a mistake, a nightmare, some unreality. I paid the rent, electric, and phone for Sarah Tudor. Washed clothes and tried them on. Polished the bottles, then flushed the contents. Watched the rain bang against the sidewalk. Touched myself until I was raw with boredom. Tried to convince myself that maybe absence was another one of Dominique's disguises.

By the time the picture outside of the windows looked like a fire, some trees still blazing and some already burnt bare, I had slinked into beige, into black. Fit my life around some of her rules; made up my own. Inverted the one about sex and money and women.

My weekends are successfully busy. While my classmates are occupied studying or perhaps partying or possibly even visiting the parents who are paying their tuition, I am working. Although if my classmates saw me in public, they would think I was merely socializing. Thankfully, such coincidences do not occur often. The faculty is more troublesome. I worry that this is a tiny town only disguised as a big city; I worry that it is a small world. I worry about finding work when I graduate. Not just because I do not have the right kind of references and contacts, but because I have the wrong kind.

My plan is impossible. I have come this far, to the second year of law school, but I have so much farther to go. Escape is a fantasy. Margaret Smyth is a fantasy. With her good grades and her low profile and her application to be a research assistant for a professor. Margaret Smyth lacks a certain sparkle; she does not make a compelling fantasy. Surely, I could do better.

Margaret, a proper and protective name. Like the precise pigment of a blanket a mother might choose for her day-old infant, admiring the shade against the baby's skin, both mother and daughter innocent of the color's cloying consequences. As if inevitable, the irritating pink of Margaret becomes the salmon of Peggy, the tea-rose of Rita, the coral of Maggie, and even the shocking fluorescence of Marbalo. Each foster parent seems to desire a unique identity, an alteration of aura. The caseworker does not make a notation of this parade of nicknames; her notes only reflect average weight and average height, competent schoolwork and a "chameleon personality."

I choose to take this judgment and bend it into necessary talents.

Developed beyond pink. The red of Melanie. The green of Colette. The yellow of Ursula. Olive. Violet. The brown of Tamara. The blue of sky and ocean and salty promises birthed in colonies of criminals who changed their lives and their names.

For each client I choose a different name. Mostly I use pages of names from a little book, *Les Guérillères,* that Dominique left behind. But some of those names are too exotic, meaning they are both too easily forgotten and too easily remembered. So I try to be careful.

Margaret is the name I chose for my competent schoolwork; it was the name closest to the student I wanted to be; a name not merely from a book but also from the closest thing I had to a past.

Like the public-school teachers the caseworker had interviewed, my undergraduate professors had found Margaret
Smyth smart, even exceptionally smart, but never brilliant. Several teachers sensed a buried potential and tried to bully and
coax Margaret. But brilliance requires both risk and passion,
and her professors could provoke neither. So they soon abandoned their efforts, judging Margaret as lacking in ambition
and begrudging her the excellent grades she continued to earn.
Some of them were surprised when they learned she was going
to law school; the most cynical of them used this information to
confirm their low opinion of lawyers. None of them asked Margaret why she had chosen law; none of them would have understood her one-word answer—Dominique—even if she
would have uttered it.

Plan for forty.

Margaret Smyth is my hope, my plan for forty. A lawyer
somewhere simple, representing battered women or consumers.
She will live in a town house, a house in another town, and
maybe have a cat. She will not pay Sarah Tudor's rent, she will
never be called Tamara, she will not wait for Dominique to
come back from her messy escape. I will be her, all the time.

Impossible.

Unless I pay close attention to the details. Unless I am very
lucky.

It is still impossible.

Anxiety rises like steam off my body; I decide to cool off in
another hot shower. I can never take too many showers it seems.
I can never take enough.

But to get to the bathroom I need to leave my back bedroom,
to travel through the passageway of my closet. It is dark. It is
always dark. Not only because there is no light, but because so
many of the clothes are black. Black is inconspicuous in the
city, but once it had seemed more dramatic than modest. Now
Margaret always chooses black. And Tamara, brown. A somber
palette, brightened by Ursula and Melanie who are difficult to
find without the flashlight, so straight and solid and lonely,
among the line of paired shoes.

The shower solves nothing.

Might as well clean for the weekend, since sleep seems as if it will be elusive. The front bedroom is first. Strip the sheets. The workers at the laundry on Columbus Avenue must think I am fastidious, if they notice at all. I like a bit of starch. I like white. I like the aura of a respectable hotel.

No need to sweep. Just take the used sheet and wipe the wooden floor. There is a scrap of paper on the floor, under the white chair. A grocery coupon. Fifty cents off. SUNLIGHT. Fresh Lemon Scent. Good on any SUNLIGHT Machine Dishwasher Detergent, GEL or POWDER. It must have fallen from one of Ann-Marie's pockets. Or out of her purse, did she bring her purse to the bedroom? She must have. The date is expired. The fine print is sinister. A Warning to the CONSUMER: Coupon Is Void if Used to Purchase Products for Resale. . . .

I crumple the coupon, but suddenly a sharp anger sputters and spins. Alone in the front bedroom, and no longer Tamara, there is nothing to curb my anger. Nothing that makes me modulate it. Nothing that can transform and transcend it.

Of course, hate has many hues. There is disdain, disrespect, disappointment. There is fear. There is jealousy, envy, and lust. I know my hate should have the shape of disdain. A minister's wife, living in suburbia, her choices limited to gel or powder, except for her Thursdays when she can choose an art gallery or a fuck, or some potato salad made fascinating by its mustard. A minister's wife, paying for sex with a woman, who is confident that giving up coffee is going to solve her problems.

But my anger is envy, Ann-Marie. I cannot pity your wasted life, only imagine what I would do with it; would have done with it. Become a librarian or an art history professor at a community college. I would have fallen in love with a dyke with bigger feet than my size elevens, a woman's basketball coach with long long legs and long thick arms and a cunt that smells like sweat and peppermint liniment. And even now, waking up married to some self-righteous minister, I'd confront him quietly and get a good settlement using the threat of scandal. I'd go somewhere like Iowa, eventually moving in with a former nun I would meet at a local woman's coffeehouse. We would have a garden in the summer, tomatoes and peppers and corn. She would show me how to quilt in winter. I would make floor-to-ceiling bookcases, using hand tools and no nails, only wood dowels. We would feed the squirrels and the birds. I would read biographies of famous woman artists and my lover would tend the fire. We would have a bright Mexican shawl on our old couch. We would have bright blue rugs, made by a local weaver, scattered on our ceramic tile floors. I would use coupons at the local grocery store and I would use them promptly and never let them expire. I would heed all the warnings; I would not be involved with products for resale. We would have a black-and-white kitchen, with a beautifully black dishwasher. I would choose powder.

Yes, I would choose powder.

# The Trip We Took
# Last February

## JEANNE WINER

An elderly man tells his wife that he's going out to do a few errands. She thinks for a minute, then asks if he'd be willing to pick up something for her.

"Sure, what do you want?" he asks, pulling on his overcoat.

"I want a big gooey ice-cream sundae."

"No problem," he says, smiling. He's got one hand on the doorknob.

"Wait a minute," she says, "I want butter pecan ice cream and hot chocolate sauce."

"Fine." He's leaving now.

"You better write it down," she says, not unkindly.

"No, I'll remember."

"Okay. I also want nuts, but no cashews. I hate cashews."

"Sure, no problem."

"Maybe you better write it down," she says, and starts to reach for the pad of paper by the telephone.

"I can remember, don't worry. Butter pecan ice cream, hot chocolate sauce, nuts but no cashews. See?"

"Well, I also want whipped cream, if it's real."

"And real whipped cream. Anything else?"

"You sure you don't want to write it down?"

"Positive. I'll see you in an hour."

The man returns three and a half hours later and hands his wife a small paper bag. She looks inside and all she sees is a bagel. She reaches in, pulls out the bagel. There's nothing else in the bag.

"So," she says, holding the bagel up toward her husband, "where's the cream cheese?"

You can think of this joke as a kind of racial equator, dividing the world into those who think the joke is funny and those who don't. Jews think it's funny; I am a Jew. My girlfriend of five years, whose name is Deidre, does not think the joke is funny; she is not a Jew.

People on this side of the equator also share a number of other things in common. For instance, we can see too many possibilities in a situation, which is not very relaxing. Since we are constantly looking ahead or to the side or behind us, we often miss the simple pleasures that exist right in front of our own two feet. And, with good reason, all of us are convinced that the world is fundamentally an unsafe place.

People on the other side, like Deidre, think of the world as a giant playground where nothing bad usually happens, and if it does, it's an unexpected surprise. I envy Deidre her world view. She has more fun than me. She worries infrequently and sleeps deeply all the way through the night. Her dreams are sometimes quirky, sometimes bland but they never seem to leave her feeling queasy about the vast collective pool of information that at any moment she might accidentally tap into while lying in that helpless state. She's wrong, of course, but I can't think of any intelligent reason why she ought to cross over and join us.

"I don't get it," Deidre said after I told her the bagel joke. "Why is it funny?"

"Well, it's actually kind of terrible," I said.

Her puzzled expression grew even more so. I felt as if I'd been suddenly transported to another planet and was being asked to explain why some Earthlings collect postcards of ugly poodles or enjoy scaring themselves half to death at horror movies.

"Look, Deidre, it's terrible that people age and slowly lose their minds, but it's also funny."

"What's so funny about it?"

"People just adapt," I said.

"So?"

"Well, that's it," I said.

The way I see it, and my parents and grandparents saw it, the world is a place where terrible things are just waiting to happen. When they do, people are forced to adapt. Given this kind of landscape, a sense of humor is not an expendable luxury; it's right up there with food, shelter, and clothing.

Because Deidre and I hold such opposite opinions about the nature of reality (she says it's like a flowing river; I say it's more like quicksand), it causes a number of problems in our relationship. For instance, vacations. Deidre likes to travel in foreign countries, especially Mexico.

"What's wrong with Seattle or Burlington, Vermont?" I used to ask. "Why not travel someplace where the water's safe to drink and we don't have to think long and hard before asking someone a simple question?" Deidre was not persuaded. "We could eat a green salad every night and wake up in one piece," I persisted. "We could count on standardized taxi fares."

But Deidre explained to me that I had two choices. I could either go with her or stay home. Because I couldn't bear to think I might be missing out on something wonderful, I've always chosen to go even though I've ended up spending some portion of each trip feeling vaguely afraid. Partly it was my imagination, which always perks up in a warm foreign climate, but partly it was to make up for Deidre. Since she isn't at all inclined to worry about anything, I've always felt compelled to be on guard for both of us. As a whole, I've enjoyed our vacations and, in actuality, nothing worse ever occurred than a two-day attack of dysentery or a stolen camera. Until last February, when something terrible finally happened.

We had rented a bungalow for two weeks in Zihuatanejo (zee-watt-a-neigh-ho), a small fishing village on the west coast of Mexico. Each morning we rose early, practiced yoga on our pink-tiled patio overlooking the ocean, ate fresh slices of pineapple and mango, and then headed for any number of different

beaches. Choosing which beach we'd go to was the first trau-
matic moment of my day.

As you might expect, Deidre wanted big waves, the bigger
the better. I worried constantly about the undertow at the wilder
(and, unfortunately, the more beautiful) beaches. Sometimes
Deidre agreed to spend the day at a peaceful cove where I could
paddle out into warm aqua-colored water and snorkel with almost no fear. It was during those idyllic afternoons that I could
relax enough to fall in love all over again. As anyone knows, it's
hard to feel romantic when you can't breathe.

We had a tacit understanding, however, that if Deidre was
willing to suffer a day or two at a safe beach, then I would be
willing to suffer the next few at whichever dangerous locations
she chose. Deidre, of course, didn't think of it that way. She just
wanted us to spend as much time as possible at beautiful, un-
spoiled (because no one in their right mind would ever go there)
beaches with huge, fun waves.

As soon as we'd arrive at one of her beaches, Deidre would
dump her bags in the sand and rush out into the wild surf.
Jumping up and down like a happy sea lion cavorting in the
foam, she'd call to me. "Come on out and play with me!" I'd
stand mute at the shoreline, dizzy with dread, and watch her
approach a twenty-foot wall of water. Every toreador eats it at
some point in his career. Surely, I'd think, Deidre can not continue tempting fate in this way without paying her dues. But
she'd wait calmly until the last possible moment, then dive deep
and come out easily on the other side. Then I could breathe
again.

"Judith, please come out here," she'd call, "this is great!"
What she never understood was how painful it was just watching her. She looked so little bobbing around in the churning
water. "Judith, please." Her words stung me because I knew
that although she was completely comfortable out there, she was
also a little lonely. If I could have stepped across that equator,
if I'd had any idea how to rearrange the basic wiring in my
mind, I would have. As it was, I couldn't even answer her.

Like many Jewish teenagers growing up in the fifties and sixties, I'd wake up at least once a month sweating from another Nazi dream. Sometimes I was simply running through a thick forest, pale yellow light flickering through the branches overhead, with the sound of soldiers panting as they gained on me. In other dreams I was sitting at a long Passover table surrounded by my relatives. Each participant held a silver goblet filled with dark red wine. Thick curtains covered the windows as we conducted the ancient ceremony in secret, risking death as we invited Elijah the Prophet to come and drink with us. Then, when we heard someone knocking at the door, we all held our breath, and I'd awaken in the familiar sweat.

Later, in my twenties, I began studying karate. Looking back, I can see that it was just one of the many ways in which I have been preparing myself for the next holocaust.

The water on that particular day in February was about 80 degrees and as blue as the sky. Since it was a Deidre day, I sat alone at the water's edge holding my detective novel while my girlfriend played in the waves. I'd read a few pages, look up and make sure I could still spot her, then continue. The sun was hot and we had just that morning run out of sunscreen. Because I was afraid that the part in my hair was getting burnt, I finally edged myself back near some rocks where it was a little cooler.

I was on the final page of my novel. The heroine untied herself at the last moment, then hurled herself through the bathroom window just as the bomb exploded. She landed, stunned, on the grass but in one piece. As soon as her elderly and adoring landlord came rushing up to her from across the yard, she managed a shaky grin. Close, but no cigar, she told him as she struggled to her feet. That's what you think, I muttered, wait until you get post-traumatic stress disorder. I closed the book and got up to find my girlfriend.

After a few anxious moments I saw her head bobbing casually in the choppy waves. Everything was okay, although she was much farther out than I'd expected. I turned and walked back to my towel. I thought I heard a cry but it was hard to tell because of the loud disco music that had just started blaring from the restaurant on the hill behind me. It was almost time to leave. I remember lying down on the towel and staring at the white sand granules in front of my eyes. I was imagining tiny organisms clinging to each speck, lasting for an hour or a day, oblivious of any other world. That's when I distinctly heard Deidre crying out for help.

*Help, help!* It was so ordinary, so matter of fact, nothing like I'd always imagined it would sound. *Help!* I ran to the water and could see a little arm sticking up against the horizon. In the last five minutes she had drifted out another two hundred yards. The undertow, the undertow had my girlfriend!

The next twenty minutes have slowed down in my mind like a movie reel played on a defective machine. Each image is indelibly tattooed into my memory bank. There's me running slow motion up and down the empty beach shouting Help me, Help me, in Spanish. Then there's a shot of me a quarter of a mile down the beach confronting a pair of lovers entwined on a red-and-white beach towel with a Coca-Cola logo printed on it.

"*¡Ayúdame, por favor!*" Help me please!

The lovers stare at me, pretend they don't understand. They obviously want me to leave.

"*Mi amiga es en la mer.*" My friend is in the ocean.

"*¿Sí?*" They finally ask. The male has his hand halfway buried down the back of the female's red-and-white bathing suit. I notice her suit matches the towel.

"*¡Es un emergencia!*" I say, flapping my arms up and down like a seagull on acid.

They tell me to call the police and turn back toward each other, dismissing me. Where's the phone, I insist, and they point in the direction of the disco music. Of course. I run on bare feet back up the beach, then up a steep grassy hill toward the restaurant. I take the fifty steps two at a time up to the main patio. The place is completely empty.

I rush through some swinging doors into the kitchen. The music is even louder back here. There is only one person, a waiter dressed immaculately in a crisp white tuxedo. He looks about sixteen, jet black hair combed straight back. He is sitting in front of an open refrigerator smoking a cigarette.

"*¡Es un emergencia!*" I say, trying to catch my breath. "*Necesito un telefono para llamar al policía.*"

"*No es possible,*" he says, checking out my thirty-eight-year-old body.

"*¿Porqué?*" My face is covered with sweat and I have a stitch in my side from running so fast.

"*Roto,*" he says.

"Broken?"

"*Sí.*" He winks at me.

I start to ask where the nearest phone is and then realize that I wouldn't understand his directions even if he deigned to give them. Damn this country. Damn their broken-down everything. This is crazy. I'm having a meaningless conversation with a horny teenager while my girlfriend is drowning.

In the next scene I am running back through the empty restaurant and down the steps to the beach. I stop at the sand and look both ways. To the right, the couple is probably fucking by now. I decide to run to the left. I am crying and shouting for help, but there is no one around. I curse Deidre but I don't mean it.

And then I see him, an older man standing in the shadow of the rocks. I half-run, half-stagger toward him. Now I can see a small green and white rowboat, which must belong to him. I arrive breathless and almost fall on top of him.

"*Necesito su barco,*" I gasp. "*Es un emergencia.*"

He holds the rope tightly in his hand and backs up as if I'm a monster from the sea. I imagine what I look like: long, wild hair tangled up like seaweed, sand and tears stuck to my face.

"*Por favor, mi amor es en la mer.*" I meant to say my friend, but I said my love. Oh well, who cares about coming out at a time like this. I make a move to snatch the rope from his hand. He backs up again, an alarmed expression on his weather-beaten face.

There's no more time left. I note the two oars in the boat. I explain the following events to myself this way: I was in an altered state. Morality was meaningless, survival everything. I didn't want to be alone on this horrifying planet without my girlfriend. I backfist him in the face and then drop a low knee sidekick to his groin. He drops the rope, I grab it and start hauling the boat into the water. He is shouting but he doesn't follow me.

I row like crazy toward the swelling waves. All those years rowing back and forth across the lake at Camp Kirby have finally paid off. Somehow I am able to time it so that the waves crash after I've passed over them. Behind the line of waves, the water is calm, blue, and gorgeous. I head toward where I last saw Deidre's arm. Nothing. I row straight out now and figure I'll just keep rowing since there's nothing to go back for. I continue calling her name.

I almost miss her. She is floating on her back in circles.

"Judith!" Her voice sounds cracked and tired.

"I'm coming, sweetheart," I yell.

I pull her into the boat. She collapses against me and cries soundlessly into my hair.

"Whew," she says finally, "I was getting very, very tired."

"Thank God, you held on."

"I knew you'd figure out something."

"I almost didn't."

"But you did."

"But I almost didn't."

"So what? You did."

This year Deidre wants us to go sea kayaking off the coast of Baja during the whale birthing season.

"It's great," she says. "You go in these kayaks and all around you the sea is the color of blood and the whales are giving birth."

"It sounds a little chaotic," I say.

"No, it's wonderful."

"But what if in the throes of birth agony, maybe not intentionally, one of the whales knocks into us?"

"They don't do that."

"You don't know that," I say, accidentally knocking our map of Mexico onto the floor.

"I'm not worried, Judith," she says, picking up the map. "Besides, I know you'll rescue me if they do."

Deidre comes up behind me and puts her arms around me. Is she kidding? Does she really expect me to perform a miracle ever again in this lifetime? Well, maybe it wasn't completely a miracle.

"I picked a survivor," she says, as if reading my thoughts. Am I a survivor? When I think of survivors, I think of cockroaches living in the walls of apartment buildings, I think of the wild cats I saw in the midnight streets of Rome, I think of 1960 Volkswagon bugs with no fenders, and yes, I think of Jews.

# *Mainstreet*

## L I N D A   S M U K L E R

Small towns    a barber pole    this is what Jake sees and
wants    it was difficult to walk into that first one    after
all it was the town Jake lived in    and there was that pale dirty
green door    not painted for years    and the sign that said Men's
Hairstyling    9–5    Mon thru Sat    but one day Jake did walk
in through the pale green door to find a long row of old men
all waiting their turn    Jake tried to seem like she was looking
for someone    then to make it seem like no one she was looking for was there so she could turn around and leave    which
is what she did    shaking her head to rid herself of the old man
smell that followed her out the door    but the sign said 6 dollars and that was better than the 13 at the beauty shop in the strip
mall where Jake had to work very hard to convince Meryl the
cosmetologist to cut her hair like Jake wanted    and why pay
13 when it was really much cheaper    free in fact    to cut it herself?    maybe because she liked Meryl's hands as they massaged
her head in the sink    maybe because at home it always took
twice as long and made a huge mess in the small bathroom
where Jake worried about her lover's complaints    little hairs
all over the sink the floor the toothbrushes the bathtub the toilet even    6 bucks    what was 6 bucks once a week?    but it was
too close to home    a place for old men and boys    Jake was a
woman moved up from the city a few years before    who
walked out that first visit to the Mainstreet Barbershop    who
drove around the country roads and small towns in her truck
and shaved her own head

* * *

Once in the middle of the work day Jake drove her truck past
the barber pole in Valie    a run-down shot-gun wreck of a town
she parked and walked into the shop    and there was the dark
mahogany paneling and there was Joe    and there was Joe's
daughter Angie at the other barber chair    and there was
Angie's Jack Russell Lucy sleeping on a bed right next to the
chair    at first Jake knew none of their names but later of course
she did    and there was that old man smell too    but not
as strong as it was at Mainstreet    and a cut cost 10 dollars
here    not 6    the barber pole seemed festive    perhaps a little
Christmas-like    and even though his daughter was working on
a client and Joe's chair was empty    Joe said I think you want
my daughter    Jake nodded without protest and waited until
Angie finished working on a man who talked to her about her
fiancé    Jake was a little worried because it was lunchtime and
she might run late for her afternoon appointment    but she
waited anyway    determined this time    she looked at the walls
papered with sepia repros of old barbershops    young men
standing out on stoops    old men too and middle-aged    Jake
liked the one painting on the wall    a painting of a table with
barber tools    everything on the table faced forward    no perspective    comb    scissors    clipper    apron    chair    mirror
one towel    when Angie finally called her over to the chair Jake
asked about the painting    Joe piped up and said I did it    A
little hobby of mine    Jake said she liked it and would love to
see others which seemed to please Joe who then said he also dab-
bled in Real Estate    Angie asked Jake what she wanted and
Jake said Short all over    she could tell that Angie thought her
hair was short already    Jake clarified    With the clippers
Down to the scalp    Angie said Okay    and Jake said I like
your dog    as if on cue the little dog got up and sniffed Jake's
pants and tried to jump onto Jake's lap    Angie laughed    she
said Get down Lucy    Lucy wagged her tail and got down and
sat on her bed watching Angie cut Jake's hair    Don't be afraid
to go too short Jake said    but she could tell that Angie was
afraid    Angie said I'll just do it this length first    Jake ob-

served the weight of the clippers in Angie's hand     heavier and more professional than the clippers Jake used at home     Angie said You can't get them like they used to make them     Dad complains all the time     and on the shortest setting Jake's hair got down to perhaps an eighth of an inch     maybe a sixteenth almost short enough     but Angie could not or would not go any further     when she was done Jake ran her hands over her scalp     her own best critic     and found some patches where the hair seemed longer     she said     It seems longer here     Angie felt Jake's scalp and said You're right     and went back to shave those parts     Jake did not check much further     she did not want to make Angie feel bad     it being the first time     Angie brushed off Jake's head and pulled away the plastic smock covering her lap     she rubbed Jake's skin hard with the towel and dug into her ears and still could not get off all the little black hairs     no easy task even with baby powder     when she was done Jake was so pleased that she finally had her first haircut at a barbershop that she walked out the door without paying she drove her truck all the way down the block before she realized what she had done and had to turn around to go back in and pay

The next week Jake came back and neither Angie nor Lucy were around     only Joe was there with an empty chair and an empty shop     so Jake sat herself down in the chair without asking and said again Don't be afraid to go too short     and Joe said Okay and began to buzz Jake's head with his clippers which seemed to shave closer than Angie's     Joe had more confidence in his hands     perhaps from the thousands of boys and men he had shaved over the years     Joe spoke about his mother and father settling in Valie from Sicily and how much he loved to paint and of course his ventures in Real Estate     Jake said she might be interested in buying something cheap in the area so if Joe heard of anything to please let her know     the door to the shop opened and Jake could see the customer in the mirror     a tall fortyish man in a flannel shirt     scraggly beard around his jaw line     he said Hi to Joe and Joe said Hi back and Jake could see the man staring at the back of her head    he sat down in a chair at the back of the shop to wait his turn and Joe said You want the back shaved? Jake said yes and Joe squeezed some hot shaving lotion out of his hot lotion canister and rubbed some on the back of Jake's neck and then dabbed some on her sideburns    she liked the way it felt    then Jack picked up his straight razor and sharpened it on the leather strop hanging on the back of the chair    he shaved Jake's neck and sideburns    wiping the excess lotion off with a towel    he brushed Jake's head hard with a bristle brush    scattering little black hairs everywhere    again there were hairs in her ears    along her chin    but Jake did not mind because this time she was going home to take a shower she remembered to pay and wondered if the two men would talk about her when she left

Angie was just coming back from lunch and unlocking the door as Jake walked up to the shop one day    once they were inside Angie let Lucy out of her arms    Lucy ran over to Jake to say hello then ran around the shop like a wild dog    Jake sat down in the chair    it had almost been two weeks since the last haircut and her hair had grown quite a bit    they talked and Angie said that she had new clippers    which could get even closer than the last    Jake said Great    Try them    and Angie did slowly working her way around Jake's head    Jake chatted with her    It looks great she said    Angie said Yep    It does the job    It makes my father nervous to cut so close you know Why? Jake asked    although she knew    He just can't    But he does pretty well Jake countered    He seems a lot better about it now than he did when I first came in here    Oh yeah Angie said    He is more comfortable    But it still makes him nervous You know he won't do those bowl cuts on the boys either    The kind where they want it shaved completely up to a certain point then the hair hangs down?    He'll say yes    but then taper the back like he thinks it should be    You figure he's been in the business for 50 years    He just doesn't care and it's hard for him to change    Me I don't mind    Jake changed the subject and asked where Angie got Lucy    Two guys in Pattenville she said

They don't really breed their dogs but they just happened to have a litter    I had been looking and everything fell into place    But these guys she said    They're so great    Luke's an interior designer    travels all over the world    and Mike stays home    They don't have kids so their dogs are like their kids    It's really great    Lucy loves to go visit    But you know I just don't get it    they have so much money!    Well it's all that 'disposable' income Jake said    No kids    But I don't have kids Angie said    and I don't have their money    But I do have a great idea for making money    What? Jake asked    Angie continued to cut and talk    You know I go up to Albany with my friend Tony    You know the bars    You should see all those cross-dressers    Now you know they have money    They have all the makeup    expensive clothes    the wigs    But my god they dress like shit    I think they need a consultant    They always have the wrong shoes and they just have to get rid of those crooked wigs    You wouldn't believe how bad they look    Jake couldn't believe she was having this conversation    here was straight-looking Angie talking about all the gay male cross-dressers she knew    Jake had been coming to the shop for quite a while and she never suspected that Angie even knew a gay person let alone frequented gay bars    she also knew that they would never be having this conversation if Joe were around    Jake's hair had a definite Mohawk effect to it at this point    Angie had managed to cut the sides away all that remained was a strip of longer hair down the middle    Well Angie    I think that's a great idea    Why don't you do it?    I should she said    I could charge 50 dollars an hour    Go for it Jake said    I think you'd be great    Jake took a chance and said    There are a lot of cross-dressing women out there too you know    Angie didn't miss a beat and continued to shave Jake's head    Yeah Angie said    It would be a great business    We should both be consultants    There are a lot of gray areas of gender out there    They all need us    Jake was floored    that Angie used the word 'we'    that she had somehow included Jake in her plans    that she understood that gender had something to do with what they had just spent 15 minutes talking about    Jake's scalp

looked done    shiny almost    Angie seemed more intense about
shaving Jake's hair than she had ever been before    examining
it closely for any stray long hairs that might have escaped her
clippers    she admired Jake's head in the mirror and then took
her over to the sink to rinse it off

Only once did Jake walk into the little barbershop in Greenport
right at the entrance to Wal-Mart    Jake was driving somewhere
and again it was convenient    shouldn't a haircut be convenient?    wasn't it one of her reasons for going to a barbershop?
utilitarian    cheap    no appointment necessary    which was
good especially if one needed a trim once a week    Jake parked
and walked in the door    a clean place    some paneling of
course    but mostly white    men's hair products on the counter
conditioner    gel    comb in dye    a tall overweight man in a
blue smock looked across the counter at her    his hair and beard
perfectly combed    not a hair out of place    slightly puffed on
top    he said Can I help you? to Jake as if he had no idea why
she was there    I need a haircut Jake said    the man stared at
her for a moment then said I don't cut women    What's the difference? Jake asked with all the confidence of her past haircuts
at Joe's    I just want it buzzed close all over    the same cut
you'd give to any man who walked in here    Mr. Entrance to
Wal-Mart said Sorry I just don't    something about his manner
made Jake wonder if he was gay    the neat clothes    the perfectly coiffed hair    the lilt in his voice    the fact that the man
did not want to deal with women at all    Jake caught herself
stereotyping the guy    just as she knew people stereotyped her
by her looks and manner    she really knew nothing about him
the barber went on to say My mother cuts hair and has a shop
down the street and we have an agreement    I can't just start
taking business away from her    but Jake would not let it drop
Look she said    Your mother would never even cut my hair like
I want it    you know she wouldn't    What's the difference?
I'm in a hurry and just want a simple haircut    the barber took
a few seconds but finally said Okay    Just this once    and Jake
had her haircut    she sat there and wondered why it was so im-

portant to push the barber to cut her hair    she could not completely answer the question except that she wanted to feel entitled to the same services that fully one-half of the country was
entitled to    she felt some victory in getting the barber to cut her
hair    even though he didn't go as short as she would have liked
at least it was even all over    it cost 7 bucks

Then one day because it didn't seem to matter anymore    because it was convenient and because her lover was shopping
down the street    Jake walked back into Mainstreet    the barber was finishing a client but no one else was waiting    the two
men paused in their conversation and the barber looked at Jake
over his half-glasses    he quickly looked back down at the hair
he was cutting    gray-white and wispy    much longer than
Jake's    a hue that matched the pale green walls    the barber's
apron too    a dull beige    the barber himself looked faded
and the same stale smell was there    old magazines    some
dimestore paintings of deer and landscapes and an old TV
Jake wondered if the barber ever turned the TV on    no nos-
talgic photos but military eagle-patterned wallpaper covered the
walls    the linoleum on the floor looked old and worn    when
the man in the chair was done he got up and paid the barber his
6 bucks    did he leave a tip?    Jake did not tip Joe in Valie
men did not seem to give tips to men    it wasn't like a beauty
shop    did Jake's mother leave a tip at that place she had Jake's
hair done when Jake was 5 or 6?    probably    Jake had just
found the old family portrait while she was cleaning out one of
her closets    there she was in a stiff short dress and patent
leather Mary-Janes    her hair pulled back from her head into
its usual ponytail    a worried look on her face    the whole family looked worried and only Grandma was smiling    red-haired
Grandma    a little mauve in the old black-and-white proof    of
course Jake's mother must have given the beautician a tip for
the fine curl she had put into Jake's hair    Jake hardly wanted
to show that picture to her lover who only knew her head shorn
Jake's lover could not even imagine that Jake was once forced
to be someone's little girl and gazed at her in wonder every time

something historically feminine was mentioned    and here now
sat Jake in what she thought was the kind of place her father
once frequented to have his hair trimmed    crew cut and thick
black glasses    in that very same picture    the days before he
began to dye his premature gray and before he went to Mom's
beauty salon to a beautician who figured out ways to hide his
bald spot    Jake's hair was silver on the sides    maybe even
white    but now shaved so close it was hard to tell    just a
shadow of hair    like the stubble of a beard    her face sharper
more masculine than that child in the picture    perhaps just as
worried

Jake stripped down to her T-shirt    she felt a little chilled in the
cool air of the barbershop    then walked over and sat down in
the leather barber chair as if she had been doing this all her life
the barber's license said his name was Joe and Jake thought all
barber's names must be Joe    and here she was sitting in Joe II's
chair with Joe II buttoning a smock around the back of her neck
and she thought to herself if you just act like you expect something then everyone else will buy into it too    the door opened
and a client came in    an old man with a cane who could barely
walk    but here he was    and Joe said Hi    and the man waved
his cane and barely looked at Jake    Jake said to Joe I want you
to cut it as close as you can get    but when Joe put the clippers
down on her head they buzzed unevenly    she could feel Joe
miss places along her skull    perhaps Joe was being careful as
he was used to cutting wispy old men hairs on brittle old men
scalps    the chair glided on some kind of ball bearing    like
smooth oil    the motion of the clippers slowly pushed Jake and
the chair around to face Joe as he cut    Jake asked Joe to go
closer    Joe got out his sideburn clippers    Jake looked around
no hot shaving cream here    no leather strop    no wonder a
haircut at this place cost 6 bucks and the shop in Valie cost 10
Joe just clipped away    leaving Jake's hair longer on top    Jake
said Could you cut it evenly all over?    Jake could tell that Joe
was trying to place her    was she some kind of religious fa-
natic?    Buddhist maybe?    he finally asked and Jake said that

she was a teacher    Joe did not blink    just gave a quiet nod and
kept cutting    Joe asked what Jake taught    Kids Jake said
and she told him what kind of kids    and Joe just nodded again
and questioned her no further    then he changed the subject
Well we're all just looking forward to the end of the week
They're predicting snow    the man sitting across from them finally said something    Marge sent me in to get it cut    It's been
a few months    Joe nodded Yep    It's that time    and the man's
white hair did look long to Jake    and his pants looked too big
the man kept talking to no one in particular    I had to walk over
here    Marge took the car away from me    Can't really see to
drive anymore    now Jake knew the man thought she was a boy
because of his limited sight    the door opened again    this time
it was Jake's lover    she looked out of place walking into the
dull room    dressed in bright green and purple    her cheeks red
from the cold outside    she smiled and looked around    Not
done yet? she asked Jake in the chair    Jake said No    Just getting started    Joe said Cold out there?    Jake's lover said Yep
Starting to snow    they seemed to like each other    this Joe and
Jake's lover who said she was leaving and would meet Jake
down at the shoe store    but before she left Jake saw her lover
look around and take in the feel of the shop    could she smell
the scent of old men as strongly as Jake could?    and would she
mind it if she did?    what did she think as she watched Joe
deftly push Jake around in the chair?    did she understand
something more about Jake?    about Joe I and Joe II and Mr.
Entrance to WalMart and all the stories Jake came home with
after her various haircuts?    would she too someday send Jake
walking to the barbershop    tempting falls on the ice    because
Jake could no longer see to drive?    and would Jake sit across
from Joe and tell him about it?    Jake's lover walked out and a
younger man and his son walked in    the boy was about six
long hair    and from the moment his dad took off the boy's coat
the boy could not stop staring at Jake in the chair    the boy
seemed to know that Jake wasn't another boy but could not figure out exactly what she was    he stared as if he had never seen
such a being and he answered in grunts to his dad's attempts to

get his attention    Jake laughed to himself    old man    little boy
Joe in his sixties    and now this middle-aged father    all here
in the barbershop    and it seemed like Joe was done and he
started to vacuum Jake's head with the vacuum cleaner he had
under the counter apparently just for that purpose    the skin of
Jake's head was stretched and sucked by the machine    and
when Joe was done Jake ran her hand over her scalp    she felt
a few rough places which she pointed out to Joe    he clipped
them back and she asked if she could use the sink to rinse off
the hairs that hadn't been vacuumed away    Sure Joe said    and
was kind enough to give her a towel    the little boy continued
to watch Jake's every move    even as the old man sat in the barber chair and Joe started to talk about the weather    Joe was
very professional    just did his job no matter who came in
Jake thought to herself that she would ask next time about the
history of the shop    how old it was and what changes Joe had
seen    but then maybe she would never ask    there was something good about talking weather and hunting seasons and
county news    about looking across the room at the dimestore
pictures of deer on the walls    about being one of the boys and
men who simply walked in and for 6 bucks got a pretty good
haircut.

# Close Calls

## WICKIE STAMPS

*I* didn't mean to kill her. After all she was my lover. Sometimes I just get mad is all," Christy said as she lit her cigarette and took a deep drag. It was my second trip up to MCI Framingham. And my second meeting with Christy. All my other clients were women who killed their abusers. Except for Christy. She was the abuser who had killed her female lover. Because Christy was a woman and a lesbian I'd made an exception and had decided to work with an abuser. I hadn't mentioned my decision to anyone in my life. Personally, I was sick of talking to people about my choices.

"It was drugs," Christy added as she swept her dirty blond hair back off her shoulder. She was wearing the type of strappy T-shirt my father and uncles used to wear. She readjusted herself in the chair and tapped her cigarette on the edge of the ashtray. Just this slight wrist movement accentuated the definition in her forearms. It was obvious that Christy spent a great deal of time in the prison's weight room. She took a second drag, heaved herself up out of her chair, and strode over to the window. I was a bit startled by how quickly she'd stood up. But Christy never did anything slowly. She stood with her back to me and stared out the window. Then she shoved her cigarette in her mouth, locked her fingers together behind her back, flexed her shoulders, and stretched. I studied her powerful back muscles and the tattoos that wrapped around her arms. Huge lizards coiled upward from her forearms, their heads disappearing into the back of her T-shirt. About a half-dozen lines of four-inch scars, obviously carefully placed, were slashed across each shoulder. As I examined her scars and tattoos I wondered if her posing before me wasn't premeditated to arouse me. After all she was an abuser which, in my eyes, meant she'd cross any boundary she could find.

"Killing her just came with the territory," she said casually as she stared out the window. "Anyway she had AIDS and wouldn't have lasted long. Gave it to herself." The last statement seem to be added as an afterthought. Christy did not seem too interested in our conversation. Like most inmates, Christy could get "good time" credits for attending therapy and showing a willingness to reform. The credits could then be applied to either days off a sentence or privileges within the prison. This often left my client's motivation open for question.

"Excuse me?" I said, not sure I understood what she had just said. I had been too caught up in studying her looks. I, who was what women often referred to as a Birkenstock lesbian—pale, slightly out of shape, and neither butch nor femme—was fascinated by the visual impact of such a masculine-looking woman. In the world of Cambridge dykes, lesbians who looked like Christy were a rarity.

She turned and blankly stared at me. "I said she gave herself AIDS." Christy's tone struck me as nasty and impatient.

"Oh," I said, uncomfortable with her attitude.

"No, not 'oh.' You don't understand. I'm not talking about how everyone gives themselves AIDS or some shit. I mean she was getting high with someone who had AIDS and she intentionally injected herself with his blood." Christy's voice was angry. She seemed annoyed at my confusion.

"Really?" I said trying not to sound too fascinated, but I was.

"Yeah, really," Christy added sarcastically. She turned back toward the window and looked out again. Like all the windows at Framingham it looked out onto asphalt and barbed wire. "Jesus, I wish they'd turn the fucking heat off," she added and gingerly touched the ancient radiator that was in front of the window. My eyes wandered down to Christy's buttocks. Like the rest of her body they were tight and highly developed. Her jeans clung to her in the same manner as the young Irish Catholic punks who dominated the street corners in Dorchester, my neighborhood. I knew I could run into trouble feeling so attracted to an inmate. Again, I decided that because Christy was a lesbian, perhaps I could help her.

"Aren't you going to say something?" she said with her back still to me. She glanced over her shoulder. While Christy was busy staring out the window I was wondering if I wasn't over-reacting to what seemed like her hostility toward me. Perhaps Christy's butchness intimidated me.

"What do you want me to say?" I asked, trying to regain my composure. I liked her looks, but she made me feel grossly out of shape and emotionally diminished by her intensity.

"Just fucking anything," she said harshly and strode over to the table where we were sitting and impatiently stubbed out her cigarette. "Just fucking anything." I looked down at her work boots and found myself instinctively curling my toes up into my Reeboks. This woman made me very nervous. I was aware that I was feeling confused about why. "What's the matter with you, are you afraid of me or something?" Christy added as she looked at me with great annoyance. I felt put on the spot. And guilty that I was so aroused. I swallowed my fear and tried to focus on our exchange. I could not figure out if I was afraid of her because she was an abuser or if her aggressiveness was frightening me.

"How do you feel about killing your lover?" I asked, trying to get our exchange back onto more therapeutic ground. Christy sat down across from me and crossed her arms over her chest. Her biceps were as powerful as any man's.

"Like killing myself," she said.

Her response surprised me. Christy did not strike me as someone who was long on remorse. From her records I knew that, after beating her lover to death, Christy completely destroyed her lover's most valued personal possessions.

"Are you telling me you are suicidal?" Christy did not strike me as a woman prone to suicidal tendencies. Murderous, yes. But suicidal? I doubted it.

"No, I just think I ought to be punished. How the fuck would you feel if you'd killed your lover?" she asked and glared at me. I wondered if she had a general dislike of women, a fact that, given she was a lesbian, confused me.

"I did." I couldn't believe my own ears. It had been a long time since I'd lied to a client.

"What?"

"I said 'I did.' " I sat completely still. I was as clueless as Christy as to what I was going to say next.

The silence lay heavily in the space between us. The exchange had given me a breather from my own confusion. And it was obvious it had taken Christy by surprise.

"You're fucking lying," Christy said.

I could see the confusion and suspicion in her eyes. I could also tell she was trying to figure out my angle. I felt like I had knocked her off guard. I suppressed a smile. I felt like I had one-up on this very powerful woman. I took a deep breath and momentarily relaxed. I considered terminating the session. Too many things seemed to be happening. But I didn't. I hated the fact that she intimidated me so much.

"You wouldn't be a goddamned counselor, sitting across from me on an act of feminist mercy if you'd killed your lover. You'd be my cell mate." She looked at me with disgust.

"Not necessarily," I said, momentarily regaining my composure and returning to the conversation. "Maybe I just didn't get caught." I surprised myself with my flip tone. It verged on being sassy.

Christy studied me. I could feel her trying to size me up. "You're lying," she said quietly but seemed fascinated by the exchange. Her eyes roved over my entire body. I felt like every nook and cranny of my out-of-shape body was completely exposed. I had never been so blatantly checked out by another woman. I wanted to tell her to knock off the cruising, but I actually enjoyed the attention. My lover Carla wasn't big on giving me sexual attention. Rather than tell Christy to cut it out, I sucked in my stomach, straightened up in my chair and, as best I could, tried to remain calm. I controlled my impulse to tuck my hair behind my ear, a habit that persisted despite the fact I had cut off most of my hair ten years ago.

"Maybe I'm lying, maybe not," I said and met and matched her gaze. A barely perceptible smile crept across my lips, a fact that did not go undetected by Christy, who seemed to be enjoying our exchange. I was aware that my behavior was edging on being flirtatious. "So, like I said, what was it like?"

Christy sized me up for a few seconds. "All in a day's work," she said flippantly. She shoved back her chair and spread her legs wide. Her blue jeans pulled tightly across her muscular thighs. I knew from her records that she had worked for several years on a construction crew. She crossed her arms over her chest and gave me an incredulous look. "Did you really kill your lover?" she asked again. She looked at me suspiciously with a slight twinkle in her eye. I couldn't help but smile. I liked her. She could be incredibly charming when she wanted to.

"No, but I know that you did and I want to know about your reasons, so . . ." She didn't let me finish.

"Have you ever wanted to?" she asked. It was a question that Christy seemed to have wanted to ask someone for a long time. There was a childlike eagerness in her voice.

"Well?" she asked and stared at me hard. I sat in my chair and considered this woman who would probably be in prison for the rest of her life. She was not the first woman I'd met with who had killed another human being. But she was the first lesbian. I hesitated in my response.

"Who the fuck am I going to tell?" she asked and tipped back her chair. Her question caught me off guard. As did the sudden increase in her anger. "And who would listen to me anyway," she added, suddenly looking extremely young and grumpy. Without warning she let her chair tip forward and banged its front legs onto the linoleum floor. It seemed like an intentional move to scare me. She seemed annoyed at the entire conversation. She reached for her Marlboros that lay on the table between us, pulled one out, tapped the end hard on the back of her hand, and jammed it into her mouth. I leaned forward, picked up her lighter, clicked it open, and held the flame toward her. She wrapped her hand around my wrist and pulled it toward her. Her hands were strong, her palms calloused. As she took a drag on her cigarette she looked over at me, held my wrist for a second longer than was necessary to light the cigarette and then released it. I was totally turned on by this strong, butch woman. By the way Christy looked at me, I was pretty sure she was aware of my attraction to her. Clearly she was interested in me. I was aware that, just like most abusers, Christy would use anything, including her good looks, to get her way. She took another deep drag on the cigarette then rested her arm back down on the table and distractedly rolled the tip of the cigarette on the edge of the ashtray. She looked over at me, waiting for an answer.

She never got one. I merely smiled nervously at this woman whose every move either aroused or scared me.

I left Framingham and went directly to see Marta, my therapist and a candidate at Cambridge's Jungian Institute. It had been a hard decision for me to reenter therapy. But for the past few months my fear level was hovering around 9.5 on a scale of 10. And I was having a hard time setting limits with people and standing up for myself. I had told the intake analyst that I would stay open to whoever they felt would be best for me. They didn't have to be queer or female, two things I'd usually required in the past. Marta Schmidt, a young, straight Jewish woman originally from New York, was who I was assigned to. Immediately we hit it off. She also had a great sense of humor.

It was Marta's idea that I meet with her after my visits to Framingham. Quite honestly I didn't know why. On the intake I'd told the analyst that my mother had been incarcerated so I assumed that Marta had based her suggestions on this fact. Also I was starting to have panic attacks after each visit.

As always the session began with a long silence. I sat in the chair directly across from Marta with my arms crossed over my chest, still angry that after so many years of therapy with droves of different therapists, I had to return. I mentioned my anger to Marta.

"Say more about that," she said.

"What's to say?" I shrugged, annoyed at her classic therapeutic response. "I'm thirty-five, I've been in therapy off and on for over ten years, I'm in recovery, I've been in treatment facilities and even battered women's shelters, and for what? To come back to therapy?" I sighed and felt rather childish. "I'm also really sick of paying so much money to get over a horrible childhood." I sat in my chair and pouted. "I'm sorry, I just thought I'd have my act more together than I do."

"What does it mean to have your act more together?"

I paused. I knew I should talk about Christy but I really didn't want to. I had conveniently neglected to mention to either my lover or Marta that I'd decided to see her. And, quite honestly, I already knew I'd made a mistake. I ignored Marta's question and sat thinking.

"I'm counseling a batterer," I blurted out. "She's a woman. And a lesbian. It's already a mess. I'm attracted to her but I'm afraid of her. I think I'm afraid of her because she's butch. I think I'm attracted to her because she's abusive." I took a deep breath and closed my eyes. I felt completely incapable of explaining to this straight woman what the hell was going on in my mind. I didn't even know if she knew what "butch" meant.

"Maybe you are attracted to her because she's attractive."

I looked up at Marta and laughed.

"That's too simple," I said and yet was relieved that maybe it was as simple as that and not some deep-seated neurosis about being sexually attracted to abusive people. "But I'm scared of her," I said.

"Usually, if we are feeling afraid, something is going on in the situation that is frightening," Marta said.

I thought about how angry Christy seemed. "Christy killed her lover. Murdered her." I waited for Marta's response.

"I'd be scared meeting with a murderer," Marta said.

"Really?" I was surprised at Marta's response. I thought I was somehow morally weak. But I plunged forward determined to convince her that I was not only a coward but confused. "Maybe

I'm just afraid of my own lesbianism. Maybe I am judging her because she is so butch. So masculine," I added, just in case Marta didn't know what butch meant.

"What does your identity have to do with being afraid of a batterer?"

"My father was very violent," I said to Marta. I knew I was jumping around "And my brother. Maybe I am projecting this onto Christy."

"Maybe you should stop reading psychology books," Marta said and smiled. I laughed. I liked her. I also liked the red lipstick she always wore. And the dark-colored dresses.

"Maybe, because I am uncomfortable with my own lesbianism, that that's why I am so afraid of Christy." My argument now sounded pretty silly.

"I doubt it," Marta said without the least bit of hesitation. "More likely, she's scary. You've had a lot of experience being around people who are abusive, so you're probably right on target. Is she acting aggressive, or does she appear extremely angry?"

"Well, I'm not too sure. But maybe I'm just judging her or something. Maybe I'm just afraid of how butch she is," I said again. "Don't you think it's possible?"

"Do you think it is different when women are abusers?"

The question threw me off. I paused and thought about it. "Well, to tell you the truth, if you had asked me that question before my last session I would have said 'yes,' but now I'm confused." I said. I felt muddleheaded. And extremely tired. "I know I am very attracted to her. I know that I am having sexual problems in my relationship. And I think I thought that it would somehow be different working with a lesbian abuser rather than a man."

"Is it different?"

"Yes, it's more confusing." I chuckled. So did Marta. I rubbed my face with my hands. I felt totally wiped out.

"Perhaps it is too difficult to work with another lesbian right now. Especially one you are attracted to. How are your sessions going with her?"

"Not well," I confessed. "They feel out of control, moving too fast. I am filled with self-doubt. I lied to her and told her I'd killed someone."

"Why did you do that?"

"I thought it might lighten the conversation or give me a chance to breathe," I said. I laughed. "I don't know my ass from my elbow right now. I don't know if I am afraid of her or if I am afraid of how I feel about her." I went back to my litany: "Maybe I'm afraid of women, maybe I'm just judgmental because she has tattoos and looks really tough. Maybe this is a triggering situation." I paused and slumped in the chair. I looked up at Marta. "She's actually really nice," I added lamely. "And *very* hot looking!" I giggled. So did Marta. We were nearing the end of our time. "So, you don't think that I'm afraid of her because of some sort of unresolved identity problem I'm having or that I don't like butch women?"

"I think working with someone who killed another human being can be frightening. Also, if you are attracted to her, it may be too difficult for you to work with her. Because you are both lesbians it may be too hard for you to get clear in your relationship with her. Especially since you are having sexual problems in your relationship with Carla. You might consider terminating working with this client."

I sat still for a few moments considering what Marta just said. Then I rocked back in my chair and looked out the window. Two crows were sitting on the telephone wire. I watched them picking and pecking at each other. I reached over, grabbed a tissue from the table and, while watching the two birds, blew my nose.

"Crows are the juvenile delinquents of the bird world," I said to Marta. She laughed. So did I. "I'm really overwhelmed. In case you hadn't noticed." She looked at me. And just smiled.

I pulled into an empty spot in front of the shelter, grabbed my bag, and, after securing the club onto my steering wheel, rang the door to the Safe Space, Jamaica Plain's battered women's shelter. A senior resident opened the door.

After checking in with the other staff, I grabbed my cup,

walked into the kitchen, and poured myself a cup of coffee. I stepped out onto the back porch for a quick cigarette. My thoughts went back to my conversation with Christy.

The only time I'd come close to a similar conversation was with a boyfriend fifteen years before. We were sitting in a bar near Fenway Park, matching each other drink for drink. Sitting in a high-backed wooden booth, we took turns threatening to either kill ourselves or each other. We played our little game in an off-handed manner. It was a disturbingly casual chat, like friends lazily discussing what they were going to do on their next vacations. I remember how turned on I was by the madness of it all. Now I wondered if I was merely attracted to my boyfriend and that, because I was drunk, tolerated his insane threats.

Then he reached across the table and hit me. And all desire went out the window. Perhaps I wasn't attracted to abusers after all. I sure wasn't after he hit me.

As a child I'd had similar bouts of psychological warfare with my younger brother Phonso, who was easy prey.

"Where's Mama?" he'd ask as he sat on the floor playing with his toy truck. I'd be sitting cross-legged in our Daddy's green overstuffed chair. Most likely I'd be reading a book, something I did a lot as a child.

"She's dead," I'd say without looking up. More likely than not she'd probably be out at the local bar drinking and flirting with some man.

"No sir," he'd say casually and continue playing with his truck. Phonso was used to my games.

"No, I'm serious, she's dead," I'd continue. "Remember when the phone rang earlier?" I'd ask, still looking at my book.

"Yesss," he'd say slowly. I could tell by the tone of his voice that he was on the verge of taking the bait.

"That was the police saying they found her body in the alley behind the bar." I'd peek over my glasses and assess the progress I was making at wearing him down.

"Liar," he'd say as he rolled his fire engine back and forth over the brown shag carpet. But, I could tell by the furrow in his brow that the fantasy of Mama lying dead in some alley was creeping into his mind.

"She's dead, I tell ya," I'd continue. "Dead as a doornail. So dead that even the maggots are finished with her." I knew this would get to him. He was always such a sissy.

I could see the image of our mother as a maggot-ridden carcass slowly working its way into his tiny mind. By now he'd slowed down rolling his truck, his shoulders had drooped and his face grown long. A few more lines and he'd be down for the count.

"Yeah, apparently she'd been in the alley with some guy and he strangled her, raped her, and gouged out her eyes. Then he threw her in the Dumpster with the rats." I was aware that the details of my story were pretty shoddy but hey, the kid had no brains and any gray matter he did have was very easily overridden by his fragile temperament.

Usually by this point I'd see the first tear drip down his cheek. He'd take the back of his long-sleeved shirt and wipe it away. Slowly he'd get up, wrap his arms around his firetruck, and walk out of the room. "I hate you," he'd mumble in between his whimpering.

"Good riddance," I'd yell after him and go back to my book. I didn't bother following him as I knew he'd just climb into his hamper, pull the dirty clothes over his head, and cry himself to sleep.

I'd go back to my book. It was one of my grandfather's old medical books, filled with drawings of skeletons with the flesh hanging off of the bones. All of the layers of flesh had numbers identifying the muscles. My favorite one was of a skeleton perched on a gravestone.

"Where's your brother?" Mama would ask when she'd arrive home.

"In the closet," I would say without looking up. Mama would sigh, put down her purse on the piano, and walk down the hall. I'd hear her open the door to his room and call out his name. Then I'd hear her open the closet door. After a few minutes she'd walk out, carrying him. He'd be lying against her shoulder, sucking his thumb.

"You were teasing him again, weren't you?" she'd accuse, sweeping back his damp hair from his face. I'd keep reading my book. Mama would walk past me and with her free hand, grab my book right out of my hands and snap it shut.

"Hey," I'd protest and, crossing my arms over my chest, sink deeper into my chair.

"You're on punishment, young lady," she'd say, tossing the book on Daddy's desk. Right before they'd disappear around the corner into the kitchen I'd make a face and stick my tongue out at him. The brat would just tuck himself in closer to Mama and suck faster on his thumb. I swear he'd have a smirk on his face. "What's the matter sugar, hmm?" I'd hear Mama say.

"How did your visit go?" Carla, who was the director of Safe Space, had walked out onto the porch to join me for a cigarette break. She must have been standing behind me for a few minutes. She already had a cigarette out and was leaning over lighting it. She took a deep drag, clicked her Zippo shut, and slipped it into her jacket pocket.

I turned toward the backyard and stared at the children playing on the jungle gym. It always felt good to see children who had come from violence free to play and laugh. I paused and just watched the children. I really didn't want to discuss Christy with Carla. I felt like I'd just get a lecture about what assholes abusers were. I also felt my relationship with Christy, including my attraction to her, was my business.

"Do you ever lie?" I asked distractedly as I continued to watch Natika and Nicole playing on the jungle gym. Their younger brother Sam was standing under the tree nearby, clapping his small hands, excitedly watching his older sisters horse around. Sam, who was being seen by play therapists at Children's Hospital, had opened up so much since he came to our shelter. I smiled as I watched him beaming at his sisters.

"You mean like the time I had an affair and never mentioned it?" she asked.

I snapped out of my reverie and turned to look at my lover over my sunglasses. I was always struck by the rich blackness of her skin. "Yeah, right," I said. Carla and I had been lovers for over six years. We'd met when we were both members of the Alliance Against Women's Oppression, a left-wing women's group. Despite the shitty sex life we presently had, Carla wasn't the cheating type. "No, I mean lie for no apparent reason," I said and turned back to watch Natika trying to coax her younger brother onto the jungle gym. She wasn't having any luck.

"People don't lie without a reason. Women, especially." Carla had joined me at the railing and yelled to Natika to leave her brother alone. "Why?" She glanced over at me. I wondered if she knew I was considering having sex with someone.

I hesitated, more to get my head clear than to measure my words. One thing I knew about Carla, nothing a human being did, including myself, ever surprised her. I also knew that Carla held a hard line when it came to abusers, male or female. She felt they seldom changed. While a member of a black revolutionary nationalist organization, Carla's husband, also a member of the same group, had gone crazy and taken her and her daughter Naomi hostage. He held them at gunpoint in their apartment until the Chicago police had teargassed the place. All of Carla's comrades had known that her husband had been beating her. All or them, arguing for the sake of the revolution and the responsibility of black women to stand by their men, had told Carla to stay with him.

"I'm working with an abuser," I blurted out. "But it's a woman."

Carla turned and looked at me hard. At that moment Natika threw a toy hammer at Sam. He freaked. Carla headed into the yard toward Natika. "Tika, I told you to stop messing with your brother," she said as she picked her way around the sandbox and past the swings.

"So you think her being a woman makes her less of an abuser? What's she in for?" Carla asked as she reached the kids.

"Murder," I said, following after her. At that moment Sam was hunkered down, rocking himself. Natika had climbed off the jungle gym and was trying to drag her baby brother by his hair toward the bars.

Carla stopped dead in her tracks. Slowly she turned, put her hands on her wide hips, and looked me dead in the eyes. "Excuse me?" she said.

I rolled my eyes and stubbed out my cigarette. "Well, she's a woman."

"So?"

"She has a right to help."

"So does a Klan member, right?" Carla was obviously pissed off. Carla usually got pissed at me when she was frightened for me.

"Miss Natika, I told you to leave that child alone!" Carla hollered and turned back toward the two fussing kids.

"I told her I killed my lover," I added. I was beginning to feel increasingly foolish.

Carla didn't even bother to turn around. "Women lie because they're trapped or they think lying will calm down their abuser." As she talked, Carla shoved her leather cap back on her head and tried to pry herself in between the kids. I wished that Carla looked more butch than she did. I felt guilty for thinking it.

"Remember that postcard you bought at the Institute of Contemporary Art?" she asked as she broke up the pair.

I searched my mind. "I'm clueless," I said. I had no memory of ever having bought a postcard when I was there.

"Your right about being clueless," Carla said as she stood up straight and arched her back. "But think about it. It was really important to you when you bought it."

The conversation ended. Carla never asked me to stop seeing Christy. In fact, she never brought the subject up again. Personally, after her comment about my being clueless, I was more than thrilled that she dropped the whole damned subject.

It would be another week before I'd see Christy again.

I went through the usual entrance routine. Name, ID, waiting for the confirmation either on the list or by the guard calling the center, emptying my pockets and dumping my belongings in the locker, occasionally a pat search, but usually not. Then buzz in through door one, wait; then buzz in through door two. Unless I was going out into the courtyard or into the cottages, something I rarely did, these were the last locked doors I'd pass through.

Christy was sitting in the Learning Center when I walked through the door. Her profile was to me. Her right arm was over the back of the chair. With the sleeve rolled up I could see parts of her tattoo on her forearm. Smoke curled up from the cigarette she held between her fingers. I watched her as she stared out the window. She ran her fingers slowly through her long hair and pushed it back over her shoulders.

Christy turned her head and saw that it was me. "Hey," she said and went back to gazing out the window at the asphalt loading area.

"Hey, yourself," I said as casually as I could and walked over to the chair across from her and sat down. Like the last time, I found myself studying her well-chiseled body.

"Like what you see?" she suddenly asked and turned to look directly at me. I was caught off guard.

"Maybe, maybe not," I said and smiled nervously. Already the conversation was out of control.

"I think maybe," she said quickly and turning toward me, leaned forward and stubbed out her cigarette in the ashtray. "I think maybe," she said again. She looked over at me, stood up abruptly, and walked over to the window. She looked out again, keeping her back to me.

"So what's up with you?" Christy asked suddenly.

"Oh, not much," I said, trying to cover my feelings with a smile.

"Kill anybody today?" she asked. She looked up at me while she lit her cigarette. Today there wasn't a smirk across her face. I swear I saw a wave of hatred sweep across her face.

"No, not that I remember," I said facetiously. My fear had resurfaced. "But the day's still young."

"I don't remember killing my lover," Christy said. "But they say it was early evening." She crossed one leg over the other and leaned back in her chair.

"But do you remember why you killed her?"

"Sure, she pissed me off," Christy said easily and stared at me. "Of course that's not what I told the attorneys or the cops." Today Christy seemed to have no problem chatting about the murder.

"What did you tell the police?" I was relieved that the conversation had moved away from me.

"Oh, I did the girl thing and cried a lot, said I was out of control, the drugs and booze, you know. And they bought it," she said as she took another deep drag then leaned her head back and made smoke rings. After she'd blown several perfect rings, each through the other, she took another drag, exhaled slowly and looked directly at me. "I enjoyed it, you know," she said. And smiled. Then her smile faded and she became serious. It was the first time she looked tired and haggard. "Do you want to know why I *really* killed her?"

I paused, unsure if I *really* did want to know. But this moment in my time with Christy felt different, more intimate. I noticed I was holding my breath. I exhaled. And realized that this is why I had wanted to work with Christy. I wanted to know why a woman would kill a woman. "Why, Christy, why did you kill your lover?"

She looked me dead in the eye. "Because she was a woman, because she loved me, because I wanted to fucking die, and she got in the way. I hated her for fucking loving me. I hated her for showing me that someone on the face of this filthy fucking earth really was capable and willing to love me. She destroyed my world. And offered me a reason to stop killing myself. I, quite simply, couldn't take the pain of being loved. It was harder than all the hatred I've had to face in my life."

I was shocked and completely unprepared for this confession. I sat motionless in my chair. Tears ran down my face. "Christy, you know I can't keep working with you. I am too attracted to you. I'm sorry."

"I know," she said and flipped her hair back over her shoulder. She stubbed out her cigarette. "Me too. I'm attracted to you. It's okay. All I really wanted anyway was to tell someone what I just told you." She put her hands to her face and rubbed her eyes. "I miss her, you know," she said as she straightened up and pulled herself back together again. "Anyway, I'll get a few privileges out of these sessions," she said flippantly. We both smiled. "Will you visit me?" she asked. Her voice sounded young and there was an eagerness in her look.

"You know, I don't know. I'm confused," I confessed. "I have a lover, we are having problems." I hesitated. "I need to think about it. If I decide not to, it's not because I don't like you. It's just that I have a lover."

"Fair enough," she said and stood up.

I could feel her eyes on me as the door to the Learning Center whooshed shut behind me.

As the guards unlocked the doors my eyes were already peeking through the plate glass windows, looking for a phone. I saw one over in the waiting area. After I got my belongings back from the guards I quickly searched my pockets for change and, finding some, dialed the number of the shelter. I recognized Carla's voice.

"Hey," I said. "It's me."

"Hey, you," she said. "Did you terminate with that client?" she asked.

"Yes, yes, I did." I could hear Natika in the background who, I assumed, was tormenting her younger brother.

"Are you all right?" Carla asked. I knew she could detect the sadness in my voice.

"Yes, yes, I am." I felt completely drained.

"Oh, by the way, you were right," I said.

"About what?"

"About fear and lying." I didn't mention that part of my need to lie was based on my fear of sexual intimacy with Christy.

"We've both been there."

"Yes, you're right," I said over Sam's screaming. I could feel the tears welling up in my throat.

"Close call, huh?" Carla said.

"Yeah," I said and wiped my eyes with the back of my sleeve.

"Well, just get in that car of yours and head on back here. I'll cook you dinner," she said in between scolding Natika and Sam. "The specialty tonight is Natika under glass." We both burst out laughing.

"See you back at the ranch," I said and hung up the phone. I dug around in my bag for my car keys. That's when I came across the postcard. I flipped it over and saw that the photographer was Barbara Kruger. Black, white, and red, it had a image of a man holding his finger to his mouth. The words "your" and "silence" were in red. The other three words were in black. "Your comfort is my silence," it read. Then I realized you could also read the red words first. "Your silence is my comfort," I read. I smiled and shoved it back into my bag. As I walked out to the car I made a mental note to talk to Carla about digging around in my belongings.

# Me and Cleo

## GWENDOLYN BIKIS

*I* first saw Cleo, my older sister's Little Sister from the Girls' Club, when I saw her play, saw her legs and arms as long as licorice sticks, so whiplike she nipped the ball out the other players' fingers, snapped and plucked the rebounds before they hit the backboard, jumped so quick it seemed there were springs in her knees. Cleo was a li'l bit darker than me and built just wiry, all tight and smooth at once. If I were to do her sculpture, I'd do it all in wire, but really I'm a painter, so no sculpture I could do would ever do her justice. Because Cleo *moved,* like silk sliding through water.

Cleo . . . I can see you with your sleek legs flying, your lanky muscles stretching tight the stripes around your socks, around the hems of your red silk, real-tight basketball shorts. . . .

Her jump shots were so smooth she could have been diving up through water, and watching her make them put me in the shivers, as though she were slithering along the most secret of my places. She'd bounce and flick that ball around a helpless tangle of legs and arms that hopelessly tried to stop her. One time, she dribbled the ball right out of some chick's fingers, then darting and springing around her, bounced the ball—I swear— right through the girl's outspread legs, catching it off the bounce before she'd even had the chance to *think* of turning around. "Smooth black is hard to attack," was Cleo's motto for her play- ing style, but it could have been for all her other ways, on all her other days, in all the other places.

"Cleo's Back," said the front of her favorite black sweatshirt, in bright pink letters. "Cleo's Gone," said the other side. Sometimes, by the time you figured out where Cleo was back *from,* she'd already be long gone. "Slick" was the word she chose to describe herself, because like everyone with the real true Player's personality, Cleo had two sides: street side, and court side. On the court, Cleo most liked to wear her lucky black-canvas hightops; but coming in off the street, she always wore new suede or leather tennis, and she cussed if someone so much as scuffed them, and fussed when someone (like our older sister Marla) merely asked her where she'd gotten them from.

"Because she knew I was actually asking her where did she get the wherewithall to get them from," Marla said.

Everybody knew that Cleo had absolutely no visible means, other than hanging round the littered, rotten-smelling courtyard of the M C Morningside Homes, hanging out supposedly empty-handed.

"But you never can tell what-all I got in my socks, or in my secret pockets," she bragged.

Man, oh man, when I think of how gone I was over that girl ... from the early spring of that summer I was visiting Marla, managing her team, until the August day she made me leave, I had one hopeless schoolgirl crush. I'd be sitting on the sidelines making like my own Girls' Club cheerleading squad, until everybody started to see who I was really cheering for. And the thing about it, Cleo didn't need more cheering.

"F that 'everybody's a star' stuff," she'd say: "I'm the only star on this team." And she'd thump her ball a couple times off the locker-room bench, as if to punch the point home. After she won her Most Valuable Player trophy, every kid on the block wanted Cleo's autograph. I remember her standing, smiling, in a mob of kids, her face still shining with sweat, the top of her royal-red jacket snapped closed over her shoulders, signing scrap after scrap of paper. "Good luck. Signed C.L."; "Happy baskets, signed Cleo." Even though she couldn't write too well, and funny as the ink pen looked, bobbling loosely in her fingers, she grinned through every minute of it. "That might be the only time you'll see Cleo happy to be holding a pen," Marla grumbled. Sometimes she'd get so discouraged with her other Little Sister.

Like anyone with an awkward name, Cleo always had plenty nicknames: C.L., Likorish, Cleo T. Cool Cleo, all of them hiding the name of—Cleotha. Cleo hated Cleotha, hated it with a red-eyed passion, hated it like she hated being stepped on. Cleotha reminded her of a "dumpty country girl with glasses," a girl who'd be afraid of someone like Cleo, so afraid she'd give up all her milk-and-candy money, let herself be kissed, then offer over her sandwich.

"I beat plenty kids up for food when I was a child," Cleo bragged. "I just had to, they was being so greedy. It ain't *polite* to eat in front of folks who just ain't got. It ain't right, so I had to start on them." Cleo rubbed her fist in the palm of her hand and shook her head in sadness that at least looked real.

"I would have given you some," I recall saying.

"You would have given me *all,* baby." She smiled then, showing off the squareness of her chin.

Cleo is an Aries, like me: sometimes we're so selfish, we don't even know we're being it. Or so Marla says. I guess Marla thinks that both of us are exactly the same—but I believe that Cleo's a whole lot worse, a lot more selfish, than me. If it was me, I would think twice about kissing someone, especially some other girl— even more, some other girl who, most likely, would not want it—but Cleo claimed she only picked the girls who'd want it. After she picked me, and after she kissed me, she told me this: "I knew you'd like it, once I did it, so I just went ahead and did." And that smile again: flashing, then closing, like the quick white glint of a pocketknife.

Cleo thought she was smooth, but she sure had one real quick attitude. Let someone step on her toes wrong, even in a basketball game, for goodness' sake, and Cleo'd go off, and I remember tears in her eyes one time, she was so hurt that she'd been made so red-hot mad by someone. I remember how she got, cutting her eyes and snarling 'bout "someone" saying this or doing that. I think, that time, "someone" had draped Cleo's jacket over their own "stinkin', sweatin' shoulders"—by pure mistake, thinking it was their own. But you sure couldn't tell Cleo that, just like you couldn't tell her that this wasn't the Training School, where everyone just naturally stole from *her,* the youngest and the skinniest of all.

That's how I knew that Cleo really thought of me as "her" girl, the game she let me wear her jacket for a whole entire two quarters. After that game, after everyone was gone, the showers dripping off and me innocently picking up the dirty towels, Cleo backed me up against the lockers, and her mouth was spicy with the taste of Good & Plenty.

Cleo never gave me flowers, never said she cared for me, and always asked for money—which sometimes she would get—so why'd I ever love her? It was all about her beauty, the way that she would press her hands all along her long, strong body, and grin at me: "Sometimes I makes sweet love to my own self," she would say. It's not too many people darker than me, and Cleo's one of them. What does it mean to put your hand beside someone's, and see how close its color matches yours, even more than your own sister's does? What does it mean to know this color, so beautiful, chose your color out of knowledge of its beauty?

By the end of August, when Marla actually called Mama to let her know that I was on my way back home, by that hot and steamy time, I'd heard the threat one hundred-thousand times: "I'ma send you back down home, Tamara." The first time I heard it it was the July night I came in drowsy, hungry, and smelling like burnt rope.

Of course I had smoked weed, and of course it was with Cleo. We sneaked it back behind the Homes where they backed up on a park that really was kind of piss-stinky. Though naturally I didn't say as much, not wanting to be called a "sissy country girl."

"I know that you afraid to go with me and get sky-high," she said to lure me, smiling in her shark-like way. Didn't she know it though? Don't nobody tell Tamara what she's afraid to do.

That day, she was wearing black suede tennis shoes, and shorts and pulled-tight kneesocks. And carrying her cap, I'm sure so I could see how neat her hair lay, all newly dressed and

styled, shaved short around her ears and back along her hair-
line. And, Lordy, she was smelling so good to me, like sweet
grease and beauty-shop powder, she smelled good enough to be
eaten; and she surely knew it too.

We settled in the sun beside the worn-out courts. Cleo
reached inside the lining of her cap, and held up a little hand-
rolled cigarette. She stretched, like to show how casual she could
be about breaking any law, not thinking this was *my* first time.
Then she yawned so wide I could see the whole way up inside
her mouth.

"Act as though you got some manners," I almost let my sister's words pass through my own two lips. Cleo liked to stretch
and scratch, to pick her teeth in public—with her fingernail
yet—liked to belch and never say excuse me. Cleo was the kind
of child that Mama would feel sorry for, would shake her head
and softly suck her teeth over.

"Think I got some matches." She was searching through her
pants pockets—though I couldn't see, with those jeans tight as
they were, how she could've fit a thing much thicker than a
folded piece of paper into those pockets.

"Look inside your jacket, Cleo," I suggested. The first time
I'd seen Cleo high, she couldn't do nothing but laugh and dance
and suck the popsicles she'd gotten me to buy for her. When she
wasn't high, Cleo made me tense and flushed, every time she
touched herself. She stroked one hand along her pants front,
while groping through her jacket pocket with her other hand,
and it made my neck tingle. It made me curious, how could one
of Cleo's hands be scrabbling even as the other one so casually,
so smoothly, was taking care of yet another kind of business?
Was it true a person could be born with hands belonging to a
criminal? Secretly, I shivered.

"Here it go," she said, pulling out a book of matches. "You
ready?" she grinned, whipping that weed cigarette from behind
her ear and holding it so I could see it.

What could Marla say to me, if somehow she found out? Was
she thinking I didn't know how much she smoked, late at night
behind her bedroom door while listening to her gospel records,

after yet another day when all her trials with others' troubles bore her down too greatly? Was she thinking she could do or say much of anything to me?

"I am a big girl now, for your information," I said out loud, to whom I wasn't sure. I was all of nineteen, newly turned that summer, on my way to college in the fall.

Cleo raised her eyebrow, struck the match, and grinned her sharp-tooth grin. "What you gonna do, babe, when I—" but she'd stopped to breathe smoke in, pulling wisps of it into her nostrils.

When you do what, Cleo? Like you the one invented the idea of getting next to me? I grinned right back and thought it to myself. Now she's handing it to me, it's smoking, and she's grinning back at me grinning back at her. ("Can't your face *do* nothing besides grin or scowl?" Marla always asked her. In answer, Cleo scowled.)

I reached out for the cigarette, which smelled exactly like the hall at Marla's, those Friday nights when she was burning Black Love incense, thinking she was hiding the true scent.

I put it to my lips and drew it in, keeping both my eyes closed tight. I drew it in and—coughed and heaved, but somehow kept my lips together tight enough to keep the smoke inside. Even I knew that was what you had to do. When I opened my eyes, still holding my breath, the world outside still looked the same. Somehow I had thought it wouldn't.

"You ain't high yet, baby sis," Cleo said, watching me while I looked around and waited. I guess I ain't, I thought, but how I'm gon' know it when . . . when suddenly I felt it—like something pulling out away from me, slow motion out from under me. And all this heat, this depth and color, rushing in at me.

"Wo-ow," I heard myself sigh. In a way, my own sounds I made, my own thoughts I had, seemed like something I was hearing. And the world seemed more like something I was looking at. "I could really paint like this," I heard myself say. It was like another depth to my perception.

"You like this, babe?" Naturally I thought she was talking bout the weed, until I looked down at her long hand and her longer fingers creeping all along my thigh. "Poppety pop," she says, arching an eyebrow. "Poppety pop my finger pop."

"Mmmmm," I said.

Cleo's hand was moving, quivering on me. "You untouched, baby sis?" she asked.

What difference could it make to her? I mean, God knew that *she* wasn't. "Sam," was what I said. Funny, I had gotten through the summer without so much as thinking about Sam, and here I'd gone and mentioned him. At a very unconvenient moment too.

She snatched back as though my leg had stuck her with a splinter. "Who the hell is *Sam?*" For someone who behaved like boys, Cleo didn't like them none too much.

"Oh," I waved my hand to show how bored I was with this topic, "This man I used to know." Used to know. I didn't like to lie like that.

"You know that man good as I know Cynamon?" Cleo asked. "Know that man all the ways I be knowing her?"

Cynamon? Was I hearing right? Cynamon was the Lady Panthers' center, who had a twitchy booty, and not a whole lot more. What-all could any one *find* to know about somebody like Cynamon? Cynamon painted her nails bright orange and looked at stories, those times she wasn't making up no even-more-stupid stories of her own about the boys she knew, away now in the Army or sometimes the Marines, and the presents they bought or were going to buy for her. Not that I ever laid my eyes on present one: "My baby Wally go' buy me a microwave and eelskin shoes and satin underthings." Now who was going to believe that, and who was going to care enough to tell her she was clear and plain a liar?

"Cynamon?" I wanted to know what Cleo knew about girls, every little bit of it, but didn't care to hear about Cynamon. "She likes boys, Cleo."

Cleo grinned. "Not no mo' she don't. Least not since I turnt her out, so's to speak."

Turnt her out? I never had understood just what "turnt out" meant, but never had known how to ask without seeming too sweet and churched and babyish. "How'd you do that, Cleo?" I heard myself ask, despite the fact of it including Cynamon.

Cleo tap-rubbed at my leg. "Turnt her in *side* out, I mean. Made her river run the uphill way." Cleo moved in a li'l bit closer to me. Even with my eyes closed I could feel her, hear her jacket leather squeaking while she shifted. "You want me tell you 'bout it, sis, or you want me to show you?"

"Mmmm, tell me first," Eyes closed, I leaned back all ready to be told. I was feeling very lazy, floating away out in the middle of a drowsy, sleepy sea. "Then show me too," I actually said. I pictured me and Cleo, floating arm in arm up to the sky on a *natural* high.

"Yeah . . ." Cleo's voice had deepened. "Yeah—I likes to ease on back and watch whiles I be poppin' 'em, watch 'em knot their brows like they in pain then smile as though they ain't and I likes to hear 'em grunt an' cry and moan an' squeak and *beg* once you got them goin' good, got 'em good and sweet and greezed."

Ooh my goodness, that was nasty, nastier than I'd ever heard her be. What would Marla say and do? I couldn't exactly see Cleo lying slapped-down on her back, but couldn't see Marla doing anything less.

"Know how I picked the first girl I ever really wanted?" Cleo asked.

"Who was that, Cleo?" I noticed I had caught my breath, the way I do whenever I feel jealous. Me, having to be jealous of a simple-face like Cynamon.

"What I mean, li'l sis, is that usually they's the ones be wantin' me, and I just goes along just for the ride, so's to speak."

"Just for the ride?" Was it the weed, or was it something else that was making my arms and legs to feel so limp and weak and warm? And making me sound so very young and stupid?

"Mm—mmm tha's right. Mmm . . . hmm. But you want to know how I picked that first girl I ever really wanted?"

"How?" I obliged by asking. How could a person tell, ever, what it was they really wanted? "Don't ask for what you want, or else you just might get it," was one thing Mama used to say.

"Don't go looking for no trouble, 'cause chances are you gonna find it," she would add.

"Who was the girl you wanted?" I asked again.

"You mean, how'd I *find* that girl I wanted? That's the question that I'm trying to answer you with, now. If I went ahead and answered it, I might be telling you about this party I had went to, deep down in the East Bee-mo' jungle, way way late at night, so late it was getting on toward early. That blue light bulb had been burning for a good long while by the time cool Cleo finally got there."

Cleo stopped, it must have been to make sure that I was listening. I hadn't stirred since she'd begun. "Mmmm *hm?*" I asked.

"So then," I heard another squeak of leather, and pictured her spreading her arms the way she did when her story got exciting to her. "I walks right in, real sharp, wid my cap politely in my hands 'cause I know it's go' be ladies there—I walks on in, and ooh wee, what right off do I see?

I opened my eyes, and I leaned so far forward, I almost fell. I propped myself on both my hands. "What did you see, Cleo?"

"I saw one whole line of ladies, baby sister, all preening and a-strolling that old hip-grind booty-shake they be using on the street, and all of it is just for me, Cool Cleo."

Cleo might have felt that she was cool, but Tammy wasn't feeling it. What I felt from Cleo was fire.

"Then up to me, comes a lay-dee," Cleo sang it. "This long-haired, light-skin lady in a evening gown with some silvery tinselish fringe along its front come strolling up to me, hip-grinding booty-shaking right on up to me, and ask me would I like a glass of wine. Which, you already know Cleo isn't goin' to refuse.

"So I sits there sipping—the lady done provided me a seat—and looking all these ladies over, all of which is wanting me, waiting just to do whatever I be wantin' them to do for me, when I sees this one in back?"

"Uh huh?" I nodded with my eyes closed, thinking all of this was sounding too wild even for a life like Cleo's. And why was it somehow sounding so familiar?

"This one look quiet, like she's hiding an' surprised to find herself in this late-night doing, and she's wondering why has she been invited? I mean, this one definitely ain't no party lady, so why she been invited here? Look to me as though she's thinkin' that, hanging back there in the corner lookin' all so quiet and so sweet.

"Then up to me, comes the lady," Cleo sang again. "The lady in the evenin' gown? She seen my glass is drunk down to its dregs. So then she start to po' some mo' of that plum wine, and then she lean down toward my ear, and then she sing to me:

*Spill that wine, take that girl—*

"Oh, Cleo," I play-slapped at her arm. "That is that *song*, Cleo." That song I should have recognized, because it had been all over the radio around '71 or '72, a couple summers before.

Cleo laughed, but then went on. "But you wan' know how I decided which girl it was that I was gon' take? I decided when that sweet girl been hiding in the back was brought right up to me by the lady in the evening gown. That sweet young thang looking giggly, like she likes me so she gots to cover it with silliness. An' there she goes, giggling even harder when I lean in toward her to touch them thick soft lips with mines. And I know, soon as I am kissing her, I know it then fo' sho': this the one. This the girl that I been wanting, this dark-skinned soft and chubby one with the real sweet features and the cute print skirts and the li'l red Keds and the oh-so-easy feelings I can see inside of, right this living minute. I can see that she the one, once I gits her in the bed, the one gon' scream an' cry more happier than she ever done in church. Because the facts is that she ain't yet had real lovin'. Ain't had *my* real lovin'."

I felt so naked, I felt X-rayed. Embarrassment had never felt exciting to me. Not before right now.

"So now I'm thinkin' I'ma take that girl," Cleo said, and

then she took me. With my eyes closed and my head all weed-smoke dizzy, Cleo took and hugged and kissed my breath away. 'Cept for that tiny squeak I loosed.

That was the real beginning, that first long tight and sliding full-tongue kiss that I gave back to her. That was the real beginning of my realizing *how* I was much more than someone else's little sister. And in those rapturous high moments I couldn't care at all about whatever people might think of to call me.

All the ways and whys of how we kissed: We kissed one time so deep, just because it felt so good, that afterwards, still dizzy, as I was dazedly signing on a form, I looked down at my hand, and I saw that I had mis-spelt my own name. Badly, in two places. We kissed one time so sweet, just because it tasted good, sneaked little dabs of lip sugar back behind the gym bleachers, so sweet that I forgot to stop, and we almost got caught by watchdog Coach Alberta: "What y'all doin' back up in there? Popping popcorn maybe?" We kissed so juicy, so flavor-full for days, sneaked inside the laundry room because the sneaking was so fun, I remember still the way her lips would feel. Luckily, because it is most likely I will never feel those lips on mine again.

Just yesterday, I was washing dinner dishes when my phone rang.

"Baby sister. What's shakin'?" It was Marla. Calling from the Girls' Club, no doubt, she was talking so street-like.

"Nuthin' doin'," I replied. "You coming home this weekend?"

"I just might. But that sure isn't the reason I'm calling. I just got a call, long distance. From Cleo."

I felt my breath leave me. Already I was certain this wasn't going to be good.

"She asked me to send her some math books." A pause. "Tammy? She called me from the Womens' Prison? They've already moved her from the jail. She's 'up against a li'l charge'

is all she'll tell me. And she's not sounding too proud of whatever it is she's been charged with *this* time. This time, sounds
like it's gon' stick."

I could see the loose little shrug that Cleo'd give, acting cool
and shucking, all the way into. . . . Into prison, this time. Before
it had just been lock-up, "diddly little county time," Cleo called
it, bragging about it in that way that people will about their trouble when it's the only thing they have.

Marla sighed into the phone. "Cleo's life has done went all to
hell and pieces, exactly how she wanted it to go. I'm not sure if
knowing where she's at is any much better than wondering if
she's dead." She let out a flat, not-happy laugh.

How does Marla think she leaves me, when she leaves me
with this news? How does she think I could even paint Cleo
when I'm left with nothing but bad news of her? Why did
Marla ever have to send me away from her?

I can't accept her there, refuse to see her matted hair, can't
stand to see her grace impeded. I see her hands clutching bars
slick with her palm sweat, I see her heart, lush red beating hard
against a too-small cage. I see her squirm beneath the weight of
dark bar shadows that fall across her body like heavy chain-gang
stripes. I see her eyes, wild and trapped inside their sockets. . . .
I see more than I can stand.

But the stories we have told ourselves and made into our
truths are all the reason we've survived. I have to make myself
believe the picture that I want to paint of her: I see her dancing
on the court again, see the floor fresh-polished so it reflects each
of her smooth movements.

"Cleo's on the fast break now," she said, while practicing her
own slide-and-glide in the locker-room mirror. I'm sitting in
the stands again and feeling the excitement as it begins to run
and ripple, like the Holy Spirit will, all through the crowd
around me, every time that Cleo sprang into her break.

I see her grinning and spinning her ball on the very tip of her
long finger: "Look! I gots the whole world in my hands!" I see
her legs climb air as she leaps up into one of her championship-
winning Playground Patented Devastation Dunks.

"Them peckerwood policies in Training School tried to keep me from almos' everything, but they never tried to keep me from makin' one of my way-up-easy jump shots." Cleo said it more than once, so it must have been real true.

"Some folks uses basketball to get themselves out," she'd say, thumping her ball on the floor, "but for me, when I'm playing, I'm already out."

We have always strained against our chains, and we would line-dance in that slave-coffle they had locked us into. And when we sing, our voices rise up that golden ladder that we keep on climbing higher, higher, like true soldiers of the Cross. It used to be that we could fly, and we have walked through fire, and the sea has even parted for us—that red and bloody water has rolled up on either side and made for us a passage safe from every danger. This is all the reason why I love us—why I have to paint us—and why I think that we are the most wonderful, most colorful, the most talented and intelligent, and the most beautiful of all people in this world.

"Refo'm schoo'?" Cleo answered me once, twirling the ball at the end of her finger. "The only good thing about it was I learned to play ball in there. The court looked like a sunken cage, but I ignored that fact. Playin' ball was what kep' me from killing somebody." And she bounced it hard against the wall.

"They try to keep us from everything that's ours in there. Because we're being *pun*ished, don't you know." I can hear her going *on:* "When I first got out of Training School, people would look at me and wonder what they could of done to me in there to make me look the way I did. Because I was looking exactly the way I was feeling. 'Quiet and deadly' someone called my temper then. Ooh wee, I was Ice-T pure-dee deadly, comin' out of there."

Then she lifted her hair, and turned her collar down, and bared her neck so that I could see the ropy scars that twisted, thick as baby blacksnakes, across her tender neck flesh.

"They held me down and done that to me with a metal-edged ruler soaked overnight in vinegar." Cleo whispered.

"Don't even try to tell me that slavery days is over."

"Uh uh uh," was all that Marla said, when I told her, and I know what she was thinking; about how an old, old wound could ache still when the weather was bad, and how a scar could thicken and pucker as it healed, yet deepen beneath the skin. "You know," she said, "when black peoples' skin is broken, they always look so wounded."

I could paint her musculature, her bare and sweaty shoulders, purple-cushioned in their shadows. But then I'd have to paint her neck, and thinking that, I lose all interest.

In all my paintings, I always try to make there be, make myself to see, a piece a patch a sweeping swatch of sky that's blue—except in Cleo's, I can't see it yet.

Cleo's gone; gone for good.

# Mykonos

## ZÉLIE POLLON

*M*aybe it was the alcohol—or the fantasy of hot sex with a perfect stranger, on an island in the middle of the wine-dark sea. Separated for too long from human touch and hungry for someone who understands that I respond to a woman's touch more than a man's, I am game.

We drink hard alcohol: ouzo and grappa—too much and too fast—and talk of our San Francisco homeland. We flirt, lowering our eyes coyly, then letting them meet just long enough to feed our anticipation. Our hands touch and our legs, hidden from view by the bar, brush against each other, then press with more force. We smile knowing smiles that break into grins. Our body language carries on a dialogue of its own; it transports us from a smoky bar filled with drunken singles on their great gay escape onto the narrow cobblestone streets that grab at our ankles as we stumble away.

She tightens her grasp on my wrist and pulls me forward. She knows where she wants to go, knows the way, and wants to get there soon. I follow, surprised by the suddenness, but eager to play.

Frolicking in the patio of a closed oceanfront restaurant, we dodge sea spray, jumping from tile-stone ground to wooden tabletop, shrieking with delight as the surf smashes against the patio wall covering us in mist. With each wave, we inch nearer to the other, pull back, then together again, awkwardly drawing close for warmth.

Her breath is of all-too-familiar stale alcohol and cigarettes, her thin blond hair sculpted into a flattop. One wandering eye makes her drunken edginess scarier—or more exciting, I can't remember.

I feel the soft fuzz of her cheek, skin melting into skin, and seduce myself into ecstasy. Passion is a strange emotion. It is anger, lust, incoherence. It is both intensely focused, vague and widespread. It is blindness.

We kiss each other's lips, softly at first, careful and tentative, caressing as we go.

Then with her back against the overturned table we pull hungrily at each other's clothing. We stop noticing the advancing tide, its arm reaching over the patio wall with each incoming wave.

I find myself lying on a banco, naked and cold in the predawn chill. My bare skin grinds into the stucco walls around me and I try to make myself more comfortable. She is leaning over me, pinning my shoulders against the side of the banco, paralyzing my attempts to move.

As I grow sober in my discomfort, she becomes more concentrated and heated in her lust, like an angry child tearing at the body of a doll, furious to find only its cotton filling.

My insides are not cotton, even to those heavy with drink and fatigue. She takes my attempts to push her away as throes of passion. She does not hear when I say "No." She is not listening. I reach to the sea for comfort.

Now neither one of us is present. She hates me for being a woman and hates herself for not being a man. I am somewhere over the Aegean trying to recall the myth. Women loving women. The conspiracy of sensual, consensual sex. The false promise of utopia betrays me, just naive and hopeful enough, romantic and desperate enough, to believe.

My numbness carries me home. I pass the bar stragglers who have yet to get laid, one of whom proposes I spend the morning with him. He has the puffy red face and swollen eyes of someone who has stared too long into the bottom of too many glasses. He looks sad and sweet, and seems hardly disappointed when I nod and say "No, thank you." I pass the workers who are preparing to start their day, opening storefronts and washing down walkways. The air is crisp and cool and I can see their breath as I pass. The fishermen have long since cleaned and cast their nets, their boats already at a distance from shore. I see them on the deep blue horizon, their colors blaring in contrast to the dry strands of yellow straw off the path in front of me.

I walk to my small room at the back of the house of an elderly baker. The room is sparsely decorated: a chair, a table and bed, a small mirror above a set of drawers, and a plate of cookies from the previous day.

As I sit on the corner of my bed facing the wall, I feel the sun rising through the window behind me heating, then burning, the back of my neck. There is a crack in the wall in front of me that runs from where the corner meets the floor, all the way up to the ceiling. At the ceiling, it starts to spread like a fan above my head, its long, thin, spider-like arms crawling slowly across the room.

I will mostly remember the colors of Mykonos: every shade of white building, yellow fields, blue waters, and the fanciful colors of tourists' outfits—oranges, greens, purples, and red. I will remember the stiff drinks and sunburnt faces, the smell of baking bread in the morning and fresh fish at night. The cobblestone walkways, the fishing boats, and the smell of the ocean. The faces of men who, with pleading eyes, ask if they can buy you a drink. These memories will be very clear to me, but I will not recall sex with a stranger. It will be months before I remember that I was raped.

# Wicked Stepsisters

## KATHRYN KINGSBURY

*I*'ve been thinking about why you would have said the things you said, Ella. Maybe it was that you were bored, or brainwashed, or maybe your life in this house trained you so well in lying that you just didn't know how to stop. Or maybe you wanted to hurt me.

Then, the other day, I was flipping through my English reader and came across this little essay about Virginia Woolf and her writing style. What it said was that Virginia Woolf thought writing in summary was inaccurate and maybe even dishonest, because our memories don't recall our lives to us in summary, but in scenes. And it occurred to me that maybe what I've been taking to be lies are really nothing so dramatic as lies, nothing motivated by malice or a desire to deceive; in fact, they're not even untrue. The stories you've been telling have all the marks of nonfiction, including the following—they are the result of a clouded memory.

Maybe, then, this explains why what you have been telling the magazines seems to me to be completely and totally false. It's because you haven't been telling them the details of our lives, but only the outlines. You've constructed our lives into a story so lacking in complexities that it's nothing more than a tale for children. You've made me into a flat character, an antagonist who only serves to highlight the impeccable qualities of the heroine.

You've managed to sum up five years into one sentence: "My father married this woman, and a few years later he died, leav-

ing me with an unloving, manipulative, abusive stepmother—
though I don't really like to use the word mother to describe
her—and her daughters, who couldn't find it in themselves to
treat me like a sister."

In all these interviews you give, sitting next to your new husband—"the King of the Big Screen," as last week's cover of *Entertainment* magazine called him—you fail to mention that you
never wanted me to be your sister. Not at all. The first time you
saw me, the first time I saw you, we both knew it: we were going
to be something much more.

I think it was two weeks after you moved in that we first spoke.
By that, I mean the first time we ever spoke alone. You and I
had spoken at dinner every night, and at breakfast, too, your father there to pry the words out of us. But I didn't like talking
around you. It sent me into too much of a panic.

The day we spoke, I was in the rose garden, lying on my back
with my eyes closed. I was paying careful attention to the fact
that I was inhaling and didn't notice the noise of footsteps or of
your breath until I felt a jab in my side.

"Hey!" you said. Your face right above mine, your eyebrows
scrunched down, making those green eyes that seemed to see
everything squint just a little. That's what I saw when my eyes
opened. I thought I was drowning.

I suppose I must have asked you what it was that you wanted,
even though I was terrified of speaking—mostly because I
hadn't brushed my teeth after lunch and I was sure it would
smell just awful to you. When I spoke I looked at your nose, especially the one small freckle on its left side. I also looked at your
lips, which were puckered shut. I wanted to pry them apart with
my eyelashes.

There was no need, though, because you started talking
again. You asked me why I was ignoring you.

I asked you to please stop leaning over me and staring at me
like that.

You said you weren't staring.

I said, "When you look at me it makes me queasy."

You said, "Thanks for the compliment."

I sat up. I grabbed your elbow. "No, no, I didn't mean it that way!" I was trembling so hard it made your arm shake. "Please don't think I . . ."

"No, I know," you said, "whenever I think about you, my stomach goes haywire." You scraped your top teeth along your bottom lip. You jumped up and ran. "Please . . . " I yelled. But you didn't hear me. I sank my ear back down against the ground and watched the backs of your sneakers arch up and hit the ground, arch up and hit the ground. They turned at the farthest bush and were gone.

I'm not sure how much later this was—several weeks, a month, maybe two. It was night. I'd just brushed my teeth. You came into my room. You closed the door behind you and turned the lock. I was sitting on my bed, pretending to myself that I was reading. I'd read the same paragraph at least five times in a row because I couldn't pay attention to it long enough to understand it. I was thinking about you.

My room was dim. I had only my reading light on. So, when you looked straight at me, your eyes seemed less threatening. I didn't look away.

You said you'd come to say good night. I said something like, "Okay." You knelt next to my bed and your eyes were there and beautiful and I closed mine and pretended I didn't know what you were about to do. What I wanted you to do.

It may have been the fastest kiss in the history of humankind, if one doesn't count the pecks that ladies and old friends use, in certain circles, to greet each other—left cheek, right cheek, left cheek—kisses so brief and faint that they often don't even involve contact between lips and skin.

As I leaned forward to kiss you again—this one, I swore to myself, would be a longer kiss, and one with open eyes—your father's voice racked through the wall—Ella, Ella, where are you? You need to sign this birthday card for your cousin.

Our faces were suspended—close to each other but not close enough—frozen by your father's call.

You blinked: I'll be there in a minute, Dad! you hollered to the ceiling and the walls and the closed door. You began to stand up, but I grabbed the waist of your nightgown and pulled you down toward me and I kissed you. The second briefest kiss in the history of the world. You had to leave.

After that, we made sure not to say good night to each other until after your father and my mother had gone to sleep.

I think we would still be going on like that today if your father hadn't died. But things got weird in the house during those months when he was in and out of the hospital. Mother seemed more bitter than usual, and watchful in a way she had not been before. We blamed it on her loneliness and fear. We did not expect her to remain that way forever.

When he died, he left mother everything, assuming that his daughter would be taken care of by his one true love, who was acquainted with his wishes and, because she loved him, must abide by them. But he did not name mother guardian in his will. That was to be taken care of in separate papers that required mother's signature if they were to be binding.

He died before she signed the papers.

It's so strange how the wishes of the dead dictate our lives.

The night of the funeral, as you lay with me in my bed, weak and asleep from all your tears, I thought I heard a noise: the shifting of a floorboard out in the hall; a sigh or a breath on the other side of my door; the clenching of nervous fingers. That night I thought I heard a whimpering anger: *Shouldn't love have died in this house with him?*

Eight days later—I remember, because it was a Monday, and the funeral had been on a Sunday—I was woken up at dawn by footsteps and swishing air at the side of my bed, then a hand on my shoulder, lips on my forehead. It was you, of course.

As soon as I started to kiss back, you stepped away. "Your mother says I have to wake you up and take your laundry." You didn't look at me, but out the window instead. "We aren't sisters anymore." You walked to the closet, opened the door, and picked up all the clothing wadded up on the closet floor. The pile went from your waist to your chin; under my panic I wondered if it smelled sweet to you. I remember mumbling things to convince you to stay: "But, please, I don't under . . . But I don't, can't you, but what have I . . . Ella. Please." But you only turned your eyes to the floor and left my room.

Over breakfast, Mother explained that it was all perfectly legal. She had consulted her lawyer extensively about the matter. She had no legal obligation to take care of you. You weren't her daughter. But you didn't want to go to a foster home, either. So she had given you another option: work for her, and she would house and feed you and add a little money on the side.

Over slices of kiwi and spoonfuls of grapefruit, mother gave me lessons on how to treat servants. Do not ask, command. Do not allow her to speak first. Never say "please."

"You aren't to go on treating her the way you have been doing," she whispered finally, scraping remnants of egg and a half shell of grapefruit to the side of her plate, and stood up from the table. "You may take my dishes now, Ella," she called to the kitchen door.

I learned to play along with Mother's new rules. I figured it would be difficult but do-able. I figured that, eventually, I'd find a way around them.

Around Mother, I simply ignored you. It wasn't that I wanted to. It was that she was watching, and I had to do what she wanted. Or she'd make sure to hurt you.

In my free time, I practiced not saying "please" and "thank you" and "if you don't mind." I practiced not saying "good night" and I practiced not saying "I love you." I practiced not saying those things because I figured if I tried hard enough to not say them, I would perhaps begin to not think them, and the feelings behind them wouldn't show up on my face unintentionally in the presence of Mother.

I learned to drop the phrases, but I never did stop thinking that I loved you, no matter how hard I tried. I just didn't say it and tried to look grim at the moments I most wanted to touch you.

You practiced, too. You were good at this game. When my mother was in the room, your face became less human and more like the leaves of clover or dandelion—gentle but ambivalent, with no visible indications of a capacity for passion. In the presence of mother, we were both what she wanted us to be: soulless and numb.

We got so good at hiding it that, even when she had stepped out of the house for a day or an evening and Sister was off riding horses or with friends and the house was empty except for just us for at least a few hours—even then, when I called you to my room and the curtains were shut and my door was locked and a chair was propped against the doorknob, and you sank onto my bed in your cleanest pair of jeans and bent over to untie your sneakers and I watched, through your T-shirt, the muscles in your back and shoulders move and your breasts sigh— even then, I had trouble leaning over and whispering to you: I love you.

So I never did. Instead, I'd wait for you to slip off your shoes and tuck them under my bed and sit straight up and look at me with your green eyes and then I'd shiver. I'd lean forward and turn my lips to your ear and I'd say, "I want you forever." And, later, when the skins of our stomachs touched and I reached for you inside, you'd lean your lips away from mine and, your eyes closed and tilted toward the space above my forehead, you'd smile and sigh, "Oh yes, do, please."

One night in spring, a few weeks after the buttercups had begun to sprout at the edges of the driveway and mother had made it one of your errands to mow them all down, the phone rang. Mother refused to take the call—"those damned phone solicitors always interrupting dinner!"—so you took a message. She didn't read it until the table was cleared of everything but cake-crumbed plates. She looked up from the note and beamed at Sister and me. One of her cousin's clients was going to have a party for his thirtieth birthday. Her cousin directs an acting agency. "Most of them show up only in cereal commercials," mother said, "but some of them are quite well known."

Sister asked who it was. Mother was still beaming. "Ken Worthy."

Ken Worthy, the macho stud in the action flicks? That Ken Worthy?

"Yes, indeed," said mother. "We'll have to go shopping for dresses. It will be a very formal event. An old-fashioned ball."

I lay next to you on my bed. It was a warm May afternoon, and we had thrown my sheets back. You lay on your back and I lay on my side, and I wrapped one arm down around your rib cage so that your breasts snoozed against my forearm. I couldn't tell the difference between what was your sweat and what was mine.

Sister and Mother were at the stables. They had left me behind because I'd told them I wanted to study for my graduation exams. They almost always believed me when I lied. Or, at least, they pretended to believe; I still can't decide whether nothing was ever said about you and me because we were master deceivers, or because they—especially Mother—were masters of self-deceit.

But that was later. On this day in May, I was calm and happy and there was no world beyond my bed. I was staring at your ear: the sharp round line that forms the top rim, and the triangle of cartilage, and your earlobe, warm and pink. I didn't notice I was whispering to you until I'd already said it: "Ella. Come to the ball."

That's how the fight began. You sighed and turned your nose toward me. Your eyes were piercing and green. Your voice was iron, and sharp. "No, it's too dangerous," you said.

I told you it wasn't dangerous at all. I told you Mother would hardly recognize you in a dress. I said there was no chance she would recognize you at a party like that where she'd be so busy kissing the asses of famous people and where she wouldn't on a cold day in hell expect to see you. Besides, what could she do to you?

You looked up toward the ceiling.

I said I would take care of everything for you. I'd buy the dress and . . .

You told me not to bother. You spat those words. Your heart pummeled fast against my arm. I shrunk away from you and turned over onto my other side, but the words kept coming right on out of your mouth: how sneaking out like that might seem like a game to me, but it wasn't for you. How if you lost this job you wouldn't be able to find another one that gave you food and a place to live. How you'd end up on welfare, how you wouldn't graduate from high school.

Of course, I didn't believe a word you said was true. If you got kicked out, I had credit cards, I had connections, and besides, you would be able to find a job after all this time working here. I knew why you were staying: it wasn't the money, it was me. Why were you so afraid of saying it?

But you were always too stubborn to listen to reason. You grabbed your clothes up from the floor and ran naked into the hallway, your bare feet padding all the way to the basement.

The week after that was strange and quiet. We were never alone—I only saw you at mealtimes, as you set the chicken cordon bleu or the rack of lamb or the bowl of sliced fruit at the center of the table. Mother was particularly joyful that week, always buzzing about the party: "Do you know, I just found out the most interesting person will be there!" and "Well, perhaps it's about time I get a new garnet ring; after all, I need something to go with my dress!" And she was always out shopping. But you and I spent no time together. I sat in my room, studying and waiting for you to visit; and you did your chores and sat alone in your room and never came.

One day, as I sat at my desk, my brain fluttering, it occurred to me: I could visit you. I could take those stairs down to the basement and I could knock on your door.

I had never seen your room before. I don't know why: my dislike of basements and the snakes and ghosts that as a child I was convinced lived there; the creaky stairs; and also, the knowledge of what it might look like—without the curtains and the Laura Ashley sheets and the mahogany mantel of my room—an embarrassment for your poverty.

I didn't knock. I turned the knob and opened the door a crack and peeked in.

The room was dark, with only one thin window near the ceiling. You had one of those humane mousetraps on the floor next to your bookcase. The bookcase had five shelves and housed your school and library books, but also your folded jeans and shirts. Your underwear and socks were stuffed into a milk crate on the third shelf up from the floor.

You were sitting on a mattress on the floor, your head bent beneath a reading lamp. You looked up at me as if this were not at all a surprise, as if I entered your room every day. You said nothing, but your face was forgiving; and even though you had not told me that you loved me in a long, long time, I swear I heard your heart whispering it to me.

"I missed you," I whispered toward the foot of your bed. I was still standing in the doorway. I wanted to step inside, but I didn't know how.

You stood up and walked toward me and took my wrist in your hand. You pulled me inside and closed the door. "Yeah," you whispered. You turned off your reading light and, for a long time, we stood still in the dark like nervous new lovers.

Later that afternoon, as we lay on your bed and started counting down the minutes until Mother was due home, you said, "I've decided. I want to go to the ball."

I took the light blue strapless I'd worn to homecoming in ninth grade and had it redone to fit you. The skirt was fuller, with purple panels added to the blue, and straps, as well. Rhinestones covered the dress like stars. You tried it on two weeks before the party.

We were in my bedroom. My ceiling light wasn't on, only the reading light next to my bed. The curtains were drawn and the room was dim and beautiful. You stepped into the dress and pulled it up over your tight-muscled thighs and your strong hips and your breasts. I zipped you up and kissed the skin where the zipper ended.

We looked at you in the mirror. You smiled when you saw yourself and you said how you looked so strange. You were the most beautiful I had ever seen you.

It was a couple of days later that I got you your shoes. I knew exactly what I wanted and went to every shoe store in town to find them. But they weren't anywhere. I ended up special-ordering them. I received them FedEx the following afternoon. I hid them in a hat box at the bottom of my closet until the day of the ball, when I snuck into your room and stuffed them into a pillowcase along with your dress. I left money for a taxi under your mattress.

I don't know what your face looked like when you found the shoes. I had already left for the ball with Mother and Sister in the limousine. I imagine you holding them to the light when you found them and watching the glass rhinestones sparkle. I imagine you putting them on your feet and dancing in circles while humming "Diamonds on the Soles of Her Shoes," smiling with a happiness so large it's on the verge of despair. I imagine you thinking how much you want me there to help you with the dress zipper.

At the ball, we had to stay far apart so no one would think we knew each other. But I always kept an eye out for you, your round shoulders and your neck becoming slender and more slender like a wrist or a plummeting raindrop as you leaned your head back to laugh and show those tough white teeth.

I danced with a man named Chuck, pleasant and of reasonable enough stature to please Mother. He wasn't famous, but he knew lots of famous people, and that in itself was enough to get him interviewed in *Vanity Fair*. He was a horse trainer and kept horses for wealthy and famous people like Ken Worthy. He talked about his connections and his job as we waltzed.

You were dancing with Ken Worthy. I wondered how you'd pulled that one off. Maybe he came up to you? He seemed to like you, in any case. You were making a good audience for him: you laughed at everything he said, and when you did, your teeth glimmered from between your frozen, smiling lips.

Two hours into the dance, you excused yourself from Ken's company and headed toward the bar. "Chuck," I said, "I think I ought to go powder my nose." I followed you.

"A glass of champagne, please," I heard you saying. Your hair was up in a coil and pinned into place with rhinestone-studded hairsticks, and rhinestone-tipped bobby pins were stuck here and there. I thought that was maybe carrying the rhinestone theme a little too far, but reminded myself that you weren't used to dressing elegantly.

"Red wine," I said to the bartender.

You looked right up when I spoke, your eyebrows surprised; but you didn't smile. "Hello," you said.

I was tempted to joke with you, to say something that would make you laugh. I wanted the same smile you'd been flashing at Ken all evening to be directed at me.

But I wasn't going to do anything so stupid as to provoke it, not with all these people around. I didn't want to risk Mother passing by, even though I knew there was, logically, nothing to worry about: the last time I'd seen her, she'd been schmoozing with some two-bit actor off in the corner of a side room, her eyelids stretched back to say, How enthralling!

So this is what I said to you: "I see you've met our gracious host." Nothing a stranger or pompous acquaintance couldn't say.

"Yes," you said. The bartender handed us each our glasses. We took smooth sideways steps away from the bar. "But no romance." You shrugged. "Still, a bright prospect for the future."

A what? I nudged you around the dance floor and down the hall to the powder room. Inside, you sat down in the pink armchair next to the armoire and mirror. I wanted to squeeze next to you, but your skirt took up too much space. I sat on the chair's arm, instead.

I asked you: What had you meant by "a bright prospect for the future"?

A silence like a tremor in the earth.

"I dunno." You shrugged. "Someone stable. Someone you'd think about marrying."

"You're joking, right?"

"Not exactly."

A silence like a stairway collapsing. I stared at the wallpaper—its small, dime-sized flowers, its clawing leaves.

But you still need me, don't you?

You said you had the future to think about, your life to think about. "Besides," you said, "I can't be happy in your house, with your mother there all the time to bitch and complain and breathe down both our necks." A pause and a laugh: "And why not marry him? After all, he shares your taste—he just loves my shoes." Giggle, giggle. You looked at your left wrist, bare but for a tennis bracelet, and said, "Oh, what time is it? My Prince Charming will be wondering where I am."

I walked you back to the dance floor, but before letting go of your arm, I whispered to you, "Will you meet me again in about half an hour? When the clock strikes twelve?"

"Oh, sure," you said.

"In the garden," I said. "Between the lilac bushes." But I didn't believe you would come.

I let your arm go and watched as you reentered the waiting arms of our gracious host.

He proposed to you on the terrace that night, just before you walked down the steps to find me. You thought he was joking, but when you laughed at him, his face became painfully sincere and he whispered to you, "You're the only woman I've met in years who hasn't been trained to forget she's human."

You coughed and then told him you would have to think

about it. You said you needed some time alone. You took off your high-heeled shoes—hard to walk on stilts with a champagne-dizzy head!—and headed toward the garden while he watched you disappear into the dark. You didn't notice until you'd reached me that you had dropped one of the shoes while walking away from the mansion.

We sat under the lilac bushes—I'd sneaked away a tablecloth and laid it on the ground so that our dresses wouldn't get stained—and you told me what he'd said, and what you'd told him. You said you'd only left him hanging in order to torture him. You fully intended to tell him yes. Later.

But don't you know that I want you more than the world, that I want you more than God, that I want you more than the things I can think to name?

Your lips were parted as if you were about to say something more, but I didn't want to hear it, so I leaned over and kissed you. We stayed like that under the lilac bushes until it had been night for so long that we no longer noticed the stars.

The reason both you and I know that Ken Worthy didn't really love you is because after the party he couldn't remember what you looked like. But he still wanted to marry you, presumably because he remembered the fact that you were beautiful, if not the unique character of your beauty itself.

The day after the ball, Mother found a short article about it in the gossip column of the newspaper. After reading off a list of this person and this person and that person who were seen there, she read this: "Among items that these members of the upper-crust accidentally left behind are three Rolexes, an emerald choker, and a glass slipper. One wonders how the lady managed to walk out the door with only one shoe. We should mention that Mr. Worthy's behavior last evening should lead one to believe that he has become quite smitten by a certain young lady in attendance whose identity is unknown to Hollywood insiders."

You snuck into my room that evening after Mother and Sister had gone to bed. I lifted the sheets for you and, as you climbed in, I told you about the article.

"Are you going to call him up to claim it?" I said.

"Oh," you said, "I think I can let him wait a little bit longer."

I meant to tell you that night that I loved you, but every time I thought to say it, I thought about how the sounds of the words were nothing like what they meant and how, if you say "love" over and over again ("loveloveloveloveloveloveloveve"), it begins to sound like "fluff." And after thinking about it that way, I could never say it to you, knowing that these words are nowhere near being exactly what I mean.

Three weeks later, Ken Worthy phoned. You picked up the phone and you heard these words: "Hello. May I speak to Ella?"

You were so unused to receiving calls at our house that you actually said, "Please hold one moment while I get her," and put the receiver down on the table before you realized the voice had asked for you.

When you picked up the receiver again and said hello, he said he was sorry he'd taken so long to call you, but the phone wasn't listed under your name and, well, you hadn't even told him your name the night of the party, so he'd had to find that out, first—which made the whole search much longer than it would have been otherwise. He said he would send the shoe over with a bicycle messenger later that day, and he was wondering if you'd thought any more about his proposal.

"Don't you think that's moving a little fast?" you said.

All right, then. He'd settle for a week at his favorite resort in Hawaii. "Lovely people there," he said.

And you, seeing what a grand opportunity this was—knowing that, if you married him, you would never have to return to this house and, if you divorced him, the alimony would be extravagant, and if you only led him on for a while you would at least be able to depend on him for food and shelter for as long as things lasted—it occurred to you that perhaps your job security was no longer as critical as it had been to you these past few years. Besides that, it was time for a vacation. "I'll call you back," you told him.

You told me all of this later at three A.M., just after sneaking into my room and shaking me awake. I smelled something familiar and warm and opened my eyes to see your silhouette sitting on the edge of my bed. "The shoe was returned this afternoon," you said, "with a note." You flicked my reading light on and I closed my eyes until I was ready to let my pupils adjust.

When I opened my eyes, you handed me the note. It was on a white note card embossed with his initials: KRW. I read the note: *I look forward to meeting you somewhere other than a party. Too many people have more than one face: the one they wear in public and to impress, and the one they wear when they are alone and themselves. With you, I finally seem to have found a woman who doesn't believe in masks.* There was more—some fancy babble about this and some sappy prose about that—but it was all so horrible and fake that I've done my best to repress that memory.

"Oh, puke," I said. "He obviously doesn't know that wasn't the real you."

"How would you know?" you said. "Just because I dressed oddly doesn't mean I acted out of the ordinary. You're just jealous."

I handed the note back to you and flicked off the light. "Let's say you did, though, act unlike yourself. His note is basically saying that's what he likes and you better as hell act like that all the time if you expect to get along with him. He's trying to control you. You'll get screwed."

"No," you said. "You didn't talk to him. He's too vulnerable to also be manipulative. It wouldn't occur to him to victimize someone."

"Not even someone half his age?"

I felt you grinning in the dark. "I'm not half his age—just a decade and some younger."

I poked my finger into your ribs and you giggled and kissed me. I backed away. "I don't understand why you're doing this," I said.

"If you spent every night in the basement, you would," you said. "I have to get away."

"You could get a job somewhere else," I said. "Something that pays well."

"Easy for someone who's never worked a day in her life to say."

"Maybe I could help you, with money and stuff," I said.

"Your only source of money is your mother."

"It was your father's once."

"But now it's hers."

Silence gaping wide. It is a hole in the earth, at the edge of which everything—my night table, our sad breathing, your sharp green eyes—teeters, threatening to fall. This hole is unforgiving and ready to swallow everything.

"Ella . . ." I whispered, afraid that the noise would knock you into the hole—and how would I be able to retrieve you then?

"No," you said. "I've made up my mind. Please—now let's talk about something else, or nothing at all. Arguing is no way to leave you."

A kiss. You kiss me and I'll do anything you say. I am no longer mine to think or worry or argue. I am yours. You are the stars flickering at me through a dank, smoggy sky.

Your leaving was unannounced to everyone but me. Not even Ken Worthy knew about it; he knew that you were coming to him, but he didn't know who you were leaving, too. He knew nothing about you. The afternoon you left, you said the same of me.

You knocked on my door. Mother was home, sunning on the terrace, but it wouldn't have mattered if she'd been standing in the hallway staring at you—you were leaving and she had no control over you now.

You entered and your eyes were red. "The limo's here for me," you said.

I wondered if I kissed you, would it empty you and make you understand finally that your life is unrealizable without me?

But when I stepped closer to you, you backed away. So I

chose words instead of actions: "I don't think you know what you're doing."

Even the outer edges of your tired red eyes smiled. "I don't think you know me quite well enough to say."

But I have known you for so long; I have thought to know many things but, of all of them, have only known you. But I was weak and tired and couldn't say the words.

"You will write?" I said.

"Write my heart out," you said. With that, you turned and left me.

In the papers, they interview you. The magazines love you. You are the rags-to-riches story, the all-American dream. They show color spreads of you and Ken Worthy in your beach house with your two Labrador retrievers, Jackie and Muff. They show you and Ken lounging on your back porch just before sunset, drinking fruit shakes from cobalt blue glasses. You tell them about your life before you found your wonderful husband—"the sweetest man alive," you call him. In all the pictures, you stare into the camera, a smile fixed onto your face. The corners of your eyes do not turn up.

You tell them about your tragic family life: your mother, "an angel," who died on your second day of kindergarten; your father, who remarried years later and died in the third year of that marriage. "The official diagnosis," you said, "was cancer. But I think he would've defeated it under other circumstances. He was almost three years into this marriage, and he realized that his new wife was nothing like my mother. He had nothing to live for. He died of a broken heart. He told me just before he died, 'Never marry just because it seems like the thing you should do. Don't marry for money or comfort or any of that. Do it for love.'" You told the reporters about the stepmother who abused you, about the stepsisters who did nothing to defend you. "The older one," you said, "actively hated me. The younger one was simply a passive co-conspirator."

They ask you how you overcame these obstacles, they comment on how difficult it must have been. You construct a fairy tale: had it not been for the help of a generous godmother, you never would have met your wonderful husband. You do not mention the role I played in your love story.

I know you are only saying these things about me to create a public image of yourself, to please the press. Because you can't tell them how much I love you, because then they would know that Ken Worthy is not the love of your life, and they'd have to stop writing articles about you two entitled "Hollywood's Happiest Couple." It would be horrible publicity. It would put a damper on Ken's career and your marital security.

Is that also why you have yet to write, Ella, why you haven't been able to pick up the phone and dial? Are you afraid of the sound of my voice, of remembering that you loved me and of how this love which you cannot control will show in your face and in those pictures of you and Ken and Jackie and Muff?

How frightened are you?

I have been without you for so long that if you put a classified in the paper for a maid, I would apply for the job. When you hired me, you could tell Ken that I was a refugee and you wanted to take me in as your own personal cause. I would speak to him in broken English. To you, I would speak in a language altogether different, a language we would invent ourselves and that only we would understand.

I would dust your grand piano, polish your floors, clean your toilets, serve your guests platters of fruit and pastries and cheese puffs. I would wash all of your silks by hand and iron them while they were still slightly damp. I would take over for the security guards when they got tired. I would stand watch against burglars and attackers while you slept in the room that you and Ken share. I would work until my skin peeled off.

I would only step out of my role when no one was looking, when the guests had gone home and your husband was out of town on a film shoot and all the curtains in the house were drawn. We would meet in the dark, where the security cameras couldn't see us. We could be who we truly are.

Life is so foggy without you. I feel like I'm breathing water.

Don't think I think about you all the time, even though I do. I try not to. I try to forget. I read, I paint, I swim. I houseclean. But it's hard to become distracted by much of anything when the world no longer exists.

I go down to your room every day, Ella. *(The quietness of the dark.)* The room is as you left it: Mother is afraid to go down there to throw your things out, and she hasn't gotten around yet to hiring someone to burn them, as she's threatened. Time passes and I wonder if she remembers that your ghost is still down there.

I have a daily ritual. I unfold and refold your pairs of jeans; I unbutton my blouse and crawl into one of your T-shirts. I sit on your mattress and turn on the reading light and stare at my hands and the rough white walls. I feed the mouse that keeps getting caught in your trap. Then, just before I leave the room, I open the trap door and it scurries away.

It makes no difference how often I let it go, Ella. It will always be caught again by tomorrow.

# Birding in Utah

## KAREN COOK

*I* had been afraid to leave home, but once I did, the relief was enormous. I'd left my dog with a friend. I had no responsibility for her, didn't need to walk or feed or even love her. I didn't miss her. I forgot my apartment: it was nearly perfect, being reasonably priced, spacious, and overlooking a park. But I hated it, the boxlike prison of its walls, the way the air outside and the trees could not enter, the endless taunting of the beautiful world that never came in to embrace the bed I restlessly slept in each night alone.

I was thousands of miles away from the daily sight of my kitchen, the long corridor that friends always envied, imagining the culinary equipment they might buy and hang, the meals they might cook. I had even given up heating milk for my coffee so I wouldn't have to scrub the pot. And I marked the passage of my life by the accumulation of round foil dishes left over from the Chinese food I occasionally took out: if I didn't rinse and recycle them, I saved them to use as ashtrays when my despair grew so great I began to smoke at home. Cigarettes made me sick, and I inhaled the bitter smoke like a penance, feeling the poisons stick to my teeth, watching the ashes piling against the shiny ridges of silver as my own nausea grew.

I had been feeling something unaccustomed for days now: a kind of joy. This was a month-long flight. I hadn't prepared for it—I only knew I was headed toward Utah, because there was a bird sanctuary there, and that I was running from X. I'd bought a battered old Nissan from a friend who swore it wouldn't get past Manhattan, but it did: it hummed. The first day I drove seven hours and arrived late at night in Virginia, where I unpacked my tent and dumped the pieces on the ground. I dug out a small flashlight and held it in my mouth, illuminating the green fabric and poles and stakes, walking around in circles until the work was done. The S-hooks that would attach the fly to the roof pole were missing, but the air was still. The world was generous and I slept well. In the morning I took a walk and saw pink flowering trees and heard a bear grunt and flee through the underbrush. I sat by a creek and opened my notebook on my knees, but did not write a word. I watched a thrush flit among the rocks.

For the rest of the trip, I resolved that I would try not to think. I would allow myself to drift, the way I did through the streets of New York City as an adolescent, a perpetual voyeur to an endless spectacle I would neither touch nor be touched by. I would watch but seek no meaning. I stashed my journal in a box in the backseat; I had already tried to write pleasure into life and failed. Instead I composed postcards. I sent one a day to my sister, to an acquaintance who liked travel, and to X, who did not love me. I wrote myself down and mailed myself away. I thought that out here I might have the courage to believe I existed even if I kept no records at all.

I drove to Oklahoma City, a sad gray metropolis where a bomb had exploded, killing hundreds. The people were gone and the building was gone; all that remained were shards of wood and metal, tattered flags, and neighboring windows without glass. I was acutely aware that I too could vanish from the map, leaving only a trail of postcards. I dialed X and hung up. I called my answering machine and listened to my voice telling me I wasn't home. I bought an apple and sliced it with my pen knife, devouring it along with moldy, melted cheese and Triscuits from a blue metal plate that slid on the dashboard. I drove hundreds of miles into the setting sun and watched a black cat dash into the tires of an eighteen-wheeler and shatter into the air. My eyes grew so tired I couldn't tell which was real, the headlights or their shadows. Insects splattered against the windshield in such numbers I had to stop at a gas station to scrape them off, thinking, against my will, that maybe every freedom kills something else.

At three A.M. I checked into a cheap room in an aging hotel on the Arizona border. The Pakistani clerk fretted over me: it was chilly, he insisted, and he banged on the door until I let him start the gas heater. As the warmth spread, I lay on a sagging mattress and contemplated the flecks of dead mosquitos on the white stippled walls. I wound and rewound my memories of the dead cat, watching it splatter forward and back, in slow motion and fast. I turned on the TV and saw killer tornadoes bearing down on towns in a videotape you could buy through the mail. I began to experience an urgent desire. I worked my fingers deep inside myself. I moaned when I came. The next night, and nights after that, I lay in my tent and tried to make up for coming fast by coming often, not caring any longer about the dirty nails on fingers I could never get clean in cold-water washrooms. I wandered through deserts, hands under my shirt, stroking my breasts. I lay on dead, dry leaves and arid stream beds, unzipping my fly, working down my underwear, thrusting my pelvis toward the sky, the penetrating heat, praying that the sun itself would fuck me.

I met a friend in Las Vegas and we traveled together. Her ex-boyfriend had stood her up out here the year before. "We'll be girls," she said. I showed her birds—mountain bluebirds, Clark's nutcracker, California quail. She bought me earrings, promised makeup lessons, showered me with lotions and conditioners. And that was friendship: She didn't want me, and I certainly didn't want her. No: only her legs, the grace with which she lowered her hands into the water when she swam, her thick luxuriant hair. I said nothing. I lay naked beside her in the sauna, my hands lightly tracing the rivulets of perspiration on my own skin, on my hips and ribs; excited goosebumps rose behind my fingertips like wake. I could no more fuck Ellen than I could fuck the sun: this was desire that could never touch anyone, hurt anyone, not her and not me.

Ellen left on a Greyhound bus in the middle of the night. I

bought coffee and stood by myself in the parking lot clutching a Styrofoam cup, trying to remember what I was doing out here. I'd come because I'd read *Refuge,* a book by a Mormon naturalist named Terry Tempest Williams. The author's mother had been dying slowly of cancer during the same years that the waters of Great Salt Lake had risen and gradually covered the shores of Bear River, Williams's favorite bird sanctuary. She would drive out there in the mornings, watch what remained, and struggle to make sense of life. Unlike Williams, I had no faith. But I had secretly hoped that if I drove to her place in Utah, if I squatted in the sand with binoculars, field guide, and coffee, I might feel it.

Two days later, I skirted Salt Lake City, a sprawling expanse shrouded in smog. I drove north toward Antelope Island, a state park in the middle of Great Salt Lake. The woman in the entry booth said that the lake had once again receded enough to permit camping. The water around the causeway glittered silver like a gate to great riches. The mountains behind me were capped with snow. A gray trail of gravel dust swirled in my mirror as I bumped toward a low grassy island, an ocher swatch with faint humps. There were no antelope here. The lone snack bar was closed. The telephones were broken. For all its promise, the place was unremittingly drab, desolate, and perfectly suited for the group of obdurate brown birds that now refused to flee from the dusty roadway in front of me. I jammed on the brakes, punched the steering wheel, and cursed.

Horned larks.

There were some birds I'd dreamed of seeing since I was a kid, just because I loved their names. This was one of them. The horns were merest tufts of feather, which made me smile. I felt chastened and ungrateful, and knew suddenly that I missed Ellen. But I had to go on. The campground was plainly visible, on a curve of shoreline with its back to the mainland, facing the impassive lake. I pitched my tent. There were no more than a dozen visitors, and every tent and camper seemed huddled against the barrenness. There was a wind, and a strong one, with clouds of insects blowing within it. I made a shelter of my bags, lit my stove, cut two hot dogs into six parts, and rolled them in their plate till they charred black, flavoring them with mustard and relish from stolen packets. I ate them sitting cross-legged in the dirt. There was no water on the island and I'd failed to replenish my bottles. I would have to wipe my dishes with a rag.

"Hey."

I looked up. There was someone looming over me. A woman with short blond hair, a billowing baseball jacket, and black trooper's shades.

"Hi," she said. "You've got New York plates."

"Yes," I said, surprised. She was holding a cup, and her knuckles were graceful and smooth.

"Well, I'm in the camper over there. Connecticut plates. Didn't you notice?"

I hadn't, actually. Well, maybe I had, but I'd expected a husband. I'd taken her for one of those hearty, adventurous types I'd seen riding contentedly on the back of his 'n' hers Harleys. Her features were a little heavy, and there was a faint fuzz on her jaw, but I liked her smile.

"Joanna," she said, pumping my hand. "Come on over for coffee."

I agreed. My heart began to beat harder. I felt a little sizzle of apprehension. Ordinarily her mannishness might have alarmed me, and I could hear a hint of brusqueness in her rough, friendly voice. But so what? I knew I was already hoping, helplessly and ridiculously, for a one-night stand, a wild escapade I'd never had. I gathered up my dirty dishes, dumped them in the hatch, and trotted across the scrubby hillside to her camper, hoping my eagerness wouldn't show. I fidgeted successfully with the latch and climbed in, noting the flimsiness of the door as it closed behind me. "I've never seen one of these before," I said brightly, and she let me inspect the minimal sink, the bed in the back near the small lavatory, the kitchen table with its two benches. A vase of yellow wildflowers stood on the table, and she pushed it away and instructed me to sit. How long was I out? What was I doing?

"I'm on vacation," I said. "I got four weeks off from work."

I told her it was hard for a city girl who only knew uptown and downtown to find her way under the big sky. I tried to make her laugh while she made the coffee. She was at the sink, her back was to me, and she was wearing shorts, which meant I could see her legs, which were almost elegant, long and hard and lean and tan. She looked like an athlete, with narrow hips and broad shoulders. Her coffee was weaker than I like, almost watery, but she asked me if I wanted flavoring: hazelnut, French vanilla. I picked hazelnut out of politeness, startled by the feminine touch. She'd unhitched the Charger and spent the day four-wheeling on the Bonneville flats. Then she'd gone in to see the Mormon Tabernacle, but the organ wasn't working, did I believe that? Joanna had cornered a churchwoman and said she'd consider living in Utah. There was only one problem.

"I told her, 'I'm gay. I don't see how a person like me is gonna fit in out here,' " Joanna said, laughing.

I told her about my day: a cave high in a mountain, with fresh, clear air and chickadees in the pines; an open-pit copper mine so big you could see it from outer space; a quick tour of the university's natural history museum. Afterward I'd searched out a woman's bookstore in the second story of an upscale mall. Very fancy, I told her, all flowered dresses and cappuccino. The gay section, I said, took up one corner in the rear of the store.

She sat back in her seat, the shiny blue jacket that said "Jo" still half zipped. She tapped her coffee cup on the table and smirked until I looked up and met her eyes. They were a delicate green.

"I thought so," she said, grinning. "Woman alone, New York plates. Had to be."

Moments later, she was pouring pink grapefruit juice into tall glasses, lacing it with vodka, swirling the ice with a playful flourish. She asked for my story. I would have been delighted to have seemed important, confident, experienced. I was employed by a famous publishing company, but Joanna hadn't heard of it. I'd stayed with my first lover for nine years. She'd wanted to stay in the closet, and for the longest time I'd been only too happy to dodge fear with comfort. There had been a few affairs since, I said vaguely, warding off some outpouring about X. X, who'd plunged her fist deep into me and shocked us both by withdrawing a hand smeared with my blood, and then made me want her so much it was terrifying. X, who'd told me I was pampered, selfish, and middle-class, and made her world seem more real than anything I had ever known. Greedy, selfish, manipulative—wonderful, goddamned X, who'd left me so long ago I should have forgotten. She'd left me stranded.

I noticed, suddenly, that Joanna was like her—tough, capable, and versatile. Just when you got used to her looking like a mechanic, she'd be sweeping you off your feet in a dress. I could guess from her swagger, her charm, the appraising way she cocked her head, that Joanna knew all that X did.

"Lately," I said, "I'm learning how to live alone."

Joanna was thirty-two, younger than me. Coming out meant nothing to her; she'd been out since she was nine. She was a security guard in a chemical plant, had been since high school. Her mother had worked there, and so had most of her extended family. The odors never left their skins. They were Czech, and they still barely spoke English. Joanna signed on for every second of overtime she could. She'd saved her money and renovated a small apartment building in the slums. She threw bottles at the junkies to make them respect her. She'd rented to a student, a Jew, and a nigger. She said that word. She bought into a car wash, and she and her partner skimmed quarters off the top. Her wife had said if she got into cars they'd break up, because Jo already worked all the time.

I couldn't imagine having a wife.

"I thought I was doing it for both of us," Joanna said. She flicked off the overhead light and lit candles. The flame flickered, and I could see the hints of creases on her face. Now her wife was gone. This spring, when an uncle who'd worked in the plant had died of cancer and left her his pension, she bought a little Mallard camper and asked for a leave. She left the car wash to her partner. Out here on the road, she'd discovered a deep fatigue. She was sick of poor people pretending they'd lost money in the machines, fed up with chemicals and nasty, lazy men who tried to make her feel cheap. She was tired of being resented for her ambition and afraid she'd gotten too hard to love. She was exhausted from being ugly. She wanted something nice.

She looked down at her hands. After she'd rinsed out the coffee cups, she'd carefully massaged them with cream. I didn't think she was used to saying these things. I could see her dream, or thought I could, the uncomplicated yearning for the small white house with the white picket fence, the tidiness and the flowers. I thought it would be condescending to tell her I was sorry, that I could see her pain, that she moved me. I asked if she often came to New York. She said she wanted to see *Cats,* but hadn't; she'd seen the Kathy and Mo comedy show, twice. She loved a sketch that sounded just like a country song, about a drunken guy who flirted madly until the prospect of matrimony was floated before him. The punchline was, "My, you look vurry vurry purty tonight."

Joanna leaned in toward me. "My, you look vurry vurry purty tonight," she said, and grinned.

It grew late, though I hadn't noticed. I hadn't drunk in weeks, but I had one drink, and another, and a third. When Joanna pulled out her minted Merits, I began to smoke. Joanna had been in the Tetons, had met two young lovers with a new tent. They couldn't keep their hands off each other. Joanna read them a story she'd written, a tale so steamy the two women had to retreat to their sleeping bag. When they returned, the three went into town and sat on saddle barstools and teased a fourth woman, a straight one they hoped might join in the game. It went on and on into the night. I fantasized about the four of them, the leather and denim and finally all the tan, bare skin by lantern light. Then Joanna told me another tale, about her ex's best friend, who'd climbed into bed and begged her for sex. Joanna did not oblige.

"Oh, she was hot," Joanna said. "What would you do?"

"I guess you did the right thing," I said.

She pointed out it was windy outside, that she herself would never sleep in a tent on a night like this. She folded down the kitchen tabletop and told me I should sleep inside. Without the table she seemed very close. I stared at the arc of her undershirt and the line of her skin. Was she flirting with me? I didn't dare believe it. Ordinarily my pride would have prevented me from deserting my tent, but in this instance I decided not to refuse. She walked me outside with a flashlight to check out the weather. It was blowing like a hurricane.

"Look what you left," she said, pointing to the car keys that in my rush I'd left dangling from the hatch. "Do you do this in the big city?"

"Wow, you really are a cop," I said, as if I weren't embarrassed. I dug my toiletries from beneath the dirty dishes. Back in the camper, I squirmed into a pair of her narrow sweats and lay down woozily on the kitchen table bed. I saw the faint dark outline of Joanna's arms, her strong shoulders, as she stripped off her shirt. I wondered if she might join me. I wondered if I was supposed to slip into bed with her—quietly, nonchalantly, or with some low sexy words. Surely X would have fucked her already. And if I were the kind of person who could get into bed with Joanna, perhaps X would still be fucking me. But what if I was wrong? What if she thought I was crazy? I lay awake and agonized, listening to the faraway sound of my tent flapping violently in the wind. Long after Joanna began to snore, I fell asleep.

"Use the shower," she said, in the morning, lighting up a Merit, a towel draped over her shoulder. No, I said; I would swim in the lake. "Have some coffee," she said. I argued I couldn't impose. "Come on," she said. She made me coffee. She handed me a bowl of oatmeal, a tasteless, pasty gruel. She gave me a cigarette. We sat in beach chairs and smoked, gazing out at the lake.

I knew I had to get in that lake, whether it was briny or clouded with flies, or I would lose myself. "You should go nude," she said. "Go skinny-dipping, I'll take your picture."

I'd have done that at night, but it didn't seem right as I watched the families in their little pickups pulling into the beachfront parking lot. It wasn't shyness, really. If only you could reach me, I thought, I lose all my inhibitions if you can get my clothes off.

"All those women," I said, on my third cup of coffee, "did you sleep with them all?"

"What women?" she said.

"You know, the ones in the Tetons."

"What do you think I am?" she said. "Do you think I'm easy?"

"No, no—I was just wondering."

"This is a *virgin* camper," she declared, waving to the sleek plastic box. It sounded like a joke, but her body looked stiff and angry.

I apologized again, for some way that I completely misunderstood the world.

"You do. You think I'm easy!" she said.

"I really don't," I answered. "What are you doing today?"

"I'm going to go check out that Golden Spike, then I have to get to Montana. I'm four days late already," she said. There was an old lover up there.

"I'm going to the Golden Spike," I said, "and then I'm going to the Tetons."

"You're going to meet all these women and you're going to invite them into your tent," she said.

"Yeah, right."

"Were you afraid when I invited you in last night?"

"Ahhh, yes," I said.

She grinned. "My, you look vurry vurry purty this morning," she said.

I retreated to my tent, where I hastily slipped on the frayed blue one-piece bathing suit I'd had since college. Then I folded up the tent and stowed it in the car. "You sure are fast," she said. I felt obscurely pleased, the way I did when X told me that I peed faster than any other woman she'd ever met. But I wasn't fast, it was just that I'd never unpacked, never unrolled the mattress and sleeping bag or blown up the little pillow, never spread out my clock and contacts and flashlight and books.

Joanna did her dishes and put them away, restored the

kitchen table, and anchored her flowers in a corner of the seat with a pile of clean, impeccably folded clothes. She took down some Tupperware and insisted on giving me a bowl of cool, red, beautifully sliced watermelon.

"That way you'll have to see me again."

"What?"

"To return this," she said.

Then she drove off to empty the septic tanks of the camper. I drove down the road to the beach, to the Great Salt Lake. I could float there, weightless. I piled my clothes and knapsack on the pebbly shore, and began to wade. I waded and waded and waded and still the water had barely reached my knees. I finally dove in and did float, in brine not much more than a foot deep. I would need to swim for miles to see if I could float with my feet down. And I might have done that, but I could see that Joanna had arrived and was sitting on the beach, arms embracing her knees, in denim shorts cut off like hot pants.

I splashed back in, nervously conscious of the hair on my legs, under my arms, along the crotch of my bathing suit. We collected my camera and she unlaced her boots and waded in. She pointed the lens down me, her jacket still puffed around her in the wind, the collar brushing against her crewcut, and snapped pictures of me floating there. I tried to smile alluringly, like a Hollywood bathing beauty. I went to the showers and tended to my body with shampoo and conditioner and all the moisturizers Ellen had left me. I brushed my hair, combing it back. I twisted on my new blue earrings. I wore the turquoise sleeveless shirt without the bra. I ignored the sensations of my nipples brushing against fabric, the inside of my arms rubbing against my rib cage, all the unnerving reminders of raw flesh. I admired my shoulders. My legs felt firm. I put on my sunglasses and glowed into the mirror.

I followed Joanna's Mallard. It was wide enough to block the view; she was all I could see. She'd told me people who drove for a living were constantly aroused; I thought of that every time I shifted gears. I'd never felt so much lust while sitting upright, not to mention while wearing a seatbelt. My center felt comically squishy. I couldn't stop smiling. When we arrived at a gas station a man in the convenience store eyed me and said, "Tell me, where's the party? I want to go." Joanna's taillight had burned out. She bought a new one, and I sat giddily in the high, luxurious cab of her truck, turning the lights on and off, trying to follow the orders she shouted over the roar of the radio I couldn't turn off. She had a giant white teddy bear in the passenger seat.

And then we drove to Promontory, Utah, where the tracks of the transcontinental railroad had been joined. It was way out of the way, on dusty roads. The two railroad companies had been so eager for land grants that they'd actually passed each other on their journeys east and west, laying track and claiming property. For nearly two hundred miles they'd run parallel, before someone had stopped them and ordered the tracks to meet. The site was irrelevant now; the trains had long since shifted to another line out in the Great Salt Lake, and the golden spike they'd hammered in for publicity had been uprooted and stored in a California museum. We watched two restored locomotives back up and down a small length of track and bought postcards and souvenir handbills and went to the bathroom, then climbed into her camper to say farewell.

We faced each other and hugged, and she kissed me. Or I kissed her. I reached for her mouth, her tongue. I'd nearly forgotten how my body could dissolve. She grasped my shoulders, slid her arms behind my back, and pulled me close. Her face had gone all soft and narrow, had lost its squareness, its hard edge. She shimmered before me, beautiful, and kissed me again. I laughed, or sighed, in delight.

"Come with me," she said. "Come with me to Elk Lake. I know a gorgeous spot, a place where we can camp."

"Yes," I said.

"Yes?" She sounded surprised. She kissed me again. And then she pushed me away, looked into my eyes.

"Can I call you?" she asked. "Can I call you when you get back to New York?"

"Sure," I said. "Yes, sure."

Suddenly I imagined her standing beside me in New York. There was an awkwardness between us. We were in Shubert Alley, momentarily frozen in the marquee lights. She had gotten splendidly, proudly dressed, in a dark suit and pink silk shirt. I was wearing jeans and worrying she might say nigger. My friends looked on in disbelief. I knew we had nothing to say.

"Wait," I said miserably. "Do you mean date me? Do you mean you want to date me when we get back to New York?"

"Never mind," she said. "We'll talk about it when we get there. Follow me. And turn your headlights on, so I know you're back there. I couldn't stand it before, thinking I might have lost you."

"Okay," I said.

I got back into my car, alone, and turned on the lights. My desire surged again and fell away. As we approached the superhighway, I saw a sign for the Bear River Migratory Refuge. In my rush after Joanna I'd forgotten it completely. I felt an unbearable ache: Here was the whole point of my trip, and I could not stop. Moreover, I would not stop, and I knew that I would never return. Egrets and glossy ibis flew over the road. Six glorious yellow-headed blackbirds sat to the right on a bale of hay. I kept my foot on the accelerator, inhaled the exhaust of Joanna's plastic Mallard, and began to cry.

Three hours later we arrived at the shore of a lake and parked between huge mobile homes. I registered my car at her campsite and she paid for it; when I tried to offer money, she said I was insulting. I drove back to the office with our site number and left a message on my answering machine giving her name and our location, in case I died here. I hoped we might have sex immediately. Instead she turned on the radio and began installing vinyl rain shields to her windows. I fetched the watermelon from my car so I could get the container back into her refrigerator. "Don't want the fruit to go bad," I said. I piled up her firewood and built a fire, as she'd asked, and popped open a Coors, a brand I detested. She began to fix dinner, frozen chicken her mother had made her, white rice, frozen Brussels sprouts that did not thaw. I wondered if the chemical plant had affected her sense of taste. I could barely swallow.

"Are you always this nervous, or is it only me?" she asked.

I wanted her to fuck me and that was that. And I didn't ever want to see her again, but that was more than I could say. Instead we talked and made marshmallows and moved closer to and away from the heat of the fire. We read Chinese tarot cards, and I drew an opposum, a creature of deceit. I asked her more and more about her life, her security job, her coin-operated car wash. When she asked about mine I said I was conflicted about my work and spent a lot of money on therapy, and there seemed absolutely nothing about me that made any sense. I remembered my job, my apartment, my dog, my hopeless and twisted love. I stood in the doorway and stared out at the lake, all the bitter fragments of the life I'd tried to leave behind swirling around me like evening gnats that would not be brushed away.

"Do you think couples can last?" she asked me.

I said I didn't see how.

"What about common goals?" she asked.

"Like what?" I snarled. "A house?"

Finally we went to bed. I once again donned the sweatpants and this time lay down beside her. It wasn't worth folding down the kitchen table. I reached for her and kissed her lips, which didn't part. I put my hand on the curve of her clothed hip.

"It's been three years since I've slept with anyone," I said.

"Three years? Jesus!" she said. She rolled over, turned away.

In the morning we had coffee and looked out at a new lake. "Look, there are white pelicans," I said. She did not look. I thanked her for sleeping with me. "Hot enough for ya?" she asked. Dressed in layers of clothing, we'd both been drenched in sweat.

"Yeah," I said.

"These days I'm into quality, not quantity."

I might have been offended, but instead I was relieved.

"No problem," I said.

I had nothing to pack, and she had chores to do. "Wait, I've got something for you," she said. I stood outside while she went into the Mallard, emerging with small sheaf of looseleaf pages, stapled together. "Here's what drove those girls back to that sleeping bag," she told me.

"My, you look very very purty this morning," I said, smiling. I couldn't wait to leave.

I haven't seen her since that bright, sunny day in Utah. I threw her pages in the car and sped off while she was still un-hooking the electric lines. But I dawdled so long at the gas station in town, trying to collect myself, that I was just paying up when she pulled in. She dropped out of the cab, took me by the shoulders, and kissed me one last time, right out there in front of the KOA and the convenience store, in the middle of redneck nowhere. Again I tasted the moistness of her lips.

"Call me," she said, and of course I never did.

But I think of Joanna sometimes. And I think of her story, too, when I am at home on my couch, looking out toward the trees. It's written in blue ballpoint, each letter careful and loopy. She calls the clitoris a pearl, pubic hair a forest, the vagina a love canal. These words make me squirm. But the third page always makes me laugh. It's blank, except for one statement:

STOP.
YOU KNOW YOU WANT MORE.

And I do. I find myself reaching for the gaps in my bathrobe, or starting to unzip my fly. Sometimes I forget completely about X. Here's Joanna in the Mallard's tiny shower, with her lovely legs. She has shed her clothes, her dark sunglasses; her skin is slick with water, her crewcut wet and soft with shampoo. I've opened the frosted glass door. I slide in behind her, along the length of her, my hands spreading lather to her smooth breasts, her rising nipples; around the flat stomach, down to her thighs. I undulate against her, gently fasten the leather straps of our har-ness, telling her how much I love her, how much I need her. I know she will turn then, and guide the smooth rubber into me, thrust gently but hard, in a beautiful rhythm that makes me begin to climb, higher and higher, up into the clear air and a place where the birds sing like a heavenly choir. I come before she's even completed that turn.

# *Strip Uno*

## JoNelle Toriseva

*I*t is ten o'clock Saturday night. Chloe, Olivia, Vita, and I are drinking cranberry tea, arguing about Kierkegaard and playing a wild game of sexually charged Strip Uno. We have only this last night together before Olivia flies to Montreal to show our nine-minute short at the film festival.

And suddenly it is her. I am pouring tea and all of a sudden she, my little sister, has arrived one whole night early. Vita pulls on her green Crew sweatshirt. Olivia yanks my first T-shirt over her head. Chloe pretends her bra is her usual mode of attire. We all turn to stare at my fundamentalist, rodeo champion, gainfully employed, semi-psychotic sister with no secrets who has arrived one whole night early.

I pour the cranberry tea into the damask tablecloth. One hand holds the yellow handle and one holds the top. Down down down pours the bright red tea.

She stands there full of impoliteness. The rudeness runs down her fingernails.

She looks at my clothes and bursts out laughing, "You look just like Dad! Those are the kind of pants that Dad wears!"

"So?" I feel Olivia standing behind me, we are breathing on cue. Vita and Chloe smile at me. They see so much. I am transparent before them.

I am not adept at fighting with my sister. We were always silent working partners. And now she stands in my kitchen, staring in open-mouthed horror at my friends and me.

I am enraged. I turn my flank—like this heavily muscled

black Angus bull we used to have. I turn, and smelling my own blood upon her eyes . . . I want to gore her. . . . How dare she question my life which has been newly shown to her? . . . but she is out of the door frame and walking into my unclean room. Vita touches my fingertips. Chloe squares my shoulders with her hands as I turn away.

My sister points to the Frida Kahlo poster over the fireplace, "Who is that?" Her eyes are wide.

"You know, she's that painter from Mexico."

She lowers her voice, "Why is she dressed like a man?"

"Why do you think?"

She shakes her head, disengages herself from the eyes in the picture, "I wouldn't know. Why would I?"

That is the last question before she collapses into silence from the heaviness of driving for days cross-country. As she sleeps my secrets string me up higher and higher from bed to chandelier to ceiling. I have had no time to cover my secrets, to arrange my housemates and the hodgepodge of construction jobs we use to finance our movies into an explanation my sister would embrace. My sister and I, we used to think the same—but falling in love changed me.

The next morning I walk quietly back into the bedroom after driving Olivia to the airport. Hannah rolls over in her sleeping bag and asks me, "Is Chloe going to miss Olivia a lot?"

"Wouldn't you?"

She looks at me, I stare back hard. I am guarding myself against her. Backs to each other, we wait for nine, ten, and eleven in the morning. She is sleeping in judgment of me.

I feel like a broken teapot. I have been shattered. And I have pasted myself back together with Crazy Glue. My fault lines are sore.

My sister is severing me from her spine. My sister—she is holding my old mind. I steal myself from her (steal, steel, steal).

Her mind gears in our mutual past of parents, rodeo, and church. What have they told her about the missing of people? About how Chloe misses Olivia?

Sin. The word slinks in her sleeping bag. Sin. Sin. Sin.

I turn over.

I burrow into my quilt.

Backs to each other the sun rises over my sister and I run through our shared history in Plentywood, Montana. A place so close to the border, we only had to stretch our arms out to touch Canada.

My sister, we would go haying. My sister, we picked rock, we sang "Amazing Grace" in church together.

We were five, we were seven, we were ten. It was night, sweet night, we were under the stars listening to wind roaring over the prairie, elk snorting in the cottonwoods, cows on the range.

I wanted my sister to grow up strong. I taught her how to climb to the top of the barn and come down quick without burning her hands.

She was traveling the rodeo circuit. She would call me late at night from strange motels, the kind that have one pay phone under a light. I could hear the June bugs hitting that light.

Me.

I'd always be leaving northeastern Montana for Mexico. Norway. Spain. Minneapolis.

My sister and I did not grow apart. We were cleft.

I was always hitting the gas, hitting the road, tearing my ticket, burning the map.

My sister has saved me several times. Once my sister and I were working cattle. We held down the calf, me on front legs, her on back, while my father vaccinated and then branded the calf. Straight arrow on left hip. That's our brand.

This calf was kicking, kicking, kicking. And I saw my sister losing him as my father swept the red iron toward the calf's flank and I reached to help my sister keep the calf down and the calf swiveled up and my father slipped and the branding iron passed my leg. Lighted my leg. Seared my right calf. Jeans tore, my skin burned, puckered, and smoked. My sister tipped the bucket of disinfectant on my leg, she dragged me to the water tank.

Waist-deep in water, the burning quenched.

Another time, we were in the north pasture and I was roping a hurt filly when the mare came at me. She reared and charged and I fell. I couldn't get any air. Dirt plugged my nostrils. In the moment before I was to be stomped into the ground, I looked up as the mare's belly arches and there was my sister, standing between the horse's hooves and me. She reached down and picked me up.

My sister would save me like that time and time again.

We worked well together. We worked well together in that other life, that life of our past, not my life now. She does not enter my present life. I am incomprehensible to her. My friends, their love for each other is wrong to her. We are consigned to hell. I buy a ticket to hell, hell, hell.

## *Visit*

The only flames I felt in Guatemala were from candles at night. In Todos Santos, high up in the Cuchumanates I was taller, lighter than everyone. One noon I was walking past the market, swinging my Mam language books and the hard clipboard holding my notes.

I passed tomatoes, pots, hats, blankets. I passed the *tienda*. And then I felt hot breath reheating the old scar on my calf and glanced down and saw a dog's fangs ready to close around my leg. Too surprised to break my stride, I hit his head with the clipboard. Out of nowhere, a basketball hit him in the side and the dog lurched off. The basketball disappeared and I kept walking in shock to the square. There, by the fountain, I sat and examined my leg. There was no blood, no teeth marks, only the shirred skin of the old scar.

A few days passed. I watered the pines in the reforestation nursery. I cooked black beans. I studied Mam nouns.

Later, three men arrived at the house. Like my sister and my father, they do not comprehend me. They cannot read my differences. After two hours of weak sugared coffee, they asked, "Where are you from?"

"How did you come here?"

"How long would it take us to walk to the United States?"

"Why weren't you afraid of the dog?"

"Can we see your leg?"

They glanced at each other nervously.

They talked to my friend. They said, "She didn't look afraid of the dog and it didn't hurt her at all. Some of the older people think that perhaps she is a *dueña de la cerra*—an owner of the mountain top come down. They want to know what she wants from us."

The next day they took me to see the diviner Don Chel. The diviner keeps time according to the Mayan calendar. He interprets illnesses, omens, dreams, messages given by bodies and the rhythm of time, the deity who names each one of the 260 days of the Mayan year. He is to bring what is dark into light.

We passed through a wall made of dried cornstalks. And walked into a room made of bricks of dried earth. They bow to the diviner. Don Chel's face was set in ancient lines. Never had I seen a man so old. He said, "This day is the holy day Eight Monkey in the year Eleven Thought."

He splashed *aguardiente* on the fire. He lits four candles. We sat on the bench together. Rain fell. A turkey walked in and out of the room. The corncob walls rustled in the wind.

He made a sharp genuflection at the altar.

The turkey brushed by me.

He said, "You may have two husbands here." He smiled.

I shook his hand. We nodded at each other and I was free to leave.

## The Now

In San Francisco, I stare at her. We are sisters. We wear a fifty-four-inch rawhide belt pulling us together at the waist. We stand at the edge of the ocean. My right arm sticks out of the mustard sweater. My sister's left arm sticks out of the sweater. The sweater has yarn like my father's chest hair on the outside.

The sweater buttons up to our chins and holds both of us perfectly.

I am at the place I began.
   I have begun.
   I am entwined. Twined. Tautly knotted to these people. My tight pulling has seasoned the ropes.
   Without asking, my sister unbuttons the sweater. Gently, she lifts my arm out and slithers her arm into the sleeve. The sweater shrinks to her, I can see the teacup underside of her breasts, I see the turtledove of her hips. She buttons the sweater straight up—the split of her ribs becoming a single white line.
   Suddenly, I am unsweatered. I shiver at the edge.
   I lean into the shore, looking down the belly of the ocean to the end of it.
   Without asking, my sister unzips the skin that holds us together.
   She is closing her eyes against me.
   She is cutting me—like the cattle.

> *She is branding me forever.*
> *I am singeing in her mind.*
>    *This is how the world*
> *did not begin*
> *was split*
> *cut in half*
> *the sister unbuttoned the other sister out of life.*
>
> *Set on fire*
> *the wooden sister*
> *burns slowly across the water*
> *she floats aflame.*

I stand on the stoop and wave good-bye to my sister as she drives off for Montana. I lock the door and climb the stairs up to the flat. The damask tablecloth snaps tight as I pull it between my hands as I sit at the table. Water boils for tea. Vita deals the cards. Uno. Strip Uno. I run my blue T-shirt like a flag from the light fixture. A testament to revealment, it hangs there, two weeks later, greeting Olivia when she returns home.

# When You Wish Upon the Moon

## RHOMYLLY B. FORBES

*T*he soft, inviting ambience of the White Raven Bookstore and Coffeehouse was even more welcome than usual as I stood in the doorway and shook cold March rain out of my hair. I took my own sweet time negotiating the maze of other slightly soggy patrons and stacks of books, some new, some used, that blocked my way to the cluster of tables and booths at the back. It would kill my tough image to appear too eager—or too angry.

Tess, the cutest waitperson in three counties, intercepted me at the dessert counter that every coffee shop places at the front of the joint to lure unsuspecting clientele into gross caloric overindulgence. Bastards.

"Caroline's here."

"Yeah, I know," I growled softly.

"She's waiting for you in your usual booth." I sighed deeply and started to move past Tess but she caught the edge of my soaked leather jacket, stopping me. "Hey, Kim? I know it's been six months, but go easy on her, please? She looks like hell. Really bad. Okay?"

I sighed again. "Yeah, okay."

My heart started to pound as I caught sight of Caroline sitting in what most of the Lexington Lesbian Nation had once labeled "our" booth. To cover my nerves, I slowly removed my jacket, hung it up on a peg nearby, and sat down across from her. The rain had made her long red-gold hair curl slightly, framing violet eyes that never failed to take my breath and soul into their depths. Her white camisole top was clinging damply to some of her, ah, most outstanding features—if you know what I mean. She was beautiful. I'm over Caroline completely.

Sure I am.

On closer inspection, I realized Tess was right. There were dark smudges under those violet eyes, as if Caroline had spent too many nights sleepless, or crying, or both. Her skin was paler than usual, making her freckles really stand out. She looked like she'd lost weight. I was confused (After all, *she'd* dumped *me*. Badly.), and I hate being confused, so I angrily blurted out the first thing that came to my mind. "Why in hell did you leave a message at my mother's?"

"I needed to see you," she said simply, refusing as always to be afraid of my bluster. "And your answering machine is still broken, isn't it?"

I had to acknowledge that it was. "So now I'm here. What's up?"

She burst into tears, melting my anger completely.

Not surprising, once I heard her story. I won't give it to you exactly as she told me, because that would require a lot of hiccups and nose-blowing and funny stares from the folks at other tables, but here's most of it:

Apparently shortly after we broke up, Caroline met a woman named Diana.

"Where'd you meet her?" I asked, trying not to show how surprised and hurt I was that she'd found someone else so quickly.

"At the Womyn's Spirit Gathering," she sniffed sadly. Figures. The last big fight we had, the one that broke us up, was when I refused to go to the Gathering with her. I didn't much feel like camping out with a bunch of weirdly named, vegetarian moon worshippers. Sue me.

Anyway, they'd been seeing each other ever since but (and this is where things started to get a little strange) only once every month or so, for two or three days in a row.

Hey, I'm a reasonably intelligent person, so I asked what I thought was a reasonably intelligent question: "Where is she the rest of the time?"

More tears. It turned out Caroline didn't know. Tess brought me a cup of cappuccino and Caroline a mug of herb tea. She glared at me as if she thought Caroline's tears were somehow my fault, then wordlessly stalked off, no doubt planning to tell every other dyke in town what a horrible person I was for hurting my ex so. Wonders for my tough butch image; lousy for my future love life.

I turned my attention back to Caroline. Further questioning revealed that no, she didn't know where Diana lived, where she worked, or her phone number.

"Hell, 'Diana' might not even be her real name. After all, none of your earth mother pals use their real name half the time. What is it they call you? Crooning Wildebeest?"

"Singing Buffalo Woman."

Whatever.

"So why keep seeing this girl? Doesn't sound like there's much in it for you." *Oh, Kim,* I thought to myself, *play your cards right and you just might get Caroline back.* Nothing like helping an ex through a bad breakup to make her want to come home to you. . . .

The way her violet eyes began to glow, I knew I'd better bludgeon that dream to a premature death right now. Apparently this Diana was everything Caroline had ever wanted, ever dreamed of. Emotionally, spiritually, Diana was Caroline's perfect lover. "When she's with me, she gives me her complete self, like there's no one else in the world for her. It's almost like she, well, worships me. I can't help but worship her right back. Even though I don't— didn't—see her but once in a while, those two or three days were enough to sustain me until she came back. I kept having this feeling that somehow she was watching over me while she was gone. Like all I had to do was talk to her and she'd hear me. It is—was—so perfect."

I had to ask. My ego told me I had to ask. "And physically?"

"Oh, Kim," she breathed, setting her steaming mug precisely

in the center of her placemat. "So beautiful. Long hair—longer than mine even, and silvery blond." I opened my mouth to say something scornful about bottle blondes but Caroline anticipated me. Damn if she doesn't know me too well. "Yes, it's natural, *all* her hair is that color. . . . And her eyes are silvery gray, too. The sex was just . . . just . . . and sometimes, you know, after? Well, she *glowed* like . . ."

"That's okay," I cut in quickly. "I don't need to know, really." I felt like shit, partly because no one likes to hear they've been replaced by the perfect lover, and partly because I was beginning to smell a rat. A big, silvery blond, straight, married rat.

Caroline would not even hear me out. "No, Kim. Diana wouldn't do that to me. I *know* she wouldn't. She couldn't."

"Oh, really? Then what are you telling me this for?"

"Because I haven't seen her in over two months, Kim. And I just know something terrible has happened." I sighed. Caroline always was a little melodramatic. "And because . . . because I was hoping you'd help me find her."

"What?" I almost choked on a big swallow of cappuccino. Not every day a person is asked to help her ex find a missing lover. "How?"

"Isn't that what you do? Find missing people?"

"You know I do. But for a *collections* agency, dammit! And look at what you've given me to go on here. No last name, maybe not even her real first name. No address, no phone number, no employer. You might as well ask me to help you find a ghost!"

"But will you help me?"

"I can't."

Caroline looked stricken. "Please?"

"No."

Then she did a very mean and dirty thing. She called me by her pet name for me, which I wouldn't tell you under torture (yeah, it's that sappy), loaded up those big violet eyes and shot an arrow right into my heart, then said "Please" again. Before I could stop myself I agreed to help her, and spent the next hour or so trying to get more concrete information on the mysterious Diana. I left feeling frustrated and disheartened by how much I didn't know, but still on the "case." I'm over Caroline completely.

Sure I am.

A week later we were back in "our" booth at the White Raven comparing notes. Caroline looked a little better, a bit more rested. Actually, she seemed about to burst, like a little kid with a big important secret.

We ordered our usual cappuccino and herbal tea from Tess, who smiled knowingly at me as she took our order.

"Did you find anything?" Caroline asked breathlessly.

I hated to disappoint her. "No. No, I didn't." I looked down at my cup, carefully wrapping my hands around its smooth warmth. "I tried everywhere. Motor Vehicles doesn't have any-one in the files matching her description, and I called the people who ran the Womyn's Spirit Gathering." I paused and gritted my teeth at the memory of *that* conversation.

"What did they say?"

It was more a question of what they *didn't* say that had pissed me off. Damn fools acted as though mundane information like legal names and telephone numbers were matters of national se-curity. Don't ask me how I found out what little I did; I'm not proud of it. "Just that no one with the legal name 'Diana' reg-istered for the event." There was more, and not only did it make me doubt my ex's sanity, I was afraid it would break her heart. In spite of everything that had gone down between us, I hated the thought of breaking Caroline's heart. Call me a softy. Actually, I'd rather you didn't.

"Caroline? No one remembers seeing anyone like who you've described at the Gathering. I couldn't find her. I'm sorry." Sorry you fell in love with a straight woman who probably has a hus-band and kids somewhere, sorry I wasn't enough. . . .

Caroline's excited voice broke into my grim wallowings. "But Kim, listen! I figured out what happened to Diana, and the fact that you couldn't find anything just proves it! Look!" She pulled a battered artsy, New Agey appointment calendar out of her backpack. My heart cringed a little at the sight of that calendar—I'd given it to her for her birthday. She opened it up and shoved it across the table at me, almost spilling her tea in the process. "What do you see?"

I didn't see anything, except a few lines of illegible scribble in Caroline's distinctively horrible handwriting. One phrase looked like it might have said "Diana Visited," but it could just as easily have said "Dolphins' Violins." Caroline must have been impatient at the time it was taking to translate her hieroglyphics, because she flipped a few pages forward and pointed triumphantly to "Divas Vivid." After being shown what I swear looked like "Dances Variety" and "Diaphragm Votes," I had to honestly admit total bafflement.

"Don't you see?" She sounded like she was explaining it to a small child. "Diana only came to me on the three days and nights of the month when the moon was dark. When it was waxing, or waning, or full, she wouldn't, or *couldn't* be with me! Don't you get it?"

Apparently not.

Caroline fished a small newspaper clipping out of another pocket of her pack. "Here," she said almost smugly. "Read this!"

### TIDAL CHANGES BAFFLE SCIENTISTS

Scientists at the National Center of Oceanography are unable to explain recent drastic changes in global tidal patterns. At a press conference on Friday, a spokesman for the Center stated, "According to our international team, all tides ceased happening two months ago. We are unable to explain this phenomenon at this time."

The cessation of ebb and flow in oceans planetwide have had a major impact on international trade and local economies, but experts are unable to predict the long-range effects.

There was more, but I didn't read it. "Yeah, so?"

"So? Haven't you looked up into the night sky lately?" Caroline looked positively triumphant. Like she'd saved the best for last. "The moon! Haven't you noticed how . . . different it looks?"

I fleetingly wondered just what was in that herbal tea. "No, I haven't noticed."

"Well, it does. It's, I don't know, too smooth, too yellow, the crater patterns are wrong. Something."

I couldn't think of anything new to say to this enlightening revelation, so I repeated myself. "Yeah, so?"

"Kim, you're not listening." How many times had she said that to me while we were together? Never mind, it's none of your business. Caroline was counting on her fingers. "One: Diana came to see me for months, but only during the two or three days the moon was in its dark phase. According to legend, the dark phase was when the Moon Goddess, who the Romans called Diana, by the way, was resting somewhere on Earth, preparing for Her next month-long trek across the night sky. Two: All tides on Earth have stopped happening. Scientists don't know why, but everyone knows what *causes* the tides to happen—the moon's gravitational pull on the Earth's oceans. So the moon must be gone!" she finished confidently. "Because if it were still there, the tides would still happen. Do you know what that means?"

"No more werewolves?" I was beginning to not believe this conversation.

"Very funny. Three: The moon doesn't look right. I called my grandmother yesterday and she agreed with me. Said it didn't look right to her, either."

"Uh-huh." I remembered Caroline's grandmother. A tiny, wizened lady with a house full of cats and a kitchen full of strange-smelling dried plants hanging from the ceiling. A genuine harmless old fruitcake.

"Besides, there's something I didn't tell you about the Womyn's Spirit Gathering. While I was there, I prayed for the Goddess to send me my soulmate." Spare me, I groaned to myself. "The next day, Diana appeared on site, and you're the one who told me no one else noticed her. But we were together

there, I swear it!" Her voice was rising, and people were beginning to stare. Great. If there's one thing I hate, next to being
confused, of course, it's people staring at me.

I decided to humor her; maybe she would calm down. "So
what you're saying to me is . . . ?"

Caroline took a deep breath, and her eyes started to shine like
a child's. She spoke slowly, almost reverently. "What I'm trying to tell you, Kim, is when I asked the Goddess to bring me
love, She decided to fulfill my wish Herself. I'm trying to tell
you that Diana, the woman I have been seeing for six months
is really Diana, the Moon Goddess, spending Her three days'
dark time or rest time or whatever in my home, in my bed, with
me!"

So much for humoring her. "You're kidding."

"I'm serious. Why do you think Her hair is silver, Her eyes
are silver?"

"You said they were gray."

"I said they were both. It's why I didn't miss Her when She
was away; She was never gone. All I had to do was look up and
talk to Her. And you know what? Sometimes She knew about
things that happened while She was gone. Like when I had to
put Buttons to sleep, She knew all about it when She saw me
again and I hadn't had a chance to tell Her!"

I hadn't heard about Buttons' passing. Damn, I was really
going to miss that cat. But this wasn't the time or place to mourn
my feisty old friend. Not when I was busy trying to keep my
ex-lover from cracking up, although I suspected I was a little
too late for that.

"What about the tides? What about the funny-looking
moon?" she continued.

"What *about* them?" I countered.

"Isn't it obvious? Someone kidnapped Diana, I mean the
moon, two months ago, on the first dark-moon night when She
was on Her way to see me, and hung a fake moon in Her place
so no one would notice what they'd done. I even know who did
it and why!" Caroline finished triumphantly.

"Do you really? Do tell." Well versed I may be in Caroline's slightly skewed perception of the universe, nevertheless even I was having a pretty hard time taking this conversation seriously. I briefly wondered who she would accuse of this heinous crime: the FBI? Interpol? Carlos the International Terrorist?

"Evil creatures. You know, bogles, hants, goblins, folk like that."

Ah. "Why?"

Caroline got a dreamy, faraway look on her face. "Because they can't stand light and when She shines in the night She keeps them from working their evil magics. She forces them to hide and spoils their spells. It's why I've always loved Her so." She stopped and looked resolutely at me. "And it's why we have to rescue Her."

"What?"

"Kim, please! I know where they're keeping Her! She's at Sinks and Rises, in the marsh near the cave where we met. We *have* to go!"

"Sinks and What?"

Caroline was crying softly. I don't think either of us cared who was watching now. "Sinks and Rises. It's where the Womyn's Spirit Gathering was. She told me. . . . She told me once that the place wasn't safe. That nothing kind lived in the marsh and She was afraid one day She would lose control. . . . Oh, Goddess, Kim. You *have* to help me!"

"No."

"Why not?" Hot tears were pouring down the cheeks of the woman I still loved. Part of my heart died behind my leather-jacket armor to see her this upset, but I was not going to help her. And as usual, I hid my pain behind a mask of anger and logic.

"Because it's beyond stupid, Caroline. Listen to yourself for a minute, would you? The moon is a Goddess named Diana who loves you and comes to Earth once a month to see you. She's nabbed by bogeymen and stuck in a swamp somewhere. And now you want me to help you rescue her? That is the most ridiculous story I've ever heard!" I stood up and threw some money on the table to cover our drinks. "You know what I think the real story is, babe? I think some weak, cowardly, married straight woman came to your festival or Gathering or whatever the hell it was, jumped into your bed, and has been lying to you ever since. Wake up and smell the herbal tea, girlfriend. You've been had."

I couldn't stand there anymore watching myself break Caroline's soul to bits. I pushed my way through the crowd of bibliophiles and fled into the cool night.

Walking after dark always soothes my spirit for some reason. Maybe if I lived in a big city I'd feel differently, but my part of town, the part near the university, is pretty safe. By the time I got to my street I felt almost normal.

"Right," I snorted to myself. "A fake moon. What's next? Elves and fairies?" The only fairies I knew personally were the ones who owned the leather shop on Lime Street. Swell guys, but hardly the gossamer wing and stardust types. Plus, I was too damn old to believe in elves, I told myself firmly. And just before I climbed the steps to my front porch, preparing to erase Caroline, Diana, and the entire ridiculous episode from my mind by the swift application of two fingers of scotch and a hot shower, I turned to look at the moon, which was just starting to glow above the budding treetops across the dark street.

It looked fine; nearly full, slightly lopsided, white with those gray patches that always looked like a howling face to me. For the first time in more years than I wanted to count I recalled how when I was a kid I used to spend a lot of time staring out my bedroom window, discussing my deepest childhood wishes and dreams with the moon, praying that someone up there would hear me. I can't even remember what I used to wish for, I thought sadly. Maybe that's why I was so hard on Caroline. Maybe I wanted her story to be true, maybe she hit a little too close to home. I felt old, cynical, and suddenly very tired. Maybe for once I just wanted her magic to be real.

Well, one thing I did remember from my own moon-gazing days was that if the moon was full enough you could see your shadow, even in the middle of the night. Hey, when you're nine or ten years old, that's pretty neat stuff. I squinted up into the night sky again and judged that there was enough showing to do the trick easily. I turned around, putting the moon at my back and looked down, expecting to see my elongated form splashed across the front steps of the house.

There was not even the whisper of a shadow where my shadow should have been.

I froze. Turned back around to make sure the moon was still there. Stupid reaction. Yeah, I know. Turned back to the steps. Still no shadow. Waited for my sane, rational, butch mind to come up with a logical explanation. When it did, I almost cried with relief.

Light pollution! That's it! Too much artificial light generated in a small city what with street lights and floodlights on campus and all. Hell, half the time I couldn't see the damn *stars* there was so much of it. "Smooth going, Kim." My voice sounded strange and unnaturally high, even to me. "Maybe you need that drink worse than you thought."

The front foyer was pitch dark as I entered the house, except for a tiny green glow that steadily blinked on and off. The glow was coming from the middle of a huge, dark mass, and I had a crazy moment when I wondered if Tinker Bell was somehow lounging on my grandfather's antique rolltop desk. Switching on the overhead light, I was temporarily relieved to discover that it was nothing more than the answering machine message light. Then it hit me.

The broken answering machine had recorded a message.

The broken answering machine that I had specifically left *unplugged* for six months had recorded a message.

Pure self-defense reflex made me grab my old hickory baseball bat from its accustomed corner by the door. Raising it with both hands like some prehistoric war club, I approached the blinking machine cautiously, very much like one might approach a large, dangerous animal. Later, I would laugh at the idea of arming myself against a small, defenseless recording device, but it sure wasn't very funny right then.

I slowly pulled the answering machine's electrical cord out

from behind the desk, praying that I would meet with resistance when the plug came out of the wall socket. No such luck. Even with the plug in my hand the little light blinked insistently, as if daring me to hit the "play" button.

So I did, thankful that there was no one else around to notice how badly my hand was shaking. Tough butch image to maintain, you know.

There was the usual clicking and whirring of the tape being rewound, the usual awful metallic beep, and then the most beautiful, warm, rich female voice I had ever heard flowed out of the cheap, tiny speaker. Holy shit, I thought irrationally, if Whoever-it-is sounds this good with that much tape distortion, I'm not sure my libido would survive hearing her in person! Her words, however, snapped me back to frightening reality.

"Kim, this is Diana. Tell Caroline I need her help. Your help, too. She'll know where I am. Hurry, child." The voice was fading rapidly, as if the caller was running out of air, or energy. "Please. . . ." And the machine beeped again, signaling the end of the message.

I looked down at the plug still gripped in my left hand.

Oh. My. God.

Caroline was right.

Oh, shit.

Yanking the tape from the machine, I jammed it into my jacket pocket and plunged into the night, still gripping the baseball bat like a savage warrior of bygone days.

I burst into Caroline's kitchen door completely out of breath and hollering like a Valkyrie. I have no idea what I was saying, but at the time it sounded an awful lot like, "Ohgodohgodohgod. Get the tape player. Yougottahearthis NOW!" Caroline was sitting at the wooden kitchen table lacing up her hiking boots when I burst in, but I must have startled the living shit out of her because she jumped up and grabbed a cast-iron frying pan off the wall and nearly brained me with it. Understandably. We faced off for a few seconds, each brandishing our makeshift weapons until Caroline realized it was me and I realized I was relatively safe and we lowered them. Caroline's expression was not terribly warm or welcoming.

She came right to the point. "What the hell are you doing here?"

"Caroline," I panted, "listen to me, please." I pulled the answering-machine tape from my pocket and held it out to her. "My answering machine was blinking when I got home. It's still broken, so I unplugged it. Someone or something left this message on my broken fucking unplugged answering machine and you gotta hear it! Now!"

She didn't say anything, just snatched the tape from my fingers and stalked into the living room. Not knowing what else to do, I trailed behind her.

Funny as it sounds, I was almost relieved to hear that rich voice pouring out of Caroline's expensive stereo system. For one panicky moment as she was turning on all the components I wondered if I had imagined the entire thing. But Diana's words coming out of chest-high floor speakers addressed most of my sanity issues. At least the ones I was processing at the moment. And let me tell you, her voice sounded even better on Caroline's top-of-the-line equipment.

"Kim, this is Diana. Tell Caroline I need her help. Your help, too. She'll know where I am. Hurry, child. Please. . . ."

Caroline punched the "stop" button with one finger. "That's Her," she said softly, "that's Diana's voice. I'd recognize it anywhere." I thought she might be crying again, but when she turned to face me, her violet eyes were clear and dry. And fiercely determined. For the first time since bursting into her kitchen, I noticed that Caroline was wearing jeans and a thick, black, long-sleeved corduroy shirt in addition to the hiking boots—a far cry from her usual Indian skirts, soft print tops, and Birkenstock sandals. Her hair was bound up in one long tight braid, a style I had never seen her wear before. I must have looked surprised. "I have to go to Her, Kim," Caroline said flatly.

"No, *we* have to go to Her."

"You're not coming with me."

"Oh, yes, I am."

"The hell you are. You don't even believe in Her. You never have. Thank you for bringing the tape, now go home and find some logical, rational, macha shithead explanation for it, have a good laugh at my expense, and leave me the fuck alone." She turned, grabbed her keys off the bookshelf, and headed for the kitchen door.

Her words made me pause for an instant. I could easily give in to what Caroline had suggested: go home, have my long overdue scotch and shower, and forget it. Or, for once in my sorry life, I could do the illogical, irrational, right thing. Not much of a choice; but one frighteningly easy to make. Caroline had called me a shithead. Was I really that much of one? Don't answer that. For the first time that night, I started to smile. I stopped at the kitchen table long enough to grab one thing, and raced out into Caroline's driveway.

She was not too pleased to see me jump into the front passenger seat of her old battered Jeep. "Look," I said firmly before she even had a chance to open her mouth, "I don't blame you for being pissed at me because I didn't believe you. I'm pissed at me, too, so don't feel special. But Diana, whoever She is, said She needed *my* help too, remember? Sorry, babe, I'm in it now."

Caroline stared at me appraisingly for a few moments, then nodded. "You're right, damn you." She smiled coldly, her eyes still unforgiving, but at least I was going with her.

"I thought you might want this," I grinned, holding up the cast-iron frying pan she'd nearly whanged me with a few moments earlier. "Figured you could scare the living daylights out of a bogle or two with it, 'cause you sure scared me!"

At that she started laughing. I joined in, but as she pulled out of the driveway, I started to get a little scared by all the unknowns of what we were about to do, so I stopped.

Now, I had no idea where Sinks and Rises was, but I was pretty sure it was out in the country somewhere and not downtown Lexington, so when Caroline turned away from Highway

Four toward the business district, I had to ask. "Where the hell are we going?"

"My grandmother's. She'll know how to rescue Diana."

I didn't say anything. At least one of us was finally acquiring some wisdom, and I was sure hoping it was me.

We sat in Caroline's grandmother's funky-smelling kitchen surrounded by silent felines and poured out our story over delicate cups of hot chocolate and thick, chewy, obviously homemade peanut butter cookies. She didn't say a word during our recital, even when we interrupted each other or both talked at once. When we finally finished, she gently readjusted the large sleeping tabby in her lap to a more comfortable position. I prayed she believed us.

"Well," she said in a quiet, matter-of-fact voice. "Sounds like you two've got some work to do. Are you willing?"

Caroline nodded right away. To my credit, I did too. Funny, Caroline's grandmother didn't look a bit surprised by our story, she mostly looked . . . proud? Relieved?

"You'll do as I tell you?" Again, we nodded. "Good." She reached into a large pocket in her apron and pulled out two small stones and two sticks. "Put the stones in your mouths and take these hazel twigs in your hands." Damned if I didn't find myself obeying the old lady. After the broken answering-machine message, I guess I was ready to believe anything. "Now, neither of you is to say a word to anybody, not even each other, until you get home safely. Because if you do, you'll be trapped there forever by those that trapped Her. Do you understand?" Again, we nodded. I was beginning to feel like one of those ridiculous toy dogs that people used to put in the back window of their cars, you know, the ones whose heads are on a spring so they sit there nodding like crazy. "Go to where you think She is, child. Drive as far as you can, but when you have to get out and walk, don't act afraid. Go out to the middle of the marsh until you find a huge coffin-shaped rock, a candle, and a cross. When you find them, you won't be far from your

Moon. Go with my blessing: may all that is good help you and protect you tonight."

It was time. We got up, each bending over to kiss her grandmother on the cheek. I was rather surprised by my instinct to do so; I hadn't much liked the old lady when Caroline and I were together. I always thought she was just too weird. So I changed my mind. Big deal.

"Kimberly?" The commanding voice stopped me at the door. I turned to face Caroline's grandmother, still sitting with the sleeping cat on her lap. "Leave the bat and the pan in the car. You won't need them. Just the hazel twigs and the stones."

The hairs on the back of my neck began to tingle uncomfortably. We hadn't told Caroline's grandmother that part of the story. . . .

How creepy was Sinks and Rises in the middle of the night? Pretty damn, let me tell you. Especially once we'd turned off the Jeep's headlights and stepped out into the woods. The dirt road we'd gotten this far on had been pretty bumpy, and I almost dropped my hazel stick trying to rub some desire-to-live back into my butt. Near as I could tell, we were at the edge of the marsh. A light mist was hovering over the ground, just thick enough to hide dangerous obstacles like fallen logs and jutting rocks. Wonderful. It was pitch-dark and totally silent, being too early in the year for frogs or crickets or other nocturnal peepers. It suddenly occurred to me that we had neglected to bring flashlights, and that's when I got really scared. Want some advice? If you can arrange your life to avoid prowling around a cold, haunted marsh in the middle of the night without a flashlight and only a small stick and a mouthful of pebble for protection, then that is certainly the way to go. Trust me.

I looked up at the nearly full moon that should have been softly illuminating the scene but wasn't, then realized that Caroline had already started to navigate the mists in front of us. I hurried to catch up with her and promptly stepped on something that felt very much like a large, rabid snake. In reality, it probably wasn't a snake, but I have this . . . thing about snakes.

Don't tell anyone. Anyway, since I wasn't allowed to talk, and I assumed that included yelling something obscene to cover my fear, I settled for gasping hard and almost swallowed my damn stone when I did.

Surprisingly, Caroline didn't seem scared at all. But then she's always been a country dyke and I've always been a town dyke. She didn't flinch once; not even when cold wet branches that felt like cold bogle fingers were tearing at our hair; not even when the light wind whispering through last year's leaves sounded exactly like hants strolling through the marsh. As we got deeper into the dense swampland, the whispers grew louder, became a murmur, then rose to a cackle. Honest. And the worst of it was I couldn't really see any of the creatures making the noise, just the occasional glint of movement out of the corner of my eye that always turned out to be a swaying branch once I really turned to look at it.

After an eternity of slogging through stuff I'm glad I couldn't see, Caroline grabbed my arm and pointed with her hazel twig. About twenty feet away was a large rectangular boulder half in and half out of the water, a dark shape against a background of white mist looking for all the world like a stone coffin. Sitting on top of the boulder was a tiny firefly, his glow flickering very much like a candle—or my broken, blinking answering machine I thought before I could stop myself. As we approached the boulder, I saw that two large limbs from a nearby tree had fallen on top of it, making a cross when they landed . . . just like Caroline's grandmother had predicted.

So, this was the place, but where was Diana? The goblins and bogles and such that had captured Her were all around us now, their little rubbery bodies and luminous eyes quite plain, even in the dark. God, they were ugly. Too ugly to really scare me; I was having a hard enough time believing they were real. And they smelled like rotten eggs. The creatures were making such a racket, yelling at Caroline and I and calling us every fag-bashing name in the book, telling us we should forget the Moon and go home, that I couldn't think what to do next. I was so pissed off I actually took a breath to holler, "Shut up, you assholes!" at them before the pebble stopped me.

I looked around. No light, no Moon, no Diana. Just Caroline standing next to me with filthy boots firmly planted about shoulder-width apart, hazel twig aimed directly at the coffin-shaped boulder, braided hair plucked loose by the bogles falling into her eyes, and a look on her face I don't ever want to see again.

The air was suddenly crackling with invisible electricity as the homophobic uglies increased their stream of verbal abuse. The boulder rocked and shuddered slightly, then settled back down in the bog.

Caroline nearly fell into the muck before I caught her and helped her stand solid again. She was sweaty and panting heavily, as if she'd just run a marathon. She made a series of gestures, then seemed frustrated when I couldn't understand what she was trying to communicate to me. The goblins and bogles were really whooping it up, dancing on top of the boulder and everything.

"Yaaaaah!" they screeched. "Failed, didn't you? Go home, little girl-lover. Ya ain't got half enough magic and you know it!"

Half enough magic. . . . Enlightenment knocks at the damndest times. Sometimes it comes after lengthy prayer or meditation in a warm, dry, incense-kissed temple, or after a round of really satisfying sex. For me, enlightenment will always smell slightly of rotten eggs, and feel like cold, wet hightop sneakers (because mine were). All at once I knew why Diana said She needed my help, what Caroline had been trying to tell me without words a moment before.

My magic was needed, too.

That thought was honestly more frightening than anything else that had happened to me all evening. I mean, I had spent most of my life wishing that magic were real, and at the same time denying any opportunity to make it real. Caroline and her cosmic friends had tried to tell me, tried to teach me, and I had been too stubborn to listen.

Well, I was listening now.

To a voice that ever so gently whispered in my head, please

help me. I wasn't sure if it was Caroline's voice I heard, or Diana's, but it didn't really matter. I turned to Caroline, caught her by the shoulders and nodded my understanding slowly so she could see me in the darkness. She squeezed my arm in acknowledgment, and together we turned to face the boulder.

The uglies suddenly got smart. They took one look at us, shut the hell up, and started slowly crawling away. Caroline resumed her previous stance. I tried to copy her as best I could, with not a clue as to what I was supposed to do next. I pointed my tiny hazel twig at that huge rock and, well, I don't know how else to describe it, but I *pushed.* I felt like I had the time my ancient pickup truck died on the highway and I'd had to push it uphill a half mile to the nearest gas station, only this time I was using my mind. I hoped I was doing the right thing.

Apparently I was, because suddenly the boulder exploded in a shower of tiny fragments. I caught a glimpse of a beautiful woman with long silvery hair lying under the stagnant water before the bright light emanating from the woman's face as she opened her eyes blinded me temporarily.

When I finally shook the spots out of my vision, all I could see was Caroline, tears of joy on her cheeks, kneeling in the cold muck and holding hands with a glowing Diana (it *had* to be) who was standing before her. The look on Diana's face as She gazed at Caroline carried more love than I thought existed in the world. They seemed to be communicating without words, because soon they turned as one to look at me. Diana came over to where I was standing in my squishy sneakers. She looked deep into my eyes and laid one warm hand against my cheek.

Thank you, child. That same impossibly rich voice echoed gently in my head. I was honestly crying too hard myself to do anything but nod, but if you tell anyone I'll deny it. Then, with one glance back to Her beloved, Diana leaped up into the air. We stood there together, Caroline and I, watching Her light travel across the night sky until it reached the false moon the bogles had hung. For a moment, if anyone on Earth had bothered to look, there were two moons hanging low over the horizon. There was a flash like a Fourth of July firework and the false moon burst into flames. As it did so, the silent marsh was filled with the painful, angry shrieks of the bogles and hants as Diana's true light flooded the clearing and scorched them where they stood.

Or cowered.

Whatever.

Caroline and I are good friends again these days. I mean, the Moon *is* pretty hard to compete with, romance-wise. And sometimes I look up at night and feel Diana's love shining down on me, too.

About a month or so after Caroline and I rescued her Lover, I was sitting in my usual booth at the White Raven reading a magazine when I looked up to see a vaguely familiar face sit down on the bench across from me.

Oh, but she was beautiful. Young, but with white hair and the most perfect, deep blue eyes I have ever seen. A body I have held in a thousand dreams but never thought could exist. She looks like Diana, I thought crazily. Tess must be putting something funny in the cappuccino. . . .

"Hi, Kim," she even *sounded* like Diana. "My name's Selene."

I sat there gulping like a fish, trying desperately to think of something to say. It didn't have to be clever, or even particularly intelligent, but my mind was a complete blank.

"My Mother said you'd probably be surprised to see me."

Inspiration. "Your . . . Mother?"

Her smile lit up her face, the booth, the whole café. I realized I had just that minute fallen completely in love with her. Oh, boy.

"Diana is my Mother. She wanted to thank you for helping rescue Her, so she asked Caroline what your greatest wish was, and here I am."

Whoa. That sounded a little too, I don't know, whorish to me. "Don't you mind?"

"Oh, no. I've been in love with you ever since you were a little girl who prayed to the Moon for someone to understand and care about you. Besides, I think you're beautiful."

Good enough for me.

Did I mention I'm over Caroline completely?

This time I think I really mean it.

# Diego & Bob

## SUE PIERCE

When Skip picked up the phone, she heard Maria— Maria, the girlfriend of Skip's ex-girlfriend Lindsay. For a moment she was quiet. Experience had taught her that when the girlfriend of the ex-girlfriend calls, complications are just around the bend. But then Skip remembered that Lindsay had gotten really sick after her last chemo treatment.

"What's up," Skip said, her voice shaky, her heart racing. "Is Lindsay okay?" She suddenly felt a sharp pain—Maria was never the one to call.

Maria seemed to hear the panic in Skip's voice, because she said soothingly, "Oh, no, there's nothing really wrong. It's just we need to go have this procedure done and the doctor has some scheduling problems and we really need to go now and"— Maria paused and took a breath—"we wondered if you could watch Diego for an hour or two. We would take him but he really doesn't like the hospital; it makes him upset."

Skip was so relieved that Lindsay was all right that at first she was only half listening to what Maria was saying. She thought about the last time she had seen Lindsay alone. They had giggled together and Lindsay had taken off her bandanna and let Skip touch the soft, shiny surface of her bald head. But when Maria got to the part about baby-sitting for Diego, Skip suddenly snapped to attention. *Jesus,* she thought, *they must have hit rock bottom on the baby-sitting food chain.*

Lindsay's pregnancy and Diego's birth had been a joyful time for Lindsay and Maria. They had named him after Maria's late

father. The new moms were more than willing to have Skip
spend time with Diego, but she had mostly stayed clear of the
boy in the two and a half years since he'd been born.

Her one major shared moment with Diego, an evening of
baby-sitting, did not qualify as a success in her mind. Because
she had gotten distracted for a moment, the newly walking
Diego and a plastic cow named Atsa Moo were able to launch
a pool party in the toilet, where Skip discovered them happily
awash. She broke up the party and ended up chasing a wet, infuriated Diego around the house trying to put dry clothes on
him. Atsa Moo had been sent diving so deep into that little cave
at the bottom of the toilet that it had to be rescued by a plumber.

Ever since then, she had found excuses for not being able to
baby-sit. The thought of going another round with Diego made
her pause for so long that Maria asked gently, "Could you do
it, Skip? I hope you don't mind the short notice. Lindsay told
me to say pretty please. She's resting right now."

*Christ, how can I refuse now,* Skip asked herself. She felt
ashamed that for a minute she had thought of not doing this for
Lindsay. *It's not like you've been doing a whole lot for them. Can't
weasel out of this one—can't be that much of a lowlife.* "No, I don't
mind at all, it'll be fine. I'll be right over," she said.

As she drove over to their house, she was thinking of how
great Maria was for Lindsay, especially now. Skip had seen
them together at parties and noted how Maria sat protectively
near and had a drink or a Kleenex ready for Lindsay at the very
moment it was needed.

That attentiveness had awakened Skip's old guilt about how
she used to abandon Lindsay at parties to flit around. Once, in
a confessional moment brought on by an excess of cocktails, Skip
had blurted out to Lindsay, "Damn, Maria is a much better
girlfriend to you than I ever was."

A short time later Skip stood in the front hall of Lindsay and
Maria's house. She covertly admired the warm tones of the Oriental rugs set against the blond wooden floors and how nicely
the wallpaper matched the painted trim. Images of her own
apartment, carpeted with magazines and clothes and furnished

with cat-destroyed furniture, flashed in her mind. Maria was saying brightly, "Well, it's a nice day. You and Diego can go to the park," as she arranged the countless accessories needed for the maintenance of a small boy.

"Here's his blankey, and his nukky and bear, and some Fruit Roll-Ups and granola bars and apple juice . . . ," Maria chanted as she stuffed a bag to bursting. Watching her swiftly and competently pack the bag, Skip felt a vague sense of panic. With her long, dark hair pulled back in a braid and her ample body, Maria seemed born to the mother role. Skip ran her hand through her own recently clipped buzz cut—*I don't even look the parental part.*

Behind Maria, Lindsay sat curled up in a chair, saying something occasionally, but mostly staying quiet. Her face was drawn and lined, and her blue eyes were underscored with deep circles. When Lindsay lifted a thin, fragile hand to reach for a glass of water, Skip felt her eyes start to fill with tears. She looked down at the floor where Diego lay making loud splatting noises with his mouth and waving a Barbie doll that was missing a limb and had an amazing porcupine-like hairdo.

Lindsay saw that Skip noticed Barbie's hair and gave a tired smile. "We were refinishing the floor and Diego stuck Bob's hair in the polyurethane," she said.

"Barbie's name is Bob?" said Skip.

"Yes, that's the name Diego made up, isn't it, sweetie?" Maria said, smiling down at him lovingly. "And we thought, why correct him? He'll have all that rigid gender stuff soon enough."

*Hey,* Skip mused, *it's cool for Barbie to get in touch with her masculine side.* Barbie had certainly been the butch hero of many of Skip's girlhood adventures. She and Barbie had walked on the moon (simulated in a vacant lot), gone surfing at the shore (Barbie spewed sand for weeks after and her hair was never the same), and had, of course, always beaten G.I. Joe at everything.

But as she looked down at Diego, her wariness dissolved into a pang of sorrow. He looked so small lying on the floor, lost in whatever kid world he inhabited. She thought, *He's really kind of homely.* He was small for his age. His fine hair lay limply on his head. He had a narrow, pale face and a large and rather runny nose.

When it was time to leave, Lindsay crouched on the floor next to Diego, took him in her arms, and murmured reassuringly into his ear. Maria picked him up and gave him a big kiss and said, "You're going to be good for Skip, aren't you?" Diego burrowed his head into Maria's chest.

Maria sang softly to the boy as she carried him out to Skip's car. As Skip drove away, Lindsay and Maria stood waving, crying, "Bye-bye, sweetie, see you soon." Diego sat in the car seat, snuffling quietly, not moving, Barbie/Bob dangling limply from his hand. Skip began to relax a little—she had heard the rumors about how Diego was either "a handful" or the "demon seed," depending on the speaker's kid-tolerance index. Suddenly, Diego flinched violently, looked around, and began to wail. Skip stepped on the gas and calculated the quickest way to the park.

As Skip drove, Diego's wails raced up and down the harmonic scale, peaking in a piercing, eardrum-damaging tin-whistle shriek. Skip frantically wracked her brain for a strategy. *This kid thing,* she thought, *I just don't have the background.*

She looked in the rearview mirror at the howling boy. Oddly enough, his keening was not accompanied by tears. His eyes seemed trained on some distant place. Barbie/Bob was being waved back and forth like a baton, in time to the wailing.

"Diego, dude," Skip said, her panic level rising. "It's okay. This is just a temporary thing." *Lame,* she said to herself, *very lame.*

Lame, Skip realized, was the operative word for her whole attitude about kids. It was one of the major reasons—possibly the major reason—that she and Lindsay had broken up.

She remembered the scenes when she and Lindsay fought about what Skip called the baby thing—just the thought of them still made her cringe.

She had loved Lindsay more than anyone in her life, but a baby—a baby was a terrifying thought, a terrifying amount of need, a fragile little creature that you could mess up for life if you did the wrong thing.

*So you split,* Skip said to herself. *But paybacks are a bitch, because here you are with the son you never wanted to have.* Diego's noise level dropped a bit, startling Skip. She looked back to see him chewing on Bob's polyurethane-spiked head. *Oh my God,* she thought, *he's going to poison himself.*

Between the chewing and the screaming, they were not going to make it to the park—disaster was sure to strike. Either Diego would choke to death or Skip's eardrums would explode. Fortunately, the parking lot of the mall suddenly appeared on her right. She whipped into the lot and pulled into a spot. She leaned over the seat and pulled Bob's head out of Diego's mouth. Diego actually looked at her for a second and then began to really cry, with tears this time.

"Hey, guy, you hungry? Want something to eat?" Skip said, trying to keep the panic out of her voice. *I am out of my depth here,* she thought.

Diego abruptly stopped crying. "Fry, fry," he said.

"Fry, fry?" said Skip.

"Donald's fry, fry!" Diego said loudly.

Skip puzzled over this bit of kidspeak. "You mean McDonald's, like Happy Meals and all that?"

Diego waved Bob vigorously. "Donald's fry, fry!" he cried.

*Okay, french fries at McDonald's,* thought Skip. *Junk-food bribery in the name of peace and tranquillity is definitely not beneath me.*

She opened the back door and wrestled with extracting Diego from his car seat. After a thrilling dash from the parking lot, during which Skip had to do some creative blocking to keep Diego from darting in front of cars, they made it into the mall.

The familiar wave of greasy onion and meat smell rolled over Skip as she sat across from Diego at a sticky plastic table. There had been a little battle at the counter. Diego had tried to lunge forward out of her arms to grab the fresh-from-the-Fryolator third-degree-burn french fries that the counter kid was dropping into the Happy Meal.

Now Diego had deconstructed his Happy Meal. The little toy car had been buried in the hamburger bun and he was carefully separating his french fries and studying each one earnestly before selecting one to poke into the ketchup. Occasionally he would thrust a ketchupy fry at the stalwart Bob, who was covered with sticky red spots.

Diego's methodical food ritual reminded Skip of an exgirlfriend who couldn't stand any scallions in her food. On their first dates, Skip would stop eating and watch, fascinated, as the woman picked and pulled delicately at her dish, dissecting out every little green bit of scallion contamination. What baffled and later infuriated Skip (among other things) was that this exgirlfriend's favorite restaurant put scallions in everything except coffee and dessert. It got to be like having lunch with Madame Curie at work. After a few months of this, though, she just wanted to scream and knock the table over because the procedure required deep concentration and did not permit conversation.

*Oh, well,* thought Skip, *at least she was better than the one who ate chicken bones.* (Though the chicken-bone eater was awfully good in bed—Skip always figured there must have been a connection somewhere.) *What is it with you?* she said to herself. *You go out with the scallion-flicking, chicken-bone eaters and complain how all these women are so weird and why can't you find a normal relationship. Then you meet nice, normal Lindsay, and, guess what—it turns out you're the weirdo.* She sighed deeply and refocused her attention on Diego. Tired of eating fries the mundane way, Diego was using Bob's spiky hair do as a french-fry pick. Bob's head was festooned with fries.

"The fry-fry rasta look—very unique," said Skip. "Uh, dude, do you think Bob really wants his, or uh, her fries like that?" She supposed this was the sort of food entertainment parental figures should discourage, but Diego gave her a stony look and continued the fry coiffure.

Skip sighed even more deeply. Suddenly she had an overwhelming urge to get high. *God, I would love to smoke some pot,* she thought, though she hadn't gotten high in ages. A cigarette, a shot of whiskey, a line of coke—any of them would do just fine. She would definitely end up an addict if she was a parent. *Clearly I am not fit for this line of work,* she thought darkly.

Diego had started sliding up and down the bench, waving french-fry-head Bob. All of a sudden, Diego lunged for Skip's soda and plunged Bob into it headfirst. Skip shouted and jumped up as the cup tipped over and cold soda spilled everywhere, chiefly on Diego. Diego froze for a minute, realized he was drenched in soda, and began to howl.

Furious and embarrassed, Skip grabbed up Diego and hauled him out of the booth. She snatched a handful of napkins and tried to dry off Diego, but the napkins just disintegrated. She finally just picked him up and carried the wriggling, screaming boy out into the mall.

"Dammit, Diego, cut it out!" she hissed at him and then felt immediately ashamed, but still furious. Diego suddenly fell silent and then, using some secret kid civil-disobedience trick, made himself completely boneless and limp and slid to the floor. He lay there, howling and clutching Bob.

Skip looked at him helplessly. She tried to pull him up but he screamed and kicked so much that she let him back down.

Diego lay on the floor, sniffling, bouncing Bob lightly on the floor. Skip crouched down next to him. *What am I doing to him,* she thought miserably. She looked up and saw people staring at her and Diego. *Oh, great, now I'm committing child abuse at the mall.*

"Diego, man, I'm sorry I flipped out on you," she said to the boy. Suddenly, she could see herself so clearly, saying, "I'm sorry . . ." to a whole succession of different tear-stained faces, or angry faces, pleading her case over a restaurant table, in a doorway, in the front seat of a car. She heard herself over and over again using that shabby little patch of a phrase to try to hold together something that she had managed to somehow make come apart.

She put her face in her hands. *I'm such a disaster,* she thought.

Then she heard a noise. She raised her head in time to see Diego go rocketing off down through the mall, making a beeline for the huge, noisy fountain in the center.

"Ahh, not the fountain," she cried, and took off after him. Visions of him flinging himself into the fountain and hitting his head and drowning terrified her. *You can drown in an inch of water,* she thought frantically—*or was it two inches?* Expanding on her nightmare, she realized that if he did drown, her total rescue training consisted of an afternoon in Girl Scouts spent trying to revive a dummy.

He was fast. Sprinting on his little legs, he ran with Bob held out before him like the Olympic torch. Skip, heart pounding, put on a burst of speed and zigzagged around slow-moving shoppers, narrowly avoiding several collisions. She reached the fountain just as Diego had one arm and one leg in, with Bob sounding the bottom of the fountain.

Skip reached down and instead of grabbing Diego and yanking him out, wrapped her arms around him and moved him back and away. This time he didn't cry or flail about—he just slid out of her arms again and lay on the tiles of the mall floor.

Skip felt exhausted. She looked at Diego. His arm was soaked. He lay next to Bob in a slowly widening puddle of water on the floor. In all the excitement, Bob's hair had gotten bent in new directions.

*Here am I in the mall with a wet boy and his doll. This is why the parent thing would never work for me. I would be so perpetually sorry, I would always be trying to catch up and to make things okay again.*

She crouched down next to Diego. He lay very still, staring off blindly into the distance. She looked at him and could see the little bits of him that were of Lindsay—the startling blue eyes, the curve of his forehead. She felt a tightness in her chest. *This must be the thing, this must be what makes the baby thing worth it.* She realized that whatever happened to Lindsay, part of her would carry on in Diego.

*What will follow me?* She felt weightless, like one of those bugs that skims across the surface of the water and barely leaves a trace. A widening ripple of sorrow washed over her.

Ignoring the stares of the shoppers, Skip lay down on the floor next to Diego and Bob and without touching Diego, curled her body around him protectively.

"Diego?" she said. The boy didn't respond, but he didn't move away.

They all lay there together quietly for a few moments. Skip stared up at the ceiling of the mall. The legs and feet of passersby loomed over her and the boy. Someone leaned over and said, "Are you okay, lady?"

Skip turned her head to talk to Diego and found herself face-to-face with Bob. She looked at the doll and said, "Bob, man, it's been a long day. You had a nice swim, now maybe we could go home."

Diego waved Bob up and down and then suddenly Diego moved in to snuggle against Skip's chest. He didn't resist when she put her arms around him and lifted herself and him up off the floor. As they walked out of the mall, Diego draped his arms around her neck and put his head on her shoulder. He snuffled quietly as he relaxed against her, his full warm weight in her arm. She could smell the milky sweet scent of his hair, mingled with ketchup and chlorine. Bob lay against her back, dripping cold water.

# The House of My Child

## EMILY FOX

*I* was seven months pregnant with my second child when I first slept with Fran. My breasts looked like a Picasso—two huge balls bobbing on my chest. Plus the veins were blue and raised. My nipples were the color of red brick, and from them oozed a sticky yellow fluid, the taste of which Fran did not like. My belly was firm and filled, and as we lay in bed, we would watch the baby moving. Fran refused to touch it. She said she loved my face.

I decided to go for Fran at dinner one night. We had been opposing counsel on a huge corporate litigation that had begun before our time but which we finally settled due to the rapport we had established between ourselves. We spoke several times a week, on some business pretext or other, and had mentioned for months that we should have lunch sometime. As the negotiations ensued, the goal turned into dinner.

From the moment I saw her, I knew Fran was gay. She looked it. And her conversation conveyed the typical compensations. She got mad at me when I told her this, but I love that lesbians know immediately that I am one. Maybe because I pass so easily in straight circumstances, with my diamond engagement ring and discussions of the kids. Of course, when I'm pregnant, nobody considers that I have any erotic life. I am seen, at best, as a woman who has been fucked. More often, I feel looked through, acknowledged only as the house of my child.

Not that I treated myself much better. Initially, I thought I just wanted Fran to come out to me. But it must have been more because I was afraid to tell her I was pregnant. I was six months pregnant at that first dinner, but she hadn't seen me recently so she didn't know. I warned her on the phone the day before. Discussing wine, I promised to buy her the bottle of her choice but said that I couldn't share it this time. She was surprised, yet responded positively with warm wishes for me and my husband. I had expected her to be turned off. I always assume that people who don't have kids think kids are disgusting. I did before I had mine and I still think other people's kids are disgusting. Mine, of course, are marvelous.

At dinner, Fran brought up the void in her personal life, a subject she had managed to allude to in the midst of our settlement negotiations. "I'm not exactly a hood ornament," she said. "Most guys are intimidated by my work and all."

"So who needs men?" I said, lobbing her one.

"Well, actually, my last relationship was with a woman."

"Yeah," I said, breathing, "tell me about it."

It had been serious and she had been hurt. The woman had been married. Fran was now unattached. This was difficult because Fran really liked sex. I had never heard a woman speak so much about sex. No woman I'd ever met seemed to think it was so important. Or so great.

I asked her if she'd been to the women's bar on that block.

"How do *you* know about that?" she asked.

"I know." I smiled.

She stared at me, suspicious.

"Okay, I saw an ad for it in a journal. Have you been there?"

"Yes."

"We should go there sometime."

"No way," she said.

"Why not?"

"Not while you're like *that.*"

"Oh, come on," I said. "Who cares?"

"*Why* do you want to go?" she asked, as if I were a voyeur.

"You know," I said. "Just to go."

I had been seeking women more or less for most of my thirty-two years. My three best friends, from college and law school, were straight women with whom I had fallen in love, hooked emotionally and intrigued, but scared off. Each relationship had taken years to resolve.

Fran was an opportunity. My circumstances were complicated, but nobody would believe what I was up to. If my actions escaped comprehension, I figured, they would escape notice. Behind a curtain of incredulity I could express myself. Suddenly, it was urgent.

The next day I called Fran to thank her. I called again on every conceivable occasion. I flirted shamelessly.

Finally Fran said that if I were not married and pregnant and somebody's mother she would take me to her favorite B&B in Key West. "Details," I teased. "But don't *you* worry about it."

We made a date to have dinner again in several weeks, after she returned from a vacation. I had no patience. I tried desperately to see her before she went away. She told me she makes time for lovers, but not friends. So I told her she should make time for me. She didn't. I contrived to be near her office one evening and rang up from the lobby to ask her for a drink. She said she was in a meeting.

"Call me when you get back," I said, trying to keep it light. Trying not to let her know that I could hardly pee anymore because the bathroom provided a place to think and I thought about her until I was too excited to pee.

Eventually, Fran called.

"All relaxed from vacation?" I asked.

"Oh, it was great," she said. "But I kept thinking about work. I kept picturing that last deposition on the insurance figures. You really were good. I meant to tell you that."

"Thanks."

"So," she said, "are we still on for dinner this week?"

"Sure." I felt my face flush. "My husband and son are at his parents' beach place so I could do Friday or Saturday."

"Oh," she said, and paused. "Well, whichever."

"Friday's good," I said.

"Okay, Friday. So where do you want to eat?" She was very into food. I told her I didn't care, but nothing fancy or pretentious. She suggested a few places that I rejected as too far away or too big a deal. I was uncomfortable sitting for a long time.

"Something casual," I said. Then I added, "I want to hug you."

We had never touched before, nor spoken about it. There was silence.

"Oh. Well. We could, we could order in. We could eat at my apartment."

I was ecstatic but stunned. I was enormously impressed by Fran, professionally. She was a partner in a prestigious law firm; I was an associate. And she was good. A tough negotiator who was secure enough to be kind. Very diplomatic. Fran was also older. The tanned wrinkles on her chest and neck conveyed a power that I had respected in women of authority throughout my life. Suddenly, these badges of experience were incredibly sexy to me. If I could touch her, I would somehow be let in on her power. I would share it and grow. As long as I'd known her, I was flattered every time Fran called me. Part of me imagined that I would have an affair with this woman but that she would never give me her home phone number or tell me where she lived. She was not at all out and so was constantly guarded.

When I got to Fran's apartment that night, she was on the phone. I stepped in. I looked around. I glanced at her. I took off my coat and then, to kill time, I examined her record collection. She had real records, not just CDs, and I looked at every one, hoping to find compatibility in our musical tastes. There wasn't much, but I found the Joan Baez album *Diamonds and Rust.* It was a favorite of mine from when I was a big Bob Dylan fan. My husband turned me on to Dylan on one of our first dates and we had gone to at least a dozen concerts together over the years.

Fran hung up the phone and approached me for the first time. It had been a month since we'd last seen each other. Our relationship had been built on the telephone, where what each other looked and felt like was within our own imaginations. Where I unbuttoned her shirt and slipped my fingers inside every time we talked, but she kept on talking. Where we couldn't smell each other. Where she didn't see my stomach growing. Where there were no physical consequences to what we said besides the flush of our faces and our own private wetness. Where we spent hours together without admitting in advance that we wanted to.

In person, we were both very nervous and quiet. Our movements were awkward. Our voices shaky. We eyed each other, but I could not look into her eyes. We approached each other slowly. Her shirt had no buttons. Her hair smelled like smoke. Her perfume reminded me of something that I couldn't remember. I stepped toward her and kissed her on the mouth.

The kiss was warm, but stiff. Quickly we separated and I took off my boots. Fran put the boots away and led me to her sofa. We sat side by side. Fran got up and asked if she could get me a drink. I told her water. She gave me the water. I told her I liked her music. I didn't actually, except for a few albums. I asked her if she could put on *Diamonds and Rust*. I told her I didn't have it on CD so I hadn't listened to it in years. I told her that my husband and I didn't listen to very much music at all since our son was born because he played with the buttons on the stereo so we had to lock it up. I told her the song "Diamonds and Rust" was about Baez's breakup with Dylan.

Fran put the album on and sat back down next to me on the sofa.

We listened to the music.

I started to cry.

Fran looked at me, helpless. "Oh, honey, why are you crying?" she asked. "We don't have to do this you know."

Tears streamed down my face. I couldn't talk.

Fran fidgeted, searching for something to do.

"This is a very sad song," I said finally.

"It is a sad song," Fran said, and she got up to take it off.

"No," I said. "Please leave it on. I like it."

We sat there.

I don't mind tears. To me they are a luxury. At home only my son gets to cry. I never even sit down alone. Yet here I was, away from my guys, sitting, not just alone, but with someone who had the time and the energy left at the end of the day to focus on *me*. I was taking a break.

Fran was losing it. She was standing up and shifting around the room, then squatting down to my height on the sofa. She was looking at me but keeping her arms wrapped tightly around herself.

"What?" she asked. "What is it?"

I didn't respond.

She stood up again and walked over to my coat. She glanced at it and then back at me. "Want to go *out* to dinner?" she tried.

I shook my head no.

"More water?" She picked up the glass.

I just sat there.

She put the glass down and shifted some papers on her desk.

"If your husband were a creep," she said, staring at the papers, "it would be much easier."

"Well he isn't," I said. "He sat through *Desert Hearts* with me. Bought me popcorn, too."

Just then, the baby belted me and I got the giggles. "And Raisinets," I sputtered, "And Diet Coke." Soon I was laughing so hard I began to snort. *"Our Bodies, Our Selves* for my fifteenth birthday. A gold bracelet when Matt was born." I held my belly and vibrated awhile, silently hysterical.

"Look," I said holding out my wrist, "this is the bracelet."

She looked. She didn't look happy.

"I'm sorry," I said, gurgling through my tears.

She didn't blink.

"Sorry," I said again, pushing a baby limb, which was sticking out my left side, back into the center. "I'll stop."

Fran studied me as if to determine precisely *which* type of sicko had landed in her living room. She tilted her head. "Have you *done* this before?" she asked.

"What?" I said, sitting up and blowing my nose.

"An affair."

"No."

"Women?"

"Not exactly."

"I thought..."

"Well I didn't," I said, and blew again.

Fran gave me another good looking over.

She was making me self-conscious. "You like my outfit?" I teased, sweeping my arm across my blue maternity pants suit. "It's my best one."

She smirked.

"Maybe this is some *hormone* thing," she said, possibly joking. Then she brightened. "Maybe you just need some pickles and ice cream like all the other nice pregnant ladies?"

"Funny," I said, letting my own smile through. "Could you come here please?" I reached over, pulled her onto the sofa and kept hold of her hand. She tried to pull it away.

"Oh, come on," I said. "I just had to, you know, adjust."

I rotated our hands so that our cupped fingers locked each other in. Then I darted my thumb back and forth across the tops of our knuckles to get her to thumb-wrestle with me.

Smiling, Fran pulled her hand out and batted mine away. Then she looked me in the eye and gave in to my arms. We held each other in a long, squeeze-out-the-world hug.

She whispered something I didn't hear.

Then our touch began to change. I kissed Fran on her neck lightly and on her face. Our mouths brushed past each other several times. Finally we met in a good, deep, kiss, lasting and exploratory.

When our eyes met again, we each broke into a shy smile.

I buried my face in her breasts and began licking them.

Then I touched her with my hands. I felt her.

She was soft.

I was soaked.

I started to climb on top of Fran right there on the sofa. Like an adolescent. But my stomach got in the way. No matter how we twisted and shifted and struggled, I could not position myself as close to her as I was dying to get. I felt like a mother lion, protective of the baby, but on the prowl. I also didn't want to crush Fran. At the time, I weighed over 165 pounds, with ten more to go until term.

"Let's go in the other room," Fran said, taking my hand.

In bed, my stomach was still awkward, but we got around it. In fact, our endurance astonished me. I had thought I had a short attention span.

Afterwards, we lay quietly for a while, each staring separately at the ceiling.

As I reached for her fingers again, I realized that Fran had avoided contact with the parts of me she considered alien.

To test her, I put her hand on my belly. She moved it.

I felt lonely, while the anger welled up. "You know, it's *me* you're not touching," I said finally. "*Strangers* feel up my stomach like I'm a petting zoo. So how come *you* can't touch me?" But just as I made my point, indignant and outraged, the baby somersaulted within me, dragging its bulging limbs across the circumference of my abdomen. Fran and I laughed together in acknowledgment that we were not alone.

Silently, then, I stroked my own stomach, trying to grab hold of a baby foot.

Fran promised to call me the next morning before noon. At 9:42, I called her.

"Hi," I said. "Remember me?"

"Hi." She laughed.

"Were you going to call me?" I asked.

"We said *noon;* it's only nine-thirty!"

"*Before* noon," I said. "Anyway, I couldn't wait."

"I'm glad you called."

"Yeah?" I asked. "So, are you free today? Can we do something?"

"Sure," she said. "Whatever you like. Your day. I know you don't get much time off."

"Well, I do have a few errands downtown, if you don't mind coming."

We met at noon and walked forty blocks south. I kept brush-

ing against Fran and playing with her as we walked. She kept
batting me away. I was giggling but she was getting angry. At
one point I actually thought she might hit me.

"Loosen up," I teased, poking her ribs.

She stopped walking and turned to face me. "You don't get
it, do you?"

"Girls are allowed to hold hands," I said, winking.

"Would you look at yourself!" she yelled.

"What *about* me, Fran?" I said, annoyed. "Dykes are allowed
to have babies, you know."

"*Dykes,* plural, aren't having *this* baby." She stomped across
the street, just making the light.

When I caught up to her, I feigned a smile. "That's what I
like about you, Fran," I said. "Your flair for drama."

I took a big breath, put my hands on my hips, and puffed out
my already ample chest. "Your *honor,*" I began in an exagger-
ated imitation of Fran's courtroom voice, "as a *representative* of
the *government* of the *United States of America,* my client simply
*cannot* be compelled to suffer the slings and arrows of life's af-
flictions, which *defendants,* the capitalist pigs, seek to *inflict.*"

"I never said that," she laughed, slapping me.

"Not much," I said. "Come on, Counsel, let's walk."

Eventually we dragged ourselves to four children's bookstores before we found the *Maisy Goes Swimming* pop-up book
that I'd promised my son. I had also wanted *Maisy Goes to the
Playground,* but apparently it was out of print. In the checkout
line Fran asked, "What are you going to tell him?"

"Matt won't care," I said. "I'll take him with me to pick out
something else."

"I wasn't talking about Matt," she said. "Or the book."

"Good luck with the baby," the cashier winked as we left the
store.

"What are you going to tell *him?*" Fran persisted, once we
were outside. "About us? About you?"

"He's my *husband,* Fran," I said. "I'm not telling him anything. Not now anyway."

# Wild Parrots
# Squalling Somewhere

## SHARON LIM-HING

*T*hey were four, moving, rippling, skimming as if one large creature born to the water. Their canoe glided over a river brightly lit with fluorescent oranges, pinks, and reds in a chemical preview of sunrise. The water also flowed a glowing green that might be algae or dumped radioactive debris from the city. From the banks, a thick, varied flora seemed to want to reach over and join hands above the water. Trees dunked mossy roots in, bushes perilously overhung the rocks to which they clung. Vines spiraled down, their cordate leaves searching for a different branch or perhaps testing the temperature of the water. Even between strong, silent oar strokes, the four women did not pause to look at the familiar landscape.

Xie Han sat in the front, and the other women followed her steady rhythm. Through the leaves, the sky was brightening on one side, screaming light and heat; the other side remained dark and starless. At the same time, the fires in the water died down, yielding to the growing daylight. Jinmei reached up with her oar and touched an indolent-looking tendril. The vine snapped around the oar like a whip. Punctuated by Jinmei's chuckling, oar and vine played tug-of-war. Eventually, a sharp crack was heard, followed by something like a breathy sigh. The oar came tumbling back into the water.

Van Dao was dotted by the arc of spray and a few drops of crimson sap. Jinmei's arm was also wet from the dripping, upside-down oar. They both wiped themselves off before any permanent damage was done.

"Why don't you just leave them alone?" complained Shinhyun.

"I just wanted to move my arms in a different way from what we've been doing for two hours," replied Jinmei.

"Look, it's bleeding," whispered Van Dao. They looked back at the thin, bloody stub where the vine had hung.

"Awww." Jinmei, now ashamed, scowled sulkily.

"They saw it was an animal, like dinosaurs were birds," mused Xie Han.

"I wonder how they reproduce, if they have flowers with pollen and stuff or if they fuck," Shinhyun wondered aloud.

"They probably entwine themselves around each other, then they fuck," said Jinmei. The four women sent laughter echoing up and down the waterway, while the canoe made waves of half-circles that came back from the banks, crisscrossed outgoing concentric circles, and rebounded against the boat with little lapping noises. Van Dao turned around and smiled at Jinmei. A voluptuous shiver traversed Jinmei. She also felt Shinhyun's hard stare in her back. Wordlessly, Xie Han resumed the same slow pace that would steadily propel them miles up the river over the next few hours.

Two years ago, Jinmei's arduous relationship with Shinhyun began. Unlike the others, Shinhyun wasn't born in the outbacks. One day, she walked out of the city and away from her privileged status as the only child of a high-ranking army officer. She kept a silence around her unsureness, that feminine mark of good breeding branded on her insides. But as Jinmei knew, even deeper was an unflinching will that got her out of her materially comfortable, oppressive lifestyle and, by herself, into the outbacks, said to be teeming with carnivorous plants, nuclear trash burning sores into the earth, marauding men riding around on the patched-up remains of motorcycles, sadistic aliens, and oversexed lesbians of color tribes. Some of those reports were true, others remained to be verified.

Jinmei had found Shinhyun in an aromatic bamboo grove that was breathing softly in the early morning mist. In the distance, somewhere beyond the trees, a clear stream was jumping over round stones and tinkling like a bell. Shinhyun was starving and covered with insect bites. There was a cut across her arm that looked like she had met up with the McCoy Rednecks, and somehow escaped.

"Hello," said Jinmei, stepping between the spare bamboo leaves. She would always remember that first sideways glance full of apprehension, which made her want to rush up and cradle Shinhyun in her arms, though Shinhyun was tall and thin. But Shinhyun's eyes also imperiously said, "Keep your distance." This, too, attracted Jinmei.

Jinmei led her home, which at that time was an abandoned wooden house reclaimed and hidden by the luxurious growth of plants. Her arms on her hips, Xie Han upbraided Jinmei for revealing their camp to a stranger, endangering them all. Yet all three women fed her and took care of her wounds. Van Dao prepared strengthening teas and healing poultices. They watched her carefully for signs of undercover cop disease. The McCoys were known to wipe their blades in plague pus. The fragile-seeming city girl did not succumb.

Besides carrying her out of the city to this haven, Shinhyun's stubborn strength had subdued many lovers, twirling them around her little finger like a string of limp seaweed. Jinmei knew this experience.

Now, iron-willed Shinhyun wanted to have a baby.

Xie Han, sitting in the back of the canoe, looked even more petite and compact than ever. The muscles that powered each stroke stuck out briefly at the apex of exertion, then sank back under her smooth olive skin. Her quick, deep strokes made noises, as if the water were grunting when parted, though Xie Han was silent, hardly even breathing hard. Sweat dotted her face.

While Jinmei sat in front as if leading the way, Xie Han watched over the three women. A kung fu teacher in a distant life and still occasionally a self-defense trainer, Xie Han liked this vantage point, which allowed her to watch over her friends without being directive. Every now and then, they would approach her to ask how to execute a flying kick that could disable an attacker temporarily. Although the three women took to lessons and discipline according to their natures, Xie Han was confident that she'd given them the ability to fight their way out of any scrape and to decommission a man with one blow. What more could a woman who cares for her friends do in this crazy life? Xie Han allowed herself a smile, and then they rounded a bend in the river.

"You wanted to move your arms in a different way. Here we are," Xie Han deadpanned.

All eyes looked up at the cascades. Curtains of moving glass spun over rocks. The roar of the falls crashed into the lighter dolloping of lazy eddies. Where the water spread out into pools near the shore, the ocher sand was visible, while on the banks ferns sprang up with a simple vitality. Droplets danced in swirling clouds, touching the women's faces, then refracting sunlight over their heads. Though not steep, the waterfalls climbed up for a good few miles. The women got out of the canoe.

"Let's rest a little," suggested Van Dao.

"Okay, but not too long. Or our muscles will get sore," said Xie Han in her kung fu teacher voice.

"Whereas what we'll do is we won't rest till we're done, then we'll be really, really sore," said Jinmei jokingly. Shinhyun shot her a withering look. Really, everything Jinmei said was so annoying. So childish and silly.

"You *know* the less we stop, the more chances we have of getting there undetected," Shinhyun remarked.

"Did I say I wanted to be pregnant? Hey, Van Dao, do you want a baby?" exclaimed Jinmei.

"I'm sick of you two bickering," said Xie Han. "Why don't you save your squabbles for when we get back?" Though she knew that Jinmei and Shinhyun had reached that sour stage that meant it was over, even if they didn't realize it yet.

"When we get back," repeated Van Dao. They all thought, *if* we get back.

Eventually, they hoisted the canoe over their heads and began a laborious trek up the hill. The path was narrow but well worn by different tribes and animals. Sometimes it traveled to the left of the waterfall, sometimes to the right, sometimes crossing over on a felled tree, sometimes over a series of white rocks rubbed unrelentingly smooth and slippery by ribbons of water.

It was during one of these crossings that Shinhyun fell. Though she knew that while carrying the canoe they were extremely visible and vulnerable, she drew a strange kind of determination from this knowledge. When she had walked out of the city, she was vulnerable then too, but she kept going. There was the blurry memory of her father removing her clothes and smiling, then a blank, and now only the words "Never again, never again," inside her head, repeated over and over like the beating of a heart, battered but still alive. Clutching the cumbersome weight of the canoe, they had been moving between rocks in sandy pits where the current tore at their legs with the force of ten angry aliens. Shinhyun stepped onto a stone that tipped over, and the water took her down. A brief panicked ride down the river. She grabbed a boulder poised over a long drop. The cool water soothed and exhilarated her body at the same time. She felt her scalp prickling from the heat of fear and adrenaline. Gritting her teeth, she ignored the precipice and negotiated her way, rock by rock, back to the relative safety of the path.

"Are you all right?" asked Jinmei, running up.

"I'm okay." She inspected her body. Graze marks on her arms and legs began to fill up with blood.

"Ooooch. We'll have to patch you up, sweets," said Jinmei, hugging her carefully. In such moments, Shinhyun became emotionally absent, waiting for the dam to subside.

In desiring you, I desired an object on which I could empty my passion, release my animal energy, smear my bruised ego. When

I desired you, I wanted to subdue you, overpower you, in fact, kill you, little by little, day by day, orgasm by orgasm. Take you, possess you, fuck you.

So it had been with her lover in the city, a junior officer in the Department of Defense. Shinhyun watched as he bent and folded himself according to her every wish and whim, accompanied by all the usual simpers and grimaces of courtship. Why do they do it? She knew that in return they hoped to reach her coolness, make her groan involuntarily, grasp and twist her entrails, control her. The contract of love.

"It's a biochemical state that lasts two years max," was how Jinmei had philosophically put it at the beginning of their relationship. "You get in a couple, you have children, and you perpetuate your society. So two years down the road, you wake up from your euphoria, saddled with a live-in lover and at least one child. Trapped! And no more of that sweet anaesthesia. . . ." For all her rationalization, Jinmei had stayed. Here, two years later, they were no longer in love, they didn't even want to have sex.

But I still love you. Jinmei and I had something there, after and beyond the reciprocal desire to dominate. And I still want a child. I'm going to have a child.

The falls past, they tumbled back into the canoe. The sun was now at its highest point. Fatigue was setting in. Yet they kept going, as long as the vegetation gave them cover.

Jinmei was not exactly tired. She had gone to further points of exhaustion. One year of drought she and Xie Han (it had been just two of them then) could not find enough food. They would wander for miles each day through brittle brown bush, looking for sustenance. On a shrunken stomach and with never enough rest, they would put one foot in front of the other under the searing sun. Both women's muscles melted away, so their cheek bones, ribs, and hip bones pushed up under dull skin. Xie Han stopped doing her morning kung fu since there was barely enough food to stay alive and keep foraging. Jinmei, taller, fleshier, and used to throwing off energy with wide gestures, dancing, and story telling, suffered more. She could not stay still, yet she was too tired to make any superfluous movements. This must be hell, she thought. During the brief warm night, the ground was hard and dusty.

Jinmei wanted to remind Xie Han now and to tell Shinhyun and Van Dao about that time of difficulty, to exaggerate and to pantomine the suffering overcome. But Jinmei knew that everyone would scold her for making noise so near the patrols. She bit her lip and concentrated for a while on the river stretching ahead. Why they were undertaking such a dangerous journey she was not sure. But the loyalty she felt toward her friends—her only family—did not permit her to think about turning back.

Finally, around a bend in the river, they saw that the banks had been shaved down to a stubble of brown grass. The area was desolate. Spread-eagled and abandoned.

The river part of their journey was over.

They hid the canoe back in the bush. The paths near the defoliated zone marked the extent of patrols' vigilance, the women knew from past missions. The canoe would be safe from other tribes as well; none usually ventured so close in. The women traveled among the trees, making a wide circumference around the city.

At sunset, they looked down from a mountainside at the valley. The city was wreathed by a dense cloud of fumes.

"It's even more polluted than when I left!" exclaimed Shinhyun. The wind brought warm wafts of exhaust and chemical residues.

"The defoliated zone has gotten wider," Xie Han pointed out.

"We only have a few more hours to the prison. Let's stop for the night." Van Dao, the youngest, was weary.

"I'll be ovulating tomorrow," stated Shinhyun.

"I am the day after," Xie Han added.

"Hey, look!" shouted Jinmei. "Dinner!" The four women ran up to a grove of mango trees. The air was alive with the buzzing of bees, the susurrus of leaves, and the smell of overripe fruit. Suddenly, they heard someone clearing his or her throat. They reached for their nunchucks.

"Good evening, ladies," someone intoned solemnly. This was followed by tittering. They looked up into the darkening boughs and saw a tribe of monkeys calmly feasting on mangos.

"Um, good evening," said Van Dao.

"What is your business here?" asked one severe-looking monkey, wiping the yellow juice from her lips with dainty movements.

"We're just passing through, on our way to the Wood and Water prison camp," replied Van Dao, on her best manners.

"On your way to prison? What crime did you commit?" Another round of giggling.

"We're looking for some sperm. Two of us want to have children."

"Oh, yes. Well, there's lots of human sperm in the forced labor camp, I have to admit that. But why go all that way? You know, Nonieko here has already fathered three offspring with female humans." She indicated a fellow monkey who was busy picking his teeth with a twig.

"Really? I didn't know that could be done."

"Yes, well, actually, only one lived to term. He was very ugly by our standards. But the mother was overjoyed. Said she was sick of men. Male humans, that is."

"Well, Xie Han, Shinhyun," Jinmei smiled mischievously, "what d'you say? It is a lot less risky than going all the way into the prison camp."

"Jinmei, you know I want an Asian baby. Not just human but Asian," said Shinhyun firmly.

"Hmmm, yes," agreed Xie Han, though she didn't want to offend the simian tribe.

"Okay, just wanted to help you out." The monkey shrugged her shoulders.

"It would be a great help if we could stay here tonight . . . and eat some of your mangos," requested Van Dao.

"Why, that goes without saying. I don't hold too many grudges. And we're not selfish like your lot, you know. Come on up! Oh, I understand. I wouldn't want to make it with some smelly human, male or female. Yes, when that biological clock ticks, you just can't help it. Thought it would interfere with my life, my responsibilities as leader, but really, you just keep going. During my first pregnancy . . ."

That night, the women slept in the trees, accompanied in their dreams by the loquacious Mulvieno, ever eager to practice the human tongues she had picked up before escaping from a cosmetics testing lab as an adolescent.

Six years old, Xie Han and all the village girls went to kung fu training at dawn. After two hours, they went to school to learn the intricacies of their language, history, and culture. Again in the afternoon more rigorous exercises before they returned home to their families. All this time, the boys stayed at home to help their fathers with domestic chores. By the time she had her first period, Xie Han was coaching younger kids who looked up to her grace and strength with awe.

Fifteen, Xie Han was practicing her specialty, the nunchuck. It was a pyrotechnical show of speed, but willfully released, the mahogany will shatter bones. Someone sneaking up behind her. She twirls around, stopped in the scorpion stance, ready to transform into the mongoose offensive.

From behind a tree peeked a small, skinny kid, who then bowed formally and broke into a shaky sea-urchin stance. Xie Han watched in puzzlement as the sea urchin did a cartwheel, executed a few comical bumblebee moves, and ended up sitting crosslegged with a silly smile on her face.

This was how serious Xie Han met playful Jinmei, an orphan from the next village over where the men went out into the world to conduct business and the women stayed inside tending the home. A few months later, the two girls—now friends till death—ran away in search of a legendary lesbians of color tribe, whispered about by men when they wanted to frighten one another on stormy nights.

Over the years, their own little tribe began to form. Young Van Dao had trailed them after they had met her people, the glowing tree tattoo tribe. Shinhyun came out of the city and joined them. And maybe soon they would have two babies.

That was good. Xie Han felt time weighing on her body like a fullness. This fullness wanted to give life to another.

Van Dao had just received a tree tattoo, sign of a complete person. Her tree was the pine, the kind that whispers, soughs, and sings in the softest of breezes and scatters tiny wooden pine cones. The scab was beginning to come off. In the dark, she could see the new skin glowing on her arm.

"Soon you will be able to marry and have your own family," her mother gushed happily. "Is there any of the boys you prefer? How about the tall one with the coconut tree?"

Van Dao didn't reply.

"Stop picking your scab or you'll give yourself scars."

One day, two women walked into the village. They looked strong and unafraid, even though neither of them bore a luminous tree of any kind. They were unaccompanied by any man. They made a few trades, while exchanging news of government incursions and pillaging tribes. The villagers were friendly but still watched them with suspicion. When the two women left the village, Van Dao trailed them.

She passed the cane and corn fields where she and her family worked year in and year out. She left behind the sacred giant banyan tree whose hanging roots had given birth to scores of other banyans and under whose boughs men and women were joined together as one. She crossed the stream that marked the end of her people's land. Then they entered the hills where Van Dao had never ventured before.

Night-blooming flowers sent messages of scent. Stars were blinking down. There were mysterious rustling in the trees, and it seemed to Van Dao that eyes whose bodies she could not see were staring at her. Unable to stand the loneliness, she bounded out of the bushes and stood in their camp, nervously rubbing her tattooed arm.

"Are you lost?" asked Xie Han.

"No. I want to go where you're going."

"Why? We don't even know where we're going."

"I want to live with you," she said shyly, looking at Jinmei.

"But, you're just a baby!" Jinmei laughed.

For years, scrupulously ignoring her questioning eyes, Jinmei persisted in treating her like a little sister. Then Shinhyun entered all their lives. Now Shinhyun and Jinmei were breaking up.

I wasn't a baby then. I'm not a baby now.

This Van Dao knew for sure, eyes shining, with the same certainty that a glowing tree tattoo marks a whole and mature human being.

They lay in the cool shade, bodies pushed up against the slight incline. They were hidden behind a barbed-wire fence and its thick hedge. A weed insinuated itself between the two barriers, its little white flowers exuding a light but intoxicating fragrance.

From their secret observation deck, they saw prisoners slowly digging up a plot of land, baked by the sun. Two guards were smoking cigarettes while they kept guns slung over their shoulders.

In the shade, they exchanged glances. There was one suitable specimen. He had bedraggled black hair and a moustache that was both long and sparse. Thin, but they could see his tight muscles as he overturned the earth with a blunt, rusty shovel.

In the glare of the sun, the guards sauntered over by the bushes, the barrels of their guns always holding the men under consideration. The women froze for a second as the back of the standard-issue boots paused a few inches from their faces.

In one clean move, Xie Han and Jinmei knocked the guards unconscious. Shinhyun and Van Dao squirmed under the fence, grabbed the prisoner, and pulled him under the hedge. The other prisoners watched in a stupor. When the women and the prisoner called Song had disappeared into the greenery, a few men also took to the trees. The others, having been there for too many decades for a forgotten or nonexistent crime, put down their tools and sat in the dust, waiting for somebody to tell them what to do.

\* \* \*

In the first few seasons with Jinmei and Xie Han, Van Dao missed her parents, her people, her tree. But she knew she could not return and be who she had now become; Van Dao had vague memories of an Aunt Lalah (a tamarind person) who lived with a woman and was shunned by everyone. Xie Han and Jinmei had been on their own for two years when Van Dao joined them, and when she walked away from her ancestors' land, she had just earned her tattoo. Van Dao's age and the fact that the glowing tree people did not practice martial arts out of a philosophic belief made it hard for her to feel an equal to Jinmei and Xie Han. She especially wanted Jinmei to think of her as a woman.

In time, Van Dao gained respect from Jinmei and Xie Han, for she knew which plants were poisonous and which healed through an infusion, a poultice, or the fruit. After all, her people identified themselves with foliage of all sorts. Always wishing to know more, Van Dao was constantly examining, picking, and sampling plants that did not grow in her village's vicinity. Many times she became very sick from ingesting unfamiliar herbs, and once she came close to death. But even that could not make her less brave; she wanted to know more, and to make this knowledge available to those she loved.

Shinhyun thought she could help her be more fertile with herbs, but Van Dao insisted that she did not know of such plants.

"Do you have a family history of . . ." began Van Dao, reading from a list.

"Forget it, we don't have time. Here," said Xie Han, handing the man a little jar. "Jerk off."

"What! You must be all out of your minds!" he objected.

"Euh!" exclaimed Jinmei. "Crappy men. You probably do it everyday anyway!"

"First you kidnap me. Then you want me to masturbate in front of four savage, perverted women. What's the deal?"

"Look," said Shinhyun in a monotone, "you give us a little sperm, we let you go. Sperm for freedom."

"Ah," he seemed to brighten up, even managed to ogle Shinhyun. "So that's it! Well, I've been in that damn camp for four years, haven't seen a women for as many, but I can still get it up. Please take your clothes off and lie down in a line." The women looked at each other. Shinhyun pursed her lips in an expression of barely contained impatience, Xie Han arched an eyebrow, and Van Dao rolled her eyes to high heaven.

Jinmei grabbed him by the rags around his neck. "In the jar, get it? If you don't want to, there are ten thousand other men in that prison who wouldn't mind giving up some of their cum for being set free."

"But you chose me!" His voice rose up in a squeal, as he disengaged himself from Jinmei's grip. "I'm not blind. You want an Asian man. So here I am, the only Asian man who's not in solitary for about one hundred square miles. What's wrong with a little natural pleasure? That way we can all enjoy ourselves."

Jinmei got out her machete and addressed Xie Han.

"Guess we'll just have to go in and get it ourselves," she said casually, fingering the blade. To Song she said, "Drop your pants."

He snarled, defeated, and snatched the jar.

"Can't a man have a little privacy at least?"

The women watched him from the corner of their eyes to make sure he wouldn't try to run away. He kneeled over the jar. After about one minute, he exhaled audibly.

Making little grumbling noises, Song retied the rope that served as his belt. He handed the jar to Shinhyun.

"They're coming," Xie Han said calmly.

"Okay, Van Dao, hand me the syringe," said Shinhyun, throwing off her clothes in a quick, nervous gesture.

Van Dao made a sharp intake of breath, alarming everyone. "I forgot it!"

"Two patrols. Backed up by a tank," Xie Han interjected tensely.

Suddenly Jinmei took the jar and consumed its albuminous contents.

"Jinmei!" shrieked Shinhyun.

Jinmei pushed Shinhyun down and blew approximately half of the liquid up her vagina. Xie Han, having understood Jinmei's intention, was already waiting, legs spread.

"Disgusting!" Jinmei exclaimed, obviously about the sperm, as she wiped her mouth.

"Let's go!" urged Van Dao.

"Thanks, Jinmei," said Shinhyun.

"Anytime," joked Jinmei as they reached for their weapons.

"Come if you want," said Xie Han to the man. "We're going outbacks."

They ran through the trees, branches slapping back, thorns clawing, peadoves taking off in a whirling of wings, frozen lizards eyes agog. Through the trees, branches waving them on, lungs gasping up oxygen, feet bouncing from speed against nervous stones crumbling down hills, buttocks propelling legs pumping through dry gullies, scrambling up hills hurting, chest and arm muscles reaching out, parting the bush, leaping flying pirouetting over webs of roots, obdurate boulders, cities of ants, tiny winding slivers of rivers. Branches folding back to hide their passage, wind rushing from seaside to seaside, wild parrots squalling somewhere, leaves shaking in laughter. Through the trees the trees the trees.

"How long has it been since you last bled?" asked Xie Han.

"About three months," said Shinhyun contentedly from behind a piece of sugar cane.

"I don't see anything yet," commented Van Dao.

"But I can feel something," answered Shinhyun, stroking her own belly.

"Please, make it a girl," said Jinmei, coconut juice dribbling off her face. She split the green coconut with a machete, scooped out the soft white jelly and gave it to Van Dao. Then Jinmei and Van Dao ran into the sea holding hands.

"Jinmei is a child herself. No wonder she doesn't want to be a parent," Shinhyun shook her head indulgently, then turned to Xie Han. "You can help me with my baby, then we can see about finding you some more sperm."

"Oh, I don't know if I want my own just yet." Xie Han was distractedly making designs in the sand holding an empty shell like a brush.

Shinhyun smiled to herself. Xie Han had been visiting Taina quite frequently.

It was strange. Years after giving up looking for the semi-mythical lesbian of color tribe, Xie Han had found them one day bathing by some falls. She came to realize they were simply a group of women traveling together, just like her own little tribe, except they were more numerous and not only Asian. There had been one particularly beautiful one, stepping out of the water. She had covered her breasts with her palms and returned Xie Han's steady stare.

Shinhyun and Xie Han reclined against a dune. Behind them, it looked as if a sleeping giant's hands had been covered by earth centuries ago. On the undulant hills, every tree in the multitude stood out as an individual; the air accentuated the leaves' different textures and colors even at a distance. The trembling verdancy hid hundreds of tribes, each living according to its own laws. Every so often a gust of wind would sting the two women with sand, then they would feel large, gritty pieces in their mouths as they sucked on sugar cane. The wind also brought the pungent smell of the open sea, salty and salubrious. They watched Van Dao and Jinmei chasing each other in hypnotic glintings on the curves of water, felt the sun sinking into their brown bodies. They listened as the waves surged in, crashed on top of one another, mixed together with churning, twirling sand and bubbles of breeze. It was the sound of single droplets of water magnified thousands of times into a lulling and exuberant roar.

# Brownstones

## DONNA ALLEGRA

*A*s much as Mother disapproved of my going out with women—"I didn't raise my child to become a bulldagger"—she welcomed me back home. I didn't give her any details, but she probably knew the reasons for my sadness. Mother's no slouch and has told me often enough, "If you knew one-tenth of what I've forgotten, daughter, you'd be in much better shape."

Almost a year passed before I did anything other than return home after working at the library, buy groceries, and hide myself in a book. I looked up only now and again to weep. I'd sometimes think, had Ellen been Black, I could have seen past the flimsy excuses. Then I'd need to clear my throat of the marinated taste of regret that lay on the back of my tongue.

One May evening I heard the Mister Softee ice-cream truck tinkle its siren song under my window and the calls of children gathering around its promise of pleasure. A whole new bunch of kids swear they own the block I grew up on and I don't know a single one who rides a bike through the backyards, plays handball in the alleyways, or jumps double-dutch on the sidewalk.

The high pitch of young voices called me from my novel. I went outside to the stoop where I could watch children living in their laughter. I'd try to see who favored butter pecan, pistachio, or banana-chocolate swirl from the ice-cream truck.

Mother was already downstairs, talking to Mrs. Singleton, but rather than join them on the stoop, I crouched on the steps. I'd never been responsive to our next-door neighbor's prodding for talk of myself or her efforts to seduce me with allusions to luscious gossip. Reputation called me shy, but the greater truth was that I didn't like Mrs. Singleton nosing around, sniffing out juicy tidbits that she'd parade as a trophy to draw acclaim to herself.

Not that I'd ever interacted a lot with any neighbors. If my school report cards read "A" in all subjects, what they left out was "Michelle does not play well with other children." I'd learned to put out a bookish and foggy air to keep people at a distance. This strategy worked better with adults than with other children.

But something did pierce me when I heard Mrs. Singleton say, "So here she comes, just as proud as can be wearing her construction boots. You'd never know it now, but Renee was the most feminine baby you ever did see; such a dainty little girl before her mother passed. In my day, no woman wanted to become a common laborer."

"Well now, Joyce, times have changed," Mother sounded conciliatory. "The women do all sorts of things they didn't used to. We always had a few doctors and lawyers, but now even they're commonplace. What's news is the women police, those girl car mechanics, and the like." I could practically feel Mrs. Singleton's frown of disapproval. I suppressed my own smile of wonder as I heard Mother press forward against the conventional reaction. "And no reason why not, Joyce. I like it when I see the lady bus driver or hear the female subway conductor."

"Well, jobs is one thing, but I want a man taking my daughter out on a Saturday night," Mrs. Singleton pronounced.

Mother said nothing to this and I called out, "Hey, Renee. How you doing?" as she waved hello to Mother and Mrs. Singleton, not seeing me sitting on the steps to the stoop. I smiled up to the handsome girl from my childhood writ large.

"Michelle? Well look who's here! What brings you back to the block? It takes all these years to come visit your poor old mother?" She winked at Mother, who put both hands on her hips, approving Renee, and looked down at me with a triumphant "Hmph."

"Mm hmm. My child gets her degree in library science, moves to Greenwich Village, and I don't see hide nor hair of her for months at a time," Mother sniffed to Renee. "But now she's back under my wing, where she belongs." She raised her eyebrows to me.

"Well, dag, Mrs. Walker. You should let the girl out for a breath of fresh air every little once in a while. I left the block when I was seventeen and came back when I was twenty-five and I never knew Michelle had even gone or come back," Renee joshed. I didn't let on that their tandem teasing delighted me.

"So what are you up to these days, Renee? How you been?"

"Time goes so fast, I just don't know some days."

"Before you two get started: Michelle, don't forget to pick up my clothes from the cleaner's before Evelyn closes. I have to get dinner started."

"All right, Mother."

"I'm heading that way, Michelle. I'll walk you down the block and we can get caught up."

As we walked, I told Renee I worked at New York University's Bobst Library and took literature classes for recreation; that I'd left my apartment, no longer wanting to live with a roommate. "I'm staying temporarily with Mother until an affordable situation comes up." Even though I omitted the severed relationship with Ellen from my story, those facts did sound plausible.

Renee told me of her apprenticeship as an electrician and her job on a fifty-story office building with men, who, in their more sensitive moments said, "Oh shit, look at this! It's a girl. How ya doin', hon?"

After stopping at Evelyn's Cleaners, we crossed the street to Renee's house and stood on her stoop reminiscing. When we were kids, Renee played with the gang around the corner. Having lived on the block these past few years, she knew more about who got married, had a city job, got arrested, had overdosed.

She snorted at memory. "You, Cheryl Marks, and Debbie Richards were in that college-bound league. By junior high, we lived in different worlds. But even before that, I could never touch you. You were always so stuck on Yvonne Hicks."

I smiled at her summation and nodded. It was true that Yvonne had been my best friend throughout elementary school days at P.S. 83. I told Renee, "Everyone else was too rough and tough for me. Come junior high, Mother sent me to Meyer Levin, that mostly white school out in Flatbush." Taking on Mother's accent, "If I can't send you back home to Jamaica to get a real education, I'll settle for second best and put you with the white children. They at least get something of an education from the schools here."

I didn't want to teach, as Mother had been encouraging me to. I cringed at the thought of all those little people expecting so much of me. "But Michelle, you'll be older and far wiser than they. Teachers make a good salary and get retirement benefits. It's a secure city job."

The way I felt about it, children were worse than adults. I felt burdened not to hurt their feelings as adults had once hurt mine. But the bottom line was that children were people—and too many at one time for my taste.

Library science, however, appealed to me. While at Hunter College majoring in a career in public books, the athletic girls began to interest, then distract me, especially in spring when the warm air made everyone giddy. At times, I'd felt dizzy with desire. A little searching through the card catalogue for entries under "Homosexual" and "Lesbian" confirmed my worries and more that I dreaded knowing about myself.

As usual, when memories breathed through me, my conversation evaporated. As if to keep us talking, Renee spoke of going to Brooklyn College to study physical education and become a gym teacher. "I put more energy into smoking herb and drinking wine than studying physiology. At the time, it just seemed like a better idea to do the rent-a-cop work full-time, ya know?" she trailed off with a sad chuckle.

"I worked as a guard in this building where the furniture had just been moved in. I got to talking with this sister who was an electrician there. She practically hounded me to get an application for her union's apprenticeship. I was pretty foggy from all the reefer I was doing, but the money sounded right and she had a trade. Nobody can take that kind of knowledge from you. I wanted that."

Renee's eyes looked as if she were taking my measure for all her dimensions. I think I passed inspection because she said, "I knew I needed to stop getting high if I was to have a shot at what I wanted in life. I decided to come home and get clean. My father had passed and this brownstone was the best place for me to grow into whatever I could be without drugs."

One of the kids playing running bases on the sidewalk sent the pink Spalding bouncing near us. Renee scooped it up and threw it back to the girl who yelled, "Thanks, Renee." Someone's record player sent the Isley Brothers' "Groove With You" wafting down the street. The melody and mood seemed to accompany what Renee said next.

"You know? I used to think it was cool and mighty to always keep my feelings down, look like I was absolutely right, never admit I made any mistakes. Now what makes me strong is that I can show some emotion, set things right when I screw up and learn something useful from it. I see myself like a river. The little streams don't seem like much, but all that water moving in one direction is where the power comes from."

I listened to the tide of emotion behind her words, fascinated by the spirit animating her. Neither of us had mentioned any boyfriends. I was pretty sure about Renee, but could she tell about me?

"Dag, it's eight o'clock! Your mother must be worried about you, Michelle. Do you want to call to tell her you're okay?"

"She knows I'm okay, Renee. I'm a woman now." I looked into her eyes as I spoke, hoping she picked up the scent of my trail. After a moment passed, I said, "Why don't you come by for dinner with Mother and me tomorrow?"

"I have a meeting with my clean-and-sober support group, but I'm clear for Friday."

So that's how we began, or rather, picked up, midstream as adult friends, no longer children on the block.

Curiously, Mother welcomed Renee. They shared a mutual

interest in current events and shared indignation over racial politics, which I gladly left them to discuss and solve without me, thank you. The year 1972 was a presidential election one, so Blacks were important to the politicians who would continue to smile and lie to get our votes.

Monday and Wednesday evenings Renee went to school as part of her apprenticeship training. Tuesdays and Thursdays she met with her clean-and-sober support people. I'd started volunteering to read stories to children twice a week at the neighborhood library on Eastern Parkway. Renee and I would touch base sometimes on the stoop and exchange stories of our days at work. I'd lost my urgency to find an apartment in the city. I liked returning home to Brooklyn away from Manhattan's crowded rush and blaring sirens.

Friday night dinners became fairly regular for the three of us. Renee's family hailed from Virginia, but she loved Jamaican dishes, so I made my variations on Mother's curried chicken, codfish, coconut-peas-and-rice recipes. Mother usually excused herself shortly after the meal, sounding almost bashful, "I'll leave you two grown girls to get reacquainted."

Once I was sure of my rising feelings, I set to work. I was subtle: a sprinkle of perfume, an open-throated blouse, a better cut of slacks on Fridays. Renee worked her side of the street as well. She brought flowers "for the dinner table." Her starched shirts and pressed pants looked like they'd arrived fresh from Evelyn's Cleaners.

When we went walking around the neighborhood, Renee took the outside lane, let me go through doors and narrow passages first, and got very vocal in return when men threw rude come-ons our way. I felt valued and cared for with this woman at my side. And worried why she hadn't made the move on me.

One Saturday, we went strolling up Eastern Parkway toward Prospect Park. Renee smiled at the white truck with the red and blue trim. The Mister Softee jingle tinkled the same tune as it had in our childhood.

"He should be around our way by seven-fifteen."

"How about a cone, Renee? My treat."

Several giggling children scooted ahead of us. They were eager, laughing, begging their mothers to let them have some ice cream.

"What do you want, Renee?"

"I'm a get me a pistachio cone," she said in a child's cadence.

"Umm, nice choice. A maple cup for me."

We had to thread our way with a crowd of children such as Renee and I once were. None of us in that boisterous group was hungry, but mouths watered in anticipation of pleasure, not yet need. The children's excitement alternated between their roughness with one another, "Hurry up, Keisha," and having to tone-down and show good manners to us big people, "Oh, excuse me, miss."

Renee played her role as sober and stable adult. "That's quite all right, Laverne. Why don't you go ahead of me in the line? I can wait." I marveled at the awe in the little girl's face because Renee somehow knew her name. I bubbled with my own tamed laughter.

We resumed our stroll through the midsummer evening up the boulevard that towering trees and tall brownstones presided over.

"Thanks, Michelle, this is great."

"Can I have a taste of yours?"

"Let me wipe this off first." Some ice cream had melted from the cone onto Renee's hand. I wanted those drippings. "No, here," I said, and guided her wrist to my mouth. I lapped from her fingers onto her palm, tongued the grooves between her fingers. I licked the sensitive area on the inside of her wrist, ostensibly to get the sweet taste of ice cream, but hoping to stir some feelings in Renee.

"Hold still, I'm not done yet," I scolded.

We both stood on the corner, near laughter.

"Want some of mine?" I offered. She nodded like a youngster, not sure her mother would allow what the child really desired. I was about to spoon some maple walnut into Renee's mouth, when a man's voice intruded.

"C'mere, sugar. I got something for you to lick only a real

man's got. You too fine and foxy to go to waste like that."

Before I could give him a piece of my mind, Renee was shouting, "You stupid broken-down, raggedy-assed, ugly motha fucka: she's not even looking at no useless low-life scuzzy piece of nothing like you. She's with me. You got that? You got anything to say about it? 'Cause if you do, I'll kick your ass from here to next Tuesday."

I had to step in front of Renee, "Baby, don't. He's not worth you getting upset. We don't have to get into his mess." I scooped my arm around Renee to steer her away.

Even if the waters between us hadn't been simmering for weeks, they were ready to boil over now. As suddenly as she had raged at him, Renee yielded to me. She quieted her words, but her eyes echoed my own anger, frustration, and longing. I piloted us along Eastern Parkway.

I brought us to the Botanic Garden. We found a bench under a tree dripping a pink and white cascade of leaves. Renee's face remained drawn tight, then she broke. "I hate those guys when they say shit like that. Where are their heads at? Do they really think you'll come running up and say, 'Yes, Daddy, I'm yours'? I wanted to beat the living daylights out of that knucklehead for talking like that to you."

I still felt astonished for having said "Baby" those minutes ago. Had Renee even heard? Did she know how I felt for her? What could she tell from the way I stroked her back, smoothed her forehead, and hugged her as she wept into the palms of her hands, elbows atop her knobby knees? She worked with the worst of men everyday; why did this one fool's taunts make my baby cry?

I felt the afternoon breeze bathing my face, the wind cradling the leaves as I sought to soothe Renee, waves of desire surging through me. She seemed calmer, her eyes still sad and dewy. I kissed the soft ebony roses unfurling from her cheeks, her perfect slice-of-moon brow, the pouting oval of her mouth. And then, I slipped my tongue between those plumped petals.

Greenwich Village is one place, but my Brooklyn hometown is quite another. Even under the cover of a curtain of leaves, we didn't feel safe to be close, to touch, to kiss, and I was streaming, ready to suckle her every body part.

"Let's take a cab to your house." When we arrived, Renee seemed disoriented after closing her front door, and I no longer felt so swift and sure. She said, "I'll get with you in a minute." She stopped briefly in the dark living room. The furnishings her parents had installed in the fifties sat mute: a large RCA Victor console in front of a plastic-covered couch, lacy doilies on the arms of potbellied chairs.

I made my way upstairs to Renee's light blue bedroom. The book case lining the far wall contained electrical texts. On the floor next to her bed lay old, worn paperbacks by March Hastings, Joan Ellis, Randy Salem, and newer, worn ones by Jane Rule, Audre Lorde, Alice Walker.

I telephoned Mother and carefully told her, "Mother, I'll be staying the night at Renee's." She hesitated a moment, then said, "All right, dear. . . . Give Renee my love."

The same Isley Brothers song that I heard when Renee and I first spoke by her stoop drifted through the warm air. I could see early evening settling outside the window. The way I was feeling, the whole night wouldn't be long enough, but we could at least begin. Renee came in and lay down on her bed beside me.

"You're not seeing anyone else?" I spoke more a request than a question, and this was only a shadow of the demand I wanted to put to her.

"Ever since I found out you were back home, I haven't been able to even look at anyone else," she said, which sounded quite reasonable to me.

I traced patterns on her hand and told her about meeting Ellen at Hunter College, going to Gay Activists' Alliance meetings, hanging out at Bonnie & Clyde's, then settling in with Ellen on East 5th Street. "I suppose I should have cultivated other friends instead of assuming Ellen's, but I didn't have the personality."

I didn't want to invoke too much memory, but I told Renee, "Ellen had a broader social network and found she wanted to be sexual outside of our relationship. I couldn't be with that. We argued the issue for weeks. When she confessed she was sleeping with someone else, I lost it and moved out the next day."

"You truly are your mother's daughter," Renee chuckled. "And your own woman too," she added hastily.

"Maybe now I could handle the situation better, but what I want is my lover's complete attention. I'm basically a home girl, Renee. I expect people to tell me the truth emotionally."

Renee nodded, taking me in. She'd been smiling throughout, listening with an ear tuned to the ebb and flow of my sensibility. It was like snuggling with a best friend when our parents had gone out for the evening. As Renee caressed me from shoulder to thigh, I felt safe to open all doors. I'm embarrassed about this, but the fact is, when I let people put their hands on my body, I develop strong attachments to them.

"Well, while you were in Gay Activists' Alliance meetings and going to Bonnie & Clyde's, I was keeping to the Brooklyn side of the bridge. I went to The Hut and The Outer Limits, being an after-hours party butch. Sometimes I'd go uptown to The Hilltop or Andre's.

"I stayed high and talked trash and couldn't figure what it was all about. I knew I wanted to settle down and be with a wife, but I couldn't see how to have that and stay high, so I stayed high. When that started hurting too much more than it was worth, and I didn't have much say in the matter ... well, I knew I'd better get some help to change my ways, or die."

Now it was my turn to give silent witness. I'd only seen Renee straight, but I could sense this was a big deal for her. There was nothing more I wanted to say and still so much yet to be spoken. I reached for her with my heart eager and my body excited, my mouth watered with both pleasure and need.

The Isleys still crooned that same love song. I could listen to it forever. From down the block we heard the Mr. Softee truck jingle its seductive call and the children gathering in excitement.

I felt like all those laughing children licking ice cream on their stoops. Laughter floated up from the street. I could afford to live here in Brooklyn.

# *Still Life*

## BARBARA WILSON

*N*o part of a city, if you've lived in it long enough, has only one history. The past is not replaced; instead, new layers of memory build up. In watercolor, this layering is called glazing. A thin wash of cobalt over crimson and over that another wash of crimson makes a different violet on the page than if the colors are mixed first on the palette and then painted on. The Seattle neighborhood of Fremont had been many things in Cory's life, but now it was the part of town where Cory's therapist, Roberta Lu, lived. Before Roberta, Fremont had been where her travel agent used to have her office, and before that, where the antinuclear group had its meetings. After Roberta, it might be anything. If there ever was an after-Roberta.

Cory had had a standing appointment with Roberta Lu for over six months now, every Thursday at three in the afternoon. She took off early from work then; it was her way of making time to think about her life. Sometimes Cory walked to Fremont, both ways, right around the north end of Lake Union, past Ivar's Salmon House and Gas Works Park, to the old-fashioned brick blocks of the small business district.

On the way there, Cory walked quickly, composing in her head all the things she wanted to tell Roberta, all the things that had happened to her that week, all the things she'd thought about. But on the way home, Cory walked slowly and thought about what she'd really said, which always surprised her and was nothing like what she'd planned.

She was walking home now. Earlier it had rained and it

would again. The air was wet, sharp, solitary. Now, in November, it would be dark by five. The lake was almost dark, deep gray-green, with a scudding of silver waves reflecting the late afternoon sky.

They'd been talking today about memory, about loss, about sex. The usual things. Cory felt she wasn't moving forward, and sometimes persuaded herself that, in fact, she was moving backwards. It used to be, when she didn't remember, that her suffering was silent and contained, something that could be pushed to the back of the refrigerator and forgotten. These days she was raw. Trying to find the words, to have the emotions that went with the words, Cory felt like she had when she couldn't read as a child, when she'd been given a heavy book full of black insects and been told to sound them out, to turn them into words.

It had been the same— only worse—with the couples counselor she and Rosemary had gone to earlier this year for a few months. That therapist, Lois Larkin, was fluent in jargon and believed that everyone else should be, too. In her mouth "incest survivor" sounded like a normal thing, like being a car mechanic or a nurse. "How do you, Cory, as an incest survivor, feel about that?" she would say. Lois had short black hair and button black eyes. She usually wore flowing cotton trousers and a striped Guatemalan shirt over a turtleneck. She was active in progressive circles, and Cory had first met her in the seventies at an antiracism workshop. "As a former Catholic, raised-middle-class lesbian...," Lois used to begin her self-examinations.

Lois and Rosemary bonded about their Catholic girlhoods and about being "partners of incest survivors," who needed to be supportive but also "to take care of ourselves around this." Sometimes Lois spoke of her girlfriend, without using her name, and told them of a book the girlfriend had read that had been helpful, or how the two of them had resolved some issue. Cory knew who the girlfriend was—she was Donna Laura—who was a cashier at the Ravenna PCC. Sometimes when Cory put her vegetables on the conveyor belt, she looked at Donna Laura, a slight, brown-haired, ordinary-looking woman in jeans and a canvas apron, and wondered about her and Lois's sex life. Lois always spoke about sex as if it were a matter of making a nice, healthy vegetarian soup. Get the recipe book out, assemble the ingredients, chop a little, blend a little, cook it up, and serve it—Delicious! Something that was tasty and good for you, too. Sex, the sex-manual kind, was unabashedly good, positive, warm, and loving. It was not mysterious, demonic, and wild. It was not harsh and strange and overwhelming, with a core of numbness that let you forget what was going on even as it happened. It was not subject to rare, unexpected moments of grace, when there was a connection, a melting between you and your lover, between you and your universe.

"Everything that has been learned can be unlearned and relearned," said Lois. And, quoting from a well-known lesbian sex counselor: "All you need is a willingness."

Going through the PCC checkout line ("Got your co-op card?" asked Donna Laura with a cheerful smile), Cory imagined Lois, bouncy and solicitous in her half of the queen-sized bed, saying, "Darling, how 'bout it? Do you have a willingness tonight?" And Donna, slight, shy, saying, "Well, as an incest survivor I don't really have desire, in fact I have fear—perhaps even revulsion—but I do feel a slight willingness. Let's go with that."

But Cory never had a willingness nowadays, forget the desire. All she seemed to have was a resistance as heavy as a boulder blocking a spring.

Talking with Roberta wasn't easy, but it was better than trying to talk with Lois. Roberta was about fifty, Chinese-American, with wild, crackly gray hair and jewelry that she said she made herself—twisted copper wire and chunks of topaz and tourmaline. She laughed quite a lot—inappropriately, Cory thought at first. Was a therapist supposed to be quite so casual and lively? Roberta shrugged off Cory asking how other women dealt with memories of sexual abuse. "How are you going to deal with them?" Roberta didn't use jargon, and even if she said, "You must have felt abandoned by your mother even before she died," it sounded like a normal person expressing sympathy, not like the calculated probe of a trained therapist.

Lois's office had rag dolls and Teddy bears sitting on the windowsills and pastel boxes of Kleenex, which Cory never used, on every table. Roberta's had a tatami mat, two rattan chairs, and a few Tibetan prayer flags on a line by the window. The room was upstairs and caught the western light if there was any. For the past two months there had been some kind of construction project going on nearby, with jackhammering.

Roberta had Cory tell her stories.

"They're not stories," Cory had protested at first. "It's just— flashes, pictures. Skin, water. A rock. Over and over, the same thing, the same sick helpless feeling. My uncle's eyes, his weird smile. The pictures just flash up; I can't get rid of them."

"The images will always have a disruptive force until they're integrated into some kind of narrative," said Roberta. "That's their power—to force their way into your consciousness. You can't get rid of them, but you can give them a context."

"I don't remember enough," Cory always began, and then she talked for an hour and Roberta had to pry her out of the chair. Afterward she had more than the sound of a rushing river in her mind, more than a sense of choking, and of breaking. She had an alcoholic uncle who had wanted to be a painter. A grandmother who had been whipped every week of her life. A mother who wore harlequin sunglasses and couldn't see what was going on.

This afternoon, just before the session was ending, they'd gotten back to sex. A jackhammer had been pounding in the background with the fury of slow progress on tough asphalt.

"Rosemary doesn't ask me about it now," said Cory. "But I know she's wondering if it will ever happen again between us. What if it's years? I know she must be thinking that."

"What if it is?" asked Roberta. "How would you feel?"

"Guilty," said Cory. "I mean, especially now that we're planning to live together."

"But hasn't Rosemary been the one to push for you to live together?"

"Yes."

"Yes?" Roberta smiled. Why was she always smiling? She looked as if she hadn't a care in the world, as if she were just hanging around in her rattan chair for the hell of it. The only thing Cory knew about her was that she was a Buddhist. "It gives a certain perspective," Roberta said once, but Cory wasn't totally sure what that perspective was.

"Rosemary says she can take care of herself," Cory said.

"How is she taking care of herself?" Roberta asked, simply curious.

". . . I haven't really asked her."

"But you don't believe her?"

Cory sulked. It was all very well for someone who believed in reincarnation to give advice. But what if you didn't? The jackhammers stopped and started; the wind crept through a crack in the window frame and set the prayer flags to rustling. Another session over in a minute and still no progress.

Roberta was patient. "But you do think everything is going to be harder when you start living together?"

"Of course it will be," snapped Cory. "I'll have it in my face every minute. My failure. It will be my fault Rosemary's not happy."

"And why wouldn't she be happy?"

"Because it's not really a relationship if you don't have sex," Cory practically shouted. Did you have to tell her everything?

Roberta was silent. She did that on purpose, Cory knew, to make a little echo in the room. Then Roberta said, "How would you feel never to have sex again?" She held up her hand, which was covered with copper and topaz. "No, not how Rosemary would feel. Not how Lois would feel. Not how every other normal person on the planet would feel."

"Relieved, I guess," said Cory finally. "Not to have to think about it anymore."

"Not to be seen as a sexual person?" Roberta suggested, looking sympathetic while also glancing at the clock.

Cory nodded. Something huge, a boulder, was sitting on her chest. She couldn't breathe for an instant. The rain of tears that happened every session but that she never predicted and never prepared for with a handkerchief, poured down her face. She wanted to say how guilty and ashamed she was, how fearful she was of losing that connection with Rosemary, and with herself, but instead, the words choked out, as Roberta handed her a box of Kleenex, "I want my childhood back."

The rain was beginning again, a drizzle that swept over her face as she crossed over University Bridge and walked quickly up Eastlake, the way she had a thousand times before. As she came up to the building where she lived, she remembered that she'd meant to tell Irene that she was leaving at the end of this month. Not leaving-leaving, but going finally to live with Rosemary and turning her apartment totally into an office.

Cory stood on the sidewalk in front of the wooden building. The sign in Irene's side-street entrance read CLOSED, but Cory could see her inside, white-haired now and stooped with arthritis, back by the cash register. When Cory had first moved in, Irene had still been in her vigorous late fifties, just retired from an elementary school library and newly widowed. She'd used her husband's life insurance to buy the building and open the small used bookstore she'd always dreamed of.

There were a few people on the sidewalk of Eastlake and the side street, getting off the bus, going into the café down the block, into the tavern on the corner. It was raining harder now, but still Cory stood there, rooted, and didn't knock on the bookstore's door. She was caught in the memory of a dream she'd had off and on for years. In the dream she was always standing on this patch of sidewalk, looking up at the windows of her apartment on the second floor. It was always dusk, in autumn or winter, that moment just before the streetlights went on, before people came home from work and turned on their lamps.

Nothing much ever happened in the dream. She stood on the sidewalk and looked up at her apartment as the evening darkened, and suddenly a lamp in her apartment was switched on, and another. One in the kitchen, one in the living room. And someone came over and pulled the curtains closed against the dark night. It was always a shadow figure; she could never see who it was, a man or a woman, a friend or a stranger. All she knew is that there was someone else now living in her apartment.

With the bitter certainty of recurrent dreams, Cory knew that there had been a terrible mistake. That she had made a terrible mistake. She had moved out, she had left the city or the country and now she had returned but was homeless. She stood on the sidewalk and watched someone else move around in her old apartment. She was homeless, and someone else was living in her home.

Never, in the dream, did Cory dare go upstairs to find out who was there. Never did she try to talk with them directly. No, she always went into Irene's shop or across the street to a pay phone to call Irene.

And their conversation was always the same. Cory begged to be allowed to live there again, and Irene said kindly but firmly, "No, Cory, you had your chance, and you left. Someone else lives there now. I'm so very sorry, dear. I would have liked to keep you as a tenant forever."

I must not leave this place, Cory thought desperately. I have to ask Irene how I can buy the building when she dies so I never have to leave it.

Someone passing by bumped into her and apologized. Cory didn't know how long she'd been standing there. The streetlights were on and the rain poured down, hard now; her hair was soaked. She ducked into the doorway of Irene's shop and banged on the glass door.

"Oh, it's you," Irene said, coming out of her back office, and opening the door reluctantly. "You gave me a start."

In the dreams Irene was a wise, kind woman, but in real life she was suspicious and often disagreeable. She never called Cory "dear." Cory always forgot this until she was in Irene's presence and the familiar complaining voice began to churn the air around her. It was customers who wanted bargains they couldn't have ("Man came around, thought I was an old fool, offered me ten bucks for that early Nancy Drew. Good heavens, I paid fifty for it; I knew what it was worth. I strung him along awhile, then I told him where to get off."), kids who wanted change for the bus, or who—Heaven forbid—actually wanted to look at, to pick up the old children's books that Irene had in her display windows. But mostly what she talked about if she got the chance was her married daughter, Joan. Joan was Irene's only daughter (Irene had a son, too, a good boy, always traveling for his company, sent her a lovely basket of fruit on her birthday), the ungrateful, selfish daughter who lived in Olympia, which was only an hour and a half away, but who hardly ever came to see her and couldn't care less if she lived or died. Cory, who'd seen Joan drive up practically every Sunday morning for the last fifteen years to take Irene out to church and then back to Olympia to have dinner with her husband and children, always nodded neutrally. It was better to keep the conversation in the old familiar paths; otherwise Irene might turn on her with those suddenly penetrating, pale blue eyes and say, "I saw a whole troop of little black children hanging around here yesterday. I thought they were going to come in the store and I'd have to deal with them."

The "troop" had been composed of Rae and Nicole's two girls and their friend Samantha, who'd come over for a special brunch one day with their mothers. Once Cory would have tried to set Irene straight, resentfully or furiously, but now she knew that Irene said things like that out of pure malice, just to see Cory's reaction.

But she hadn't raised the rent in almost ten years, and every Christmas she gave Cory a tin of home-baked cookies.

How could such a mean-spirited woman specialize in children's books? Cory wondered for the millionth time. How could Irene keep books that children loved behind the window and in locked glass cases? Cory let her fingers run over the books on the front table. They had heavy cloth covers with gilt-stamped titles or thick board with an illustration pressed on. Just touching the covers brought her back to some safe place where she could rest a little. She picked up a shabby old volume of Robert Louis Stevenson's *A Child's Garden of Verses,* with illustrations by Jessie Wilcox Smith. The cover illustration showed a golden brown path leading into the distance, hedged in by tall, dark green trees, closed off by an intricate wrought-iron gate. Inside, on the thick rag pages, were more color illustrations, of pensive, dreamy, English-looking children in short frocks and trousers, and singsong verses in large type:

> *"I should like to rise and go*
> *Where the golden apples grow."*

"It's not in very good shape," said Irene suddenly. "Except for the illustrations. Some people would cut out the illustrations. Why don't you take it? I know you wouldn't cut them out."

It was this sort of generosity from Irene that always caught Cory off guard, that kept her dreaming about Irene, wanting something from her.

She blurted out, "You know Rosemary?"

Irene nodded. Her pale blue eyes sharpened, expecting the worst. "Of course. She bought that nice first edition set of the *Little House on the Prairie* books for her niece. She knew a bargain. Though I'm sure I gave her too good a deal. What happened to her?"

"Well, I'm thinking of moving into her house in December. I wouldn't give up the apartment," Cory added quickly. "I'll just use it for an office. It's practically only an office now."

"Well," said Irene coolly, moving away, fussing with the books on the table. "I guess people move on. Times change." She frowned at the Robert Louis Stevenson book in Cory's hands, probably regretting she'd offered it.

"I'll still be upstairs almost every day," Cory protested. "I don't want to move on. It's really important for me to stay here. I love this building, I love the view."

"When I die, they'll tear the whole thing down, put up condominiums," Irene predicted savagely. "This is valuable property; Joan will make the most of it."

"Maybe I . . ."

"It's worth at least a million dollars. Oh, she'll have a ball, after I'm gone. But maybe I'll surprise her. . . ." Irene was start-

ing to go into one of her tiresome rants when she suddenly
stopped. "You're soaking wet, Cory, go on upstairs. You look
like a homeless dog. I'm not going to throw you out, for pete's
sake!" She turned away in irritation, but not before Cory caught
something in her eyes, something she'd seen before and not understood. Love, with no means to express itself except anger.
"Haven't you paid me rent every month right on time for I
don't know how long? I guess I should raise it, now that it's
going to be just a business. Yes, I should have raised your rent
a long time ago. Heaven knows, your office has been here all
along, you're probably making a fortune up there. I'm soft, far
too soft."

But as Cory was backing out of the store, Irene barked, "It's
not a big secret, you know, you and Rosemary. She's a nice girl.
Knows a bargain when she sees one. Show her that book I gave
you. And don't cut the illustrations out!"

Upstairs, the rain battered the windows facing the lake. Cory
turned on all the lights. She would be moving in three weeks,
and had promised herself that she'd start going through her
things tonight, beginning with her paintings. She'd been stuff-
ing them in boxes for years; now it was time to sort them out,
to throw them out. She put on Pablo Casals playing Bach's cello
suites, and set to work.

The early watercolors were spheres and cylinders and ovoids.
Red apples with blue shadows; green apples with reddish shadows. Lemons on purple plates, grapefruits in blue bowls, bananas that looked like boats and boats that looked like bananas.
Studies in cool and warm colors, with attention to core shadows and cast shadows.

That was her unself-conscious period, during the first joyful
months of painting, encouraged by her first teacher. But then
had come Intermediate Watercolor and Madelyn the photo realist, who could make water in a glass, sun on a wall, dew on a
petal, rust on metal look like the real thing. Cory flipped
through her paintings from Madelyn's class. One box alone was
full of still lifes of glass and liquids. Most were moderately suc-

cessful studies; some of the best had the evocative stopped-time feel of Madelyn's own paintings. Here was one, a memory preserved from the past, intact. Two jars of fruit, pears and apricots, sitting on a rough pine counter in front of a window. Raindrops beaded against the small panes of glass; in the background was a blur of wet green trees. The sliced pears were a translucent jonquil in a syrup of champagne; the apricots were whole, big as peaches, poppy-bright. The labels, hand-scrawled, read AUGUST, 1986. Rosemary had written them. It was the summer they'd gone to Eastern Washington for two weeks, their first summer together. A hot summer, with long afternoon naps, lovemaking, bushels of fruits at the roadside stands for eating and canning. In the mornings Cory had taken her sketch pad out on walks; in the evenings they read to each other from the books they found in the cabin, dog-eared natural history books by Sally Carrighar and Aldo Leopold. In the afternoon sometimes there were brief storms, like the one Cory had caught in this painting.

A still life, caught forever, gone forever.

She put it down and picked up a study for a portrait of Nicole, pregnant with Ayisha, their first child. After Madelyn, Cory had taken a class with Joe, whose specialty was people standing around Seattle streets under umbrellas. He had a stall at the Market and made a good living off the tourists, who thought the umbrellas were cute and so Seattle. Cory painted urban streets then too, and portaits. Nicole, round and dark and pleased, Rae, burstingly proud, with Ayisha, and then Aja. Portraits of Rosemary, too, with her hair getting longer, and her body getting more comfortable to her, that Rosemary nevertheless claimed made her look too fat. There was even a self-portrait. Cory hadn't thought it looked like her; a few years later, she liked it better. The gray had already started coming in; the green eyes looked wary, but still hopeful of getting everything right.

Next was a box of skies. That had been the period of weekend workshops with Justine, who said, "Anything goes here. Let your color sense guide you. What's your inner palette telling you to paint? What are the colors that speak to you? No, don't tell me. Show me. Paint me anything," said Justine, and then paused a beat. "Just not one of those dull gray Seattle marinescapes." Cory had laughed self-consciously with the rest, wondering if they too had sketchbooks brimming with masts and sails and seagulls appearing out of the mist.

All through her intermittent painting career, through the fruits and vegetables, through the glass panes and glass jars, through the portraits and urban scenes, Cory had kept painting Lake Union, her lake of tugs and drawbridges, houseboats and kayaks. Her urban lake she saw every day and never tired of seeing. But even the lake, her marine views, looked different according to which teacher she'd had and which technique she'd been practicing at the time. Madelyn the photo realist used a strict, slow glazing technique. She drew a pencil outline, sometimes in a grid pattern, carefully on the page, then began working in small areas, laying on thin washes of transparent pigment, sometime letting them dry naturally, sometimes using a hair dryer. Madelyn worked with a controlled system of wetting and drying the paper; she built up layers, a dozen or three dozen washes of color that did not seem to thicken, but to grow more and more translucent. Her colors were never muddy, and rarely ran together. Justine taught painting in a completely opposite way. She soaked her paper, both sides, with clear water and splashed on color, held the paper up to make the color run, sponged and dabbed and smeared. Not for her the patience of the slow glaze; not for her the cordoning off of small sections kept separate from each other.

Justine painted wet on wet. Tentacles of indigo reached into swirls of rose and made an atmospheric cloud of violet; a stroke of Windsor blue webbed through lemon yellow to become green, the spring green of new-leafed trees, Justine said, and quickly sketched in a few decisive lines for a trunk and branches. Justine's students were rarely as successful as Justine herself—painting wet on wet needed as much control as dry-brush or glazing—and their work tended to be blurred and splotchy, with water marks from uneven drying. "It's a sunset," they told Justine hopefully. "Love your energy." She always smiled. Some of Cory's best—and worst—paintings came from this time. "Catch the spirit of what you see," Justine said. "Don't try to pin it down. Let us see the movement of the universe." Where Madelyn's glassy still lifes had a melancholy clarity, Justine's skies and forests moved and kept on moving.

After an hour Cory had thrown away no pictures; she was painting a new one. She wasn't working from a photograph or a still-life setup, and certainly not from any view, for the night was howling wet and dark outside her windows. It was *A Child's Garden of Verses* that had inspired her, and yet she wasn't copying the cover. She wanted to paint something from memory, memory touched with imagination. She wanted to paint a pebbled path leading to a garden, but not one hedged in by dark English oaks. She wanted to paint bougainvillea and roses, jacaranda and mimosa trees, an apricot hung with golden globes of fruit. "I should like to rise and go, Where the golden apples grow," she hummed, taking out her tubes of paint. "Find your palette," Justine had always told them. "Find what colors speak to you." And Cory had chosen viridian and Prussian blue and indigo for her own. She had watercolor pads full of radiantly deep Northwestern skies and waters. But now she squeezed out all her yellows on the plastic palette, her reds, her brighter blues. Now she painted, not what she saw before her, or what she had ever really seen, but what she knew was there. A garden, with a gate that could be closed against the outside world, where she could walk at will, perfectly safe, in the midst of the flowers that flowed magically from her brush.

"I saw your lights," said Rosemary at the door. "Your apartment was all lit up. I just got out of the office and was on my way home. I thought I'd see if you wanted to go out to eat, or get some take-out. Unless you've eaten already."

Rosemary knew that Thursday was therapy day, and that sometimes Cory sat and cried all evening, that sometimes she needed to talk, that sometimes she needed to be bodily taken out of her apartment and made to eat something. She seemed astonished to find Cory painting with the music turned up. Now it was Mozart's Clarinet Concerto.

"It's a garden," said Cory. "I got the idea from a book Irene gave me. But I haven't put the gate on yet."

An Indian yellow path led smoothly under a rosy arbor, magenta bougainvillea on one side, peacock-blue jacaranda and yellow mimosa on the other. She didn't really remember what mimosa or jacaranda flowers looked like, so she had had to improvise, in the way of Justine, splashing on color instead of worrying about detail. In the foreground there were the beginnings of an apricot tree, with heart-shaped leaves and golden fruit.

"Wow," said Rosemary, "this jumps off the page."

"It's not finished," said Cory. "There's the apricot tree, the gate. . . ." She stood back, unsure. The gate would be a problem, now that she'd put the apricot tree in the foreground. She'd meant to paint the gate French blue with a small dry brush, copying Jessie Wilcox Smith's intricate design with fleurs-de-lis. Maybe not closed, maybe half open. She needed the gate, as Justine would say, to give the painting definition—"and so you can reassure people that you can paint something that looks like something." But how could she put the gate in front of the apricot tree, and if the gate was behind it, then the apricot tree would be outside the garden.

Cory put her brush down, caught up in one of the logistical problems that seemed always to come with spontaneous paintings. Which was more important, the apricot tree or the gate? She could feel her energy suddenly running out. It was almost eight o'clock and she was starving.

"Oh, don't put in a gate," said Rosemary. "Don't touch it. It's beautiful. Really, it's like an illustration in a children's book. Someplace you'd love to wander in and explore."

I did explore it once, Cory almost said. It was my world. But that wasn't quite true. For the last two hours she'd been inside this painting. It was still her world.

"You should frame some more of these," said Rosemary, turning to the paintings spread out over the desk. "I have lots of wall space." She picked up the watercolor of the pears and apricots. "1986," she read from the label. "August. That was such a hot summer," she said, and blushed. She tried so carefully not to make comments that could sound suggestive.

How did she take care of herself, Cory thought. And what did it cost her? What did she do with her desire to touch and be touched, with her hunger to be loved not just for her "good personality," but for her body? Did she have to shut off everything, like Cory did, because it was too painful to feel? The guilt flashed up, but more than that, sorrow. Sorrow for both of them, once children in their free and easy bodies, now adults who had to be careful and patient with each other. It hadn't always been that way with them. Sometimes the gate had been open. She had a flash of memory, not white skin in green water this time, with its weight of nausea, but something bright and fleeting: creamy, freckled skin, golden-brown hair, the round heft of belly and thigh, hot wetness between their two skins. The way the warm rain of that summer storm had poured down the windows of the cabin, with the sun right behind.

A still life was always a picture of inanimate objects. In the painting the pale gold of the sliced pears, the rich velvet of the orange apricots pulsed through the translucent jars. Madelyn had taught Cory to keep the color values rich and concentrated, contained by transparency, almost within reach, almost real in a stopped-time memory. But Justine would say, Break the glass, let the color out. Cory imagined the two jars smashing, the pears and apricots spreading across the page, soaking and staining the paper to the very edges.

She wanted her hunger back. Where had it gone? Hunger, not just desire, hunger for the whole of life, for a whole life. For a long time, color had been bottled up in a still life; the river had been surging through a space too narrow for it and echoing against the sheer canyon walls. She heard the roaring in her ears and willed it to become something else, not the river but the ocean. A wave coming that she could master, that would not drown her but would embrace her, would fling her up to the top of the frothing crest and, for an instant, hold her there, let her be there.

Rosemary was still bent over the boxes of paintings. She was wearing a warm brown sweater with a boat neck. Her neck and shoulders were bare, creamy, honey-freckled, as she bent over the paintings, pushing back her brown curls with one hand. A sliver of black lace curled sleepily in the corner of the sweater's opening.

It would be so simple to put her hand on that shoulder and turn Rosemary around. All she needed was the willingness to think wave not river, hunger not sex, love not anything else. Now, she told herself. Now. Turning Rosemary around, turning the hazel eyes toward her, pressing the soft mouth on hers, breaking the glass, painting wet on wet to the edges.

# Nothing in Common

## LYNNE YAMAGUCHI

*K*issing her that first time was a match igniting in slow motion. Crossing the room to stand before her, the hardwood hard under my soles, the air between us reshaped as my hand rose to the pebble warmth just behind her earlobe: here was the match lifted from its mates, the box slid snug into its lid, the match head poised over the striker band. Then the tip's succumbing to the grit, the pungent hiss of sulfur: her lips, impossibly gossamer, opening to mine, sending through my chest a slow scald, subcutaneous. Combustion then, an eruption of heat, light, carbon, dancing as on the head of a matchstick as we stood kissing, aflame.

How could either of us have known in that moment the hunger of that fire; how could we have known the old-growth acreage it would consume? All we knew then of desire was a match's flare, a candle's slow exhalation, the consolation of coal in a season of cold; no conflagration. How could we know that what lit that night would turn inferno?

I had noticed her months before we actually met, at dyke dances off campus, at occasional fund-raisers for women's organizations, once at Hotshots on a Friday night. By the time we did meet, in the computer room at Campus Copeez at the beginning of the semester, I knew that she was a poli-sci major, that she baked bread for a living, that her lover of three years drove a metallic gray, late-model Japanese subcompact with Pennsylvania plates, and that she didn't smoke.

But she swore: "Oh, shit" were her first words to me, followed immediately by "What the hell does 'System overflow' mean?" I explained, helped her reboot, and coaxed her to lunch. By the end of the week, soup, sandwiches, or the special had become a routine. My lover was happy I'd found a new friend.

From the start, we had nothing in common. Even our sexuality, our shared dykedom, seemed of different time zones—literally, perhaps, as nearly a decade separated us in age, and our respective comings out spanned almost two. She liked Queen Latifah, macaroni and cheese, Naiad mysteries; I preferred the Queen of Soul and Streisand, brown rice, poetry, physics. The idea of biking or even an evening stroll tired her; political debate tired me. So what kept us meeting, talking, leapfrogging the gaps and silences between us?

Curiosity, I could answer. Instinct, perhaps, in hindsight. Fate, if I could believe in destiny.

Pheromones.

My private mission.

Over my decades of loving women, desire had become for me a compass, an instrument guiding me over the terra infirma I traveled seeking home. Desire was my microscope, telescope, particle accelerator firing into the subatomic spaces of the human cosmos, in search of data words left out: The taste and texture at the corner of a certain woman's lips. The breath of sweat in the pale of another's neck, in the groin's undulant grace. The arc of a lover's feet sweet against my face. The rim-to-rim fit of two pelvic bowls in a slow fish; the exact interleaving of thighs.

My investigations were selective but thorough. And as the observed reveals the nature of the observer, I'd discovered that desire—not only sexual, but perhaps always ultimately so—was more than a means of locating myself in the world, more than an instrument only: it was for me, rather, the measure and the measured; compass and landscape; barometer and weather.

But so many questions remained, chief among them what I couldn't know: What was desire for other women? How did it feel to others; what answers did it yield them?

I talked about desire with everyone I could.

Passion became my passion.

I still can't explain why my inquiry, always personal, this time became utterly so. I know only that by the end of the semester, I wanted to know every nuance of this woman's desiring: what shape it made in her mouth, the angle it assumed in her pelvis, at what decibel it rang in her cells. Did she gaze on other women as I gazed on her bent head, longing to push off from shore, to float the flow of that naked nape down the shallow rapids of her spine? Did the sight of a woman bending over a desk across the room ever cause her to look away, feeling the flesh of that cleft peach on her tongue, its soft burst under pressure, the sticky juices rubbed into that pubic beard?

Could another woman's glance thrust breath from her like that of one's fingers' sudden bloom inside her?

Did music played at a certain rhythm and a volume too loud for thought open her thighs and set her walls to pulsing?

No, I didn't ask, not like that, not so nakedly. But her answers to the questions I did ask—about her first kiss, her first love, her first lover, her current love; about food and music and what pleasured her; about monogamy, her fantasies, her expectations for the future—told me that whatever desire was for her, it was not her own weather.

I imagined luring her outdoors, into a new climate.

When the semester ended, along with my TA-ship, she got me hired at One in the Oven, the bakery where she worked. There, aproned and perpetually floured, we danced a courtship dance amid the counters and tray racks. Comically self-conscious in our posturing, we were still flirting with fantasy then, neither of us quite reaching for the other, both yet ignorant of the mutuality of our attraction.

The end of ignorance arrived sweating, out of breath, in hot July: I went to her one searing evening to talk, and when my longing spilled from me like beads from a broken string, she bent to help me pick them up! And helping me, spilled her own, admitting she wanted me too. Oh, her hand on my thigh, pledging its heat through the thin cotton.

But faith: we were faithful. We were in love with our lovers, after all, and cherished the prospect of long, rich lives with them. Heady as this new attraction was, this beginning, we agreed, would also be the end. Friends: we would remain just friends.

I left. I walked out her door, elated and wistful, and was four steps homeward when she called me back inside.

There came that kiss then, and another, and another—one, when I finally did leave, for every delirious step down the long staircase from her apartment to the street.

Of course we told our lovers; of course they were upset. And we vowed that nothing more would happen, hiding our hunger from ourselves even as our lovers watched the same flame flicker in our two faces. Our relationships floundered, rebounded.

We continued to want.

At the bakery, her presence surrounded me like heat from the ovens. Morning after morning, I listened for her arrival, her muffled greetings to the counter staff. Waiting for the double doors into the kitchen to open, I could feel the want begin its leavening, its ferment rising in me throughout the day.

The nature of our work—all about appetite, its enticement and fulfillment—made the days that much harder. Spooning salt into the mix of dry ingredients at a neighboring counter, I could taste, even with my back to her, the sinewed line of her neck. Sourdough was a vinegar ache at the back of my throat, a moan waiting for her answer. Sugar was the tongue's longing; cinnamon, the lips'. And in my hands, the dough swelled belly soft, yielding to my touch, opening a cave around my hand.

How, in that heat, steeped in that fresh-baked fragrance, could I keep my hand from the curl falling into her eyes; how, reaching to tuck it behind her ear, could I not linger, catching my fingers in her mane? How, when she reached to wipe a smudge of flour from my face, could I keep my cheek from leaning into her palm? How could I not follow her oven warmth when she squeezed by, not open my arms to her when she opened hers for a hug?

How could we have thought that hugging would smother those coals?

At home, away from the ovens, away from her, still the heat lit my face. My lover and I could talk of little else. She was hurt; she was afraid; she understood, but couldn't I work through my feelings without sleeping with someone else? My sexuality was changing, awakening in new ways, but couldn't we change together? Wasn't our passion enough, after all these years? We made love fiercely, urgently. Riding orgasm after orgasm until my body could give no more, I remembered all the ways in which no one knew my body, and my soul, better.

Wanting consumed me. Desire, my compass, was failing me, its needle spinning as at magnetic north.

Evenings, I threw myself into polishing my thesis.

Nights, I awoke in darkness feeling the fit of my hand in her.

At lunch, and sometimes after work, we talked: no potential affair has ever been discussed more thoroughly. We talked to talk ourselves out of wanting. We talked to talk through the wanting. We still had nothing in common; we still wanted to stay with our lovers, who also wanted us, but who were meanwhile being ripped apart, as we were, by our longing for the other.

Mostly, though, selfishly—for what could be more selfish than desire?—we talked to savor the wanting, this miracle that had astonished us both with its bounty.

What we'd found in common was desire.

Would we act or wouldn't we? Was this feeling worth the risk to our relationships? Each had to decide for herself, but we were also deciding together.

There came another kiss, the night she tried to decide for me that we would not be lovers. We had debated, argued, processed until we were both exhausted beyond reason. She was ready to sleep with me, had arranged with her lover to do so. I couldn't decide, couldn't choose; blackness yawned on either side of me. Finally, she'd had it: the uncertainty was blistering all of us; she would end the uncertainty.

For a moment I couldn't hear over the blaze that roared up inside me. I crossed the room to her, took her face in my hands, and surrendered to the inferno.

What our lovers each in her own way said was: Go, find her; finish with her and come home.

We tried.

The next Friday we each showed up at work with a packed bag. After work we drove together to a Super 8 two towns away. A long weekend, we'd been granted, Friday to Monday: three nights, two and a half days, to work each other out of our systems.

In our motel room, she could hardly look at me. Our chance had come, and we both were too tired and hungry and scared to seize it. What were we doing and who were we to each other? The questions hung like fog in the air between us. To find each other, we'd have to risk losing our way.

We started slow. We stood between the beds and kissed. We lay down and kissed, first on one bed, then on the other, fully clothed. We shared a sub we'd brought with us from work. She took a shower, came out dressed for an evening in. We kissed some more, still dressed. We reinvented kissing, practicing our skills until I could feel my lips begin a second skin. When, finally, the coals were banked just so, we opened, slowly, the draft to more air, undoing buttons, then zippers, one at a time. And when I found her skin, suede over a belly puppy-taut and trembling, awkwardness fled; wonder took over.

Her pleasure when she found my breasts was audible, as was my answer.

Her wetness—"It's a gift," she quipped—shook me to my soles.

When she lifted her face, rapt and jubilant, from my armpit after licking her way up my ribs, something in my chest cartwheeled.

We dressed only to go out for food, which we brought back and ate. We read a little—she, the paper; I, poetry—watched a little TV. She slept. I watched her. I laid myself along her length and slept with her.

We kept waking to each other, easing from sleep into sex as easily as into dream. In light or in darkness our hands found each other, our bodies opening, enfolding, holding each other. Touching became autonomic, an organismic cycle of reach and response, unselfconscious as breathing. And skin became our medium: like dolphins reveling in a game of surfaces, we dove, singing deep; leapt, lungs guzzling air, praising horizon.

Beneath the shimmering surface, though, swam unease. As pleasurable as our touching was, it—*I*—felt curiously passionless. By Sunday, our last full day together, I could no longer avoid my sense that something was missing. Reluctantly, I reached beneath the surface for answers, and what my hands found was fear.

The thing I lifted into the light was brittle, jagged: Had I imagined the fire I'd felt between us? Had she felt it too? Did she feel its absence now? Could we stir it, let it burn? Would she run? Would she feel it? Had it already died for lack of fuel or air or common ground?

I fingered fear's barbs and edges throughout the morning, testing its whet in conversation with her over brunch. When we came back to our room, the brittleness had beat us there. I sat on the far bed alone and closed my eyes. Now or never; choose or lose. I lit a candle and watched my fear curl into ash. Then I stood, and went to her, and pulled her to her feet. From my core let I light, incandescent; it swallowed us both in its fountain.

We made love then, literally: forged it from salt and flesh and sinew in the heat of that passion. We made love out of hunger, molten, cast, and cooled: a bronze, Rodinesque; muscular, and hard as rage. From need we wrought a base, hammered, dense; from longing, belonging, transfigured in the flame.

On my hands and knees, I opened myself up, and took her in, and gave as I'd never given before. "More," I kept asking, till her hand throbbed in me like my own heart.

And the scent of womb filled the room—sheets, mattress, carpet saturated with our spill.

Baptized in her abundance, I immersed myself in her until every cell knew love as loss arrested. And suffusing the love, grief, the capillary layer beneath the skin of desire.

There wasn't time enough.

Late Monday morning, ten minutes before checkout time, we kissed in the parking lot, got in our respective cars, and drove home to salvage what we could of our relationships, now charred, smoking ruins.

How does the story end? It hasn't. More than a year has passed since that first kiss; nine months since the last. We each, jointly and separately and repeatedly, have tried to let go, to cut a break that would check the wildfire. We've hurt each other, hurt ourselves, hurt our lovers. The longing still leaps and burns between us.

I finally quit the bakery in March after too many excruciating months of longing shackled; I start a real, if temporary and entry-level, teaching job in the fall. She and her lover are still trying. My lover and I have abandoned the old structure and begun the long, hard task of digging a new foundation in new ground; we don't know yet whether we're building one home or two.

Was it worth it? What did we gain?

Yes, with sorrow, to the first. To the second, she as yet has no answer.

Mine?

What remains with me is as tangible as bread: what my hands will never forget: The abode her bones made, spare and fragile. The substantiality of flesh. The shapes her whole made in my hands: orb, burl, trunk, bowl, ridge.

The whole her shapes made.

The whole we made; the something we made of nothing. What we shared, finally, in common:

This love.

# Listening to Lauren

## SHELLY RAFFERTY

*E*very day I wake up wondering what accident will happen
to me. I know I can't predict or control my fate. Lightning
could strike me. I could drive off a cliff. I could fall in love. Or I
could fall out. . . .

The smell of coffee assaulted me; Lauren apparently liked it
strong. As I staggered to the kitchen, socks shielding my tender feet from the cold hickory floor, I already knew I would regret my first cup.

"Pour me a big one, would you?" My voice was scratchy, the
result of our shared minibinge the night before. Lauren had already collected the Miller ponies; next to the counter, the J & B
bottle stuck its smelly, stale neck out of the trash.

"Oh, you're up. How are we doing this morning?"

I ground the heel of my hand into the soft space above my
right eye. "Don't ask." Lauren pushed a large mug in front of
me. I took it. In spite of last night's excesses, she looked re-
markably fresh scrubbed in a hooded Rutland sweatshirt and
jeans. But then again, she had been drinking wine. Only two
glasses, as I recall.

"Take anything in it?"

I shook my head. I deserved to get it black. I glanced around
the spare Adirondack living room. In the loft, I could see that
the bed Lauren shared with Joah was empty. "Where's our girlfriend?"

"Down at the dock. Taking her constitutional."

At the sliding glass doors, the steam from my coffee immediately clouded up the space in front of me. I swiped at the glass with the sleeve of my flannel nightshirt, and gazed down at my ex-lover Joah, her slight figure standing unmoving at the foot of the little platform, a model of Presbyterian resignation. She was wearing the Army jacket I had given her years before. "It looks cold out there," I murmured.

Lauren's cup thumped gently on the table behind me. "You couldn't get me out in it."

"I think you're going to lose your dock," I observed. Already the lip of the small platform was being nosed up by the swelling lake. "This damn thaw is buckling the ice like there was some giant garden mole underneath."

"You guys really worked hard on that. How long will it take us to get you to come back and build another?"

I ignored her subtle complaint. Last summer, I had looked forward to the challenge of carpentry—it had kept me out of harm's way. Wary of her lover, and of Joah herself, I had busied myself with measuring lumber, cutting it with the circular saw, and setting bolts for the boat hoist. Much of the time I had been waist-deep in the June-cold lake, numbing myself from the reality of Joah's newly constructed life. It was good work, staying my temptation to revisit the many inside jokes and silent staring that had been common between Joah and me.

"You seem awfully complacent about letting it go."

"What's to be done? The neighbors say the lake hasn't been this high in thirty years, and who knew this freakish thaw would come? Last week it was ten below." Lauren pushed air away from her dismissively. "I can't be prepared for everything."

"We should stake it, at least drive some chain through the H-poles. I'd hate to see you lose the frame," I said, without much enthusiasm.

"Joah and I sank some cinderblock before we put the boats up in September. That frame's as good as planted there. Where's it going to go, anyway? It's cast iron, remember? We'll be able to save it. But the deck's going to go. I noticed a crack at the back board yesterday."

"I suppose you'll want a bigger one next time."

"That would be nice." Lauren smiled. "The new and improved model."

"Joah used to hate the cold."

Lauren tilted her head courteously. Dull daylight glinted off the barrette in her wavy, brown hair. It matched the short amber crystal that dangled from her left ear.

I continued. "Every year she complained. As soon as Christmas was over, she was ready to pack away the shovels and sweaters. The snow was only good for yuletide, that's all. Just for atmosphere."

"She doesn't seem to mind it much now," said Lauren. "Or maybe she just doesn't notice it."

I turned back to the small table and cleared some room for my coffee cup. I pushed aside the box from Clue, a game Joah had endlessly refused to play with me years earlier. Even as Lauren had suggested it last night, I had cringed, expecting Joah's characteristic disdain. But she had surprised me. "Okay," she had agreed nonchalantly, leaning across the table with her beer pressed to her mouth. Her arched eyebrow was not lost on me. "And I'll kick your ass, too," she'd warned mischievously. We'd played twice. Joah won both times.

Lauren sat down opposite me. "When are you heading back?"

Considering my throbbing head, I wasn't exactly thrilled about making the drive to Boston, but I had clients to see in the morning. "I'll want to get on the road before dark," I said. "Probably after lunch. Around two, I guess."

We both looked out the doors again. The mist hung in a steamy curtain, barely rippling in the still, frigid air. "I've got to go into town in a while. We're out of milk."

I appreciated Lauren's conscientious attention to her groceries. I knew that she was telling me that I would have some time to spend with Joah, alone. And for the first time in my life, I wasn't sure I wanted it.

\* \* \*

"Computer Diagnostics and Troubleshooting. May I help you?"

"Hey, it's me."

I grip the phone tightly, because Joah has not called me in several months, and that has been good for me, but I am frozen in the fear that she is calling me to tell me horrible news.

"What's up?" I ask, trying to be cool.

We exchange the required pleasantries before I finally muster the courage to call her bluff. "There was perhaps something you wanted?" My Yiddish inflection is affected, but harmless. It is an old joke between us.

"We're having a thaw. The lake's rising—that is, the ice is. Sort of a surprise." She pauses. "We're going to lose our dock."

She means our dock, the one she and I built last summer.

"Shit."

"Come up and watch?" An invitation. How odd. Joah never invited me anywhere.

"How are the roads?" The Vermont countryside could be a treacherous drive in winter.

She ignores my question. "Actually, you could help me. I want to take the deck off the frame. Maybe we can save it."

For a moment I am nearly dumbstruck, because Joah has never asked me for a thing. But already I know I will go, because it is in my nature to want to figure out what she means, what she is trying to tell me. "I don't mind helping you, but what about Lauren?" I ask. "Isn't she around?"

"She's had the flu," Joah answers, a little too quickly. "She's not been feeling too well. Listen, can you come tonight? Lauren and I will be here all weekend. If you want to bring someone. . . ."

"I'm single. Again."

"Well, then." She waits a beat. "Come anyway. It'll be all right."

I know it won't be, but I drive up anyway.

"She's out there every day, isn't she?" I gestured to the yard. When Joah and I lived together, I had gradually—if reluctantly—gotten used to her daily disappearances. In the beginning, we would walk together, but eventually, after her cancer had been discovered, I knew she wanted to walk alone. And I let her. Even at the height of her chemotherapy, when the retching and nausea had become as predictable as sunrise, Joah insisted on walking.

"I think she's commiserating with God."

"She's talking to someone," I agreed. I leaned back in my chair and listened to the rumble of my cranial bones rubbing against each other. I had earned the damn headache. "Man, I drank too much last night."

"Do you want some Advil?" Lauren's expression registered genuine concern. She was a strange-looking woman: a handsome, deeply lined face, a bright, full mouth set in a friendly jaw. Overall, she seemed thinner than I remembered her, her hair a little grayer.

"That would be great."

From a corner cupboard, Lauren found the white plastic bottle. As she opened the cupboard door, I couldn't help noticing several amber plastic vials of pills. Were those the vestiges of breast cancer treatment: Tamoxifen? MS Contin? I was puzzled, but I kept my counsel. Joah's remission had been total: in the year before she left me, her mammogram had been completely clear. I dismissed my worry: the pills had to be old.

Lauren struggled a moment with the childproof cap, before dumping the salmon pills next to my coffee cup. On what appeared to be a second thought, she dosed herself with two.

I looked toward the yard again. "I miss her," I said slowly. "Maybe I shouldn't tell you that."

Lauren shrugged. "Say what you want to. I'm not the censorship board."

"I guess that after six years I should have her out of my system." I took a deep breath. "But I don't."

Lauren seemed unmoved. "You don't need my permission to miss her. I'm sure your breakup was difficult."

"She seems happy with you."

"Do you think so? She's always been hard to understand."

I couldn't keep a wry smirk off my face. "And I thought it was just me."

Lauren turned her head, allowing her chin to drop slightly. Her voice was warm, understanding, absolutely devoid of defense. "Well, at some point, I just gave up trying to figure her out."

"And I never did."

"You might be a lot happier if you could."

"I know."

I got to my feet and found the coffeemaker; another cup couldn't do any more damage than had already been done. Without asking, I leaned over Lauren's shoulder and poured her a refill, too.

"Maybe it's just me," I began again, sitting down. "I never thought she would leave me. I thought my life was perfect. I mean, we loved each other, and I know she loved me, even though she wasn't beyond teasing me." What was I doing? Did I want Lauren to make Joah's leaving me make sense? "We were even going to move to Vermont," I added wistfully. "I still have the real estate books, the maps. Before Joah got sick, I had our whole lives planned out."

Lauren lifted her coffee and drew a few sips off the cup.

Completely inscrutable. I had no idea what she was thinking.

"You know, I don't know why Joah left me," I said quietly. An invisible hand reached up and throttled my throat, wringing strange tears out of my shaking voicebox. "After all these years, I still don't know why Joah left me."

Our hands lay several inches apart across the table, but Lauren leaned in and grasped my wrist lightly. "Cancer changes a lot of things."

"I know that."

"No," said Lauren slowly. "You witnessed that."

"I saw it changing her." There was anger in my voice. How well did I remember? The lump, that morning, when I came out of the shower and she was still in bed, her head turned toward the window. I picked up my slip and pulled it over my head. I knelt on the floor to look for my other shoe, and I saw it on Joah's side. I crossed the room, and suddenly recognized the look on her face, her hand on her breast, the expression of terror. *It's here. Just like it came for my mother. Now it's come for me.*

I shrugged and shook my head. "She's probably told you the whole story."

"Not really. She doesn't seem to want to talk about it."

"She never did." I felt my jaw tensing again. "Anyway, she survived, for Christ's sake."

"Yes."

Once again I got to my feet and went to the glass doors. I could see Joah painstakingly pacing at the edge of the yard, on the shoreline. Every now and then she would stop, lean over, scrape with a piece of bark or stone, and throw it out onto the chunky ice. I could have stood there for hours, watching her move. Every inch of her was still familiar, her hesitant, almost uneven gait; her sure hands; the small of her back. The way her shirt collar wrinkled askew under the Army jacket.

Abruptly, I turned. "She's not going to tell me, you know."

"Tell you what?"

"Why she left me."

"Maybe she can't. Maybe she doesn't know."

"There's a reason for everything," I muttered. "You know, one day when I got home from work, Joah wasn't there. That wasn't unusual. I figured she was out drinking with her nursing buddies. But later, she called home. I need to be separated from you, that's what she said. A few days later she came and got her clothes. For about a month I tried talking to her, but she was terse with me, uncommunicative. Then she disappeared. She didn't want to save our relationship. She just wanted to be left alone. I couldn't do anything."

"Until me," said Lauren.

"Yeah, until you."

"Joah's a mystery."

I looked again in the direction of the yard. "That she is," I said. "That she is."

Lauren turned sideways in her chair and got to her feet. Last night's treacle of Scotch—or whatever remnant there was— burned a new hole in my upper intestine. I crossed my arms behind me, and let the cold glass doors hold me up. "I'm jealous of you."

A small exhalation of surprise from Lauren. "Really? Don't be. I'm sure Joah still loves you."

"But she lives with you."

The dishrag made halfhearted semicircles on the vinyl tablecloth. Lauren's voice was gentle. "I know you aren't trying to accuse me," she began. "What do you want me to say? She's different than she was; you know that. You're still in love with something she used to be—"

"But I stayed with her," I interrupted. "All through that whole fucking scene. Through the biopsy, the radiation, chemotherapy. All the tests, everything. When she thought Death was knocking on the door, I did not waver. I went to the support group. I talked to the doctors. I did everything I could. I never gave up. I knew she could beat it." I suddenly felt exhausted, and threw myself into the chair again. "Shit. I keep asking myself, What did I do wrong?"

Suddenly, Lauren stopped. "Do you really want to know?"

"What I did wrong? Of course."

"You didn't get cancer."

"Don't be ridiculous."

"And you're angry that she survived."

That was true, I admit it.

As long as there was cancer, Joah needed me. "All right, I know where you're going with this. I'm not angry that she survived. Clearly that had nothing to do with me."

"You didn't really think you were going to cure her?"

"She could have stayed," I said stubbornly. "I did."

"You think she owes you something for surviving."

Was that it? "I'd have done anything to make her happy."

Lauren smiled. "And what would you do to make yourself happy?"

I was dumbstruck. "I don't know," I answered softly.

My boots made a peculiar *squick squick* as I trudged down through the yard. It was full of weeping grasses and decaying hillocks of charcoal-dusted snow.

"Hey. What are you doing?"

Joah turned her head toward me, looked at me hard. God, she was beautiful: her chestnut hair glistened in the damp January air, her steamy breath exhaled in a halo of translucent vapor, and her depthless eyes penetrated mine.

I tried to brush off the meaningfulness of it all. "Your girlfriend's gone off to town. I've got to leave soon, myself."

"Yeah."

"We're gonna lose the dock."

"If the lake doesn't take it, the wind will, I guess."

"Lauren says you anchored the uprights. Smart."

Again, the little puff of vapors. "That was your idea. You told me to do it before you left last summer."

I stepped toward the foot of the dock. "These back boards are splitting already. Looks like the sealer we put on didn't do much good." An ugly crack had rent its way halfway through the length of the first board. I kicked at it. A jagged piece of sand-laced white paint broke off and skittered across the slush.

"The lake's pretty unforgiving, I guess."

For a moment we stood in silence. The wind was picking up, a healthy, cool breeze that pushed the fog behind us through the trees.

"Hammond opened the dam this morning, but I think it's too late." We both looked toward the end of the lake where the DEC ranger lived. The previous summer, his nightly canoe drift-bys had marked quitting time during dock construction. One sweltering evening, just as we had put up the hammers and saw, he'd come ashore, accepted a beer, and pronounced our work sound.

"Northern lights tonight," he'd promised. Long after he'd

gone, I'd watched and waited. Eventually Joah fell asleep by the
fire, her absence apparently ignored by Lauren. I had waited
until sunrise, scanning the skies from horizon to horizon, wondering when the great miracle would occur. But it never appeared.

I tugged absently at the loose scarf around my neck. It was
getting colder. "Did you ever see that aurora borealis?" I asked
Joah.

"August. I saw it in August. Accidentally, really. Lauren had
left the fire going over there"—she pointed to a circle of rocks
past the boat hoist—"you know, like we always do. Anyway,
the wind was rattling the windows. Woke me up. When I
looked out, I could see that the fire had stirred up again, so I
came down to put it out. And there was the aurora borealis, just
as pretty as you please, swaying like a big theater curtain."

"I still haven't seen it," I muttered regretfully.

"We can still get this deck off the frame," she said suddenly. She
was squatting in the gravelly slush at the foot of the dock, studying the creaky press of the ice against the uprights. "If I could
just get the bolts loose, I might be able to pull the nine-foot section off the front end, and drag it back to the beach." She stood
up. "I need the wrenches, bolt cutter—right?" I nodded in the
direction of the toolshed, which stood several yards away in a
little grove of pines. Joah led, I followed.

"Joah, this is crazy. The ice won't hold you."

"It might. The water's only four or five feet deep there, isn't
it? I remember you measuring with the yardstick to make sure
we had enough draft for the boat."

My hand was on Joah's arm. "Just let it go. We'll build another one next summer."

"Look," she said, agitated. "What about all of our work? We
busted our asses building that thing. You can do what you want,
but I'm not giving up that easily. You can either help me or
watch, I don't care. Now, come on."

Before I stepped out on the ice, I made sure my barn boots
were laced up tight. I looked out across the small lake: there

were some dark patches, to be sure, and every few minutes we heard the telltale snap of another ice fault letting go in the thaw. But at my feet, the ice looked solid. Where it crowded under the dock, the blue-green pushed up through the boards, bowing the floor like a flexible plastic comb. In theory, all we needed to do was to loosen the long eye bolts: back, middle, and front.

"This is too dangerous, Joah. Look at how tight the front joint is." Joah placed one foot in front of the other and stepped ahead warily. "If you get a wrench on that bolt—it'll pop. You could lose a finger."

She was halfway to the end of the dock. "There has to be something we can do."

Oh, Joah, I thought. Some things just can't be fixed. "We could just wait," I said. Carefully, I placed another foot forward.

"If we wait, and we lose it, we'll never know if it could have been saved. Come on, show some guts." She turned. "Just a few more steps," she almost whispered, extending her left hand for the upright at the end of the dock. I saw her gloved hand reaching, slow, deliberate, as if to grasp the post by its metaphorical throat. I was right behind her, my own hand almost at the tapered waist of her jacket when the ice gave way under her outer foot. "Oh, Jesus!" She went down on her shoulder, as her leg punched a hole through the slippery surface. The bolt cutters were still gripped in her gloved hand. A sharp crack sent a resounding pain through my hip as I hit hard.

Joah lay in a peculiar twist in front of me, a whole leg and more disappeared into the sloshing, icy darkness, the other turned curiously outward like a useless, broken wing. From the way she struggled, I could tell she wasn't touching bottom. Her hands scrabbled in vain for a handhold, black water spilling around the edge of her jacket and soaking her sleeve.

She stared at me speechlessly.

"Drop the bolt cutter!" I shouted at her. Startled to her senses, she shook off the tool and reached for me. Desperately, she threw herself forward. Our forearms grappled and slipped like oily wrestlers. I scrambled to my knees.

"Pull me up! Pull me up! I can't get any leverage!" Her teeth were already chattering, her face was white. With all my strength, I threw her arms off, and grasped the open front of her jacket and yanked the two of us backward. Up she came, extracted from the shadowy, dripping maw, all of her seized in my fierce clench. As she fell toward me, her drenched leg splashed silvery cold across the space underneath us. My head banged on the ice.

For an instant I had her, the grimy chest of her jacket gripped in my fists, her arms around my neck, both of us breathing hard. I felt a sweat break out across my forehead.

"You all right?" She was so slow to answer that I almost shook her. "Joah."

"My boot's full of water."

"You're okay. You weren't in any danger of drowning." I paused. "You could have pulled yourself out."

Joah raised herself slightly; I could feel her breath on my face. The cold from her clothes was already soaking through mine. "I'm not so sure," she said, as a tear suddenly slipped off her cheek and onto my lip. Slowly, I tasted it, I knew it, I remembered it. Then I closed my eyes, relaxed my hands, and let her go.

We backed off the ice slowly, abandoning the tools to the churning hole behind us.

There's never been a day when I haven't wanted Joah waking next to me. I've never forgotten the silk of her limbs, the curve of her waist, the moist warmth of her breath exhaled against my neck, just after we have finished. But I know too, that these sensations are memories. Now darkness finds her wakeful, a finger silently tracing down a sleepy jaw, the back of a hand caressing a shock of graying brown, a mind never focused on what could be, but only on what is.

I had packed my bags after my shower: they waited next to the front door like patient dogs. Joah was asleep on the couch, bundled up in two blankets and an afghan. She hadn't touched her tea.

I took a last look around the small house. It was an elegant house, simple, clean, with many windows. For a moment, I knew I could go, get in my car, leave Joah behind me. And I understood in that same moment, that she would be safe. She would go on surviving. She never did need me, really. She'd always said that. Only now, I believed her.

In the loft, a lumpy comforter reminded me that Joah slept there, that Lauren slept there, and that I did not.

Sadly, I turned back to the kitchen. My head was pounding again; my feet ached with cold, still. A few more Advil for the road would do the trick.

I opened the cupboard. There it was, among the crowded amber bottles.

I reached up for the Advil, and knocked a tall plastic vial to the counter. I was right. It was Tamoxifen. A new prescription.

Lauren's.

# Skin Queen

## REBECCA LAVINE

*I*t was my pal Hester who said to me, "You know what your problem is, Gracie—you're a drag queen trapped in a woman's body. That's your problem."

We were getting ready to go out to the Klit Kat, which is Hester's favorite club but not one I really like. The girls there never smile, never actually look you in the eye. Most of them seem younger than my baby sister, Melissa—in fact, they look young enough to be in high school—and lately it seems every one of them has more than one facial feature pierced. But it's rare enough that Hester and I both get the night off on a Saturday. And as you know, there aren't a lot of choices, even living in the city.

I was trying on mesh net leggings I had found in a bargain barrel at the vintage store down the street. The material felt slippery and soft. I said to Hester, "I don't really see why that's a problem."

Hester, looking intently in the mirror, lifted her chin and dabbed at her mouth with her pinkie. She had just gotten a haircut, and her curls were springing out like tight little smiles all over her head. She was one to talk about drag queens—her outfit was more femmed up than mine. Aside from a bra and miniskirt, she wasn't wearing much more than a pair of polkadotted heels. "You're gonna to be cold in that," I said to her.

She ignored me, continuing to probe her face with her fingers. "I'm not saying it's bad, Gracie," she said. "But maybe it's why you don't get that many dates."

We've had this conversation before, the one about dates, I mean. It's Hester's theory that if you are as femme as I am, you have to be aggressive to get dates. But she also gets on my case about my house, how it's decorated like a gay boy's, with velveteen wallpaper and a zebra-striped couch. She wants to know what I'll do when I bring someone home. All this time she's been asking me this, have I ever brought someone home? To punish her for bringing it up again, I kicked off my heels and went looking for my combat boots. Hester backed away from the bathroom's full-length mirror and followed me through the clacking beaded curtain into my bedroom.

She tossed herself onto my bed, pulling one of my wigs out from underneath her. "I only say these things for your own good, Gracie," she told me, propping her feet up on the wall under my Billie Holiday poster. " 'Cause, girl"—she stretched her arms above her head, tilting her eyes suggestively upside down toward me—"we gotta get you laid."

I reached over and tugged on Hester's curls, but gently. It's not that I mind her pushing me to get out more. Somebody's got to look out for my welfare; and it's true I've gone much too long without getting any. But sometimes I feel like that part of me is worn out; out of shape from lack of use.

Sometimes I wish I'd never brought Hester back home with me after work that first time. I'd been on the job only about six months before she showed up. On her first day, she took off a yellow vinyl bikini, avoiding the hands of any man who wasn't holding a tip. Back at my house, sharing a bottle of Rémy Martin that she had swiped from the package store across the street, we had exchanged stories about the first time we walked into a strip joint; about the men who thought we'd give them blow jobs if they bought us drinks; and of course about who else at work liked girls funny.

Since then, Hester has always been telling me I have pretty repressed ideas for a girl who makes her living taking off her clothes and who spends her nights looking for other girls whose clothes she can take off, and maybe she's right. Hester is the only person who understands the loose sensation of power you get when you're onstage and those men are watching you like a goddess. But when the moment comes for me to meet a woman, Hester next to me, her hand pushing into the small of my back, I feel dusty inside. I don't even know how to say hello. Later I'll tell Hester, "She wasn't that cute," or, "She didn't act interested," and I feel all twisted up, because this is something I know Hester doesn't understand.

Hester propped herself up while I put on my makeup. I like the bedroom mirror because it is the most streaked and dim. "Well, sugar," I said, putting on the red leather coat I bought myself for my twenty-seventh birthday, "maybe there's room for only one Don Juanita in this town." After all those furtive encounters in alleyways and under bridges, by the time my last lover left her girlfriend for me we didn't seem to want each other anymore. We spent three years together hardly ever doing the nasty; and by the end, when I was kissing her, all I could think about was getting the lock fixed on the door and did one of us have our period. Twenty-seven and I'd only had three lovers. Hester doesn't know that about me. She thinks I'm a bit more worldly.

"Oh, please, Gracie, you can't pull that one with me," Hester said, hauling her long body off my bed. "You are one sexy chick and you know it."

I shrugged. It was time to go.

We climbed up out of my basement apartment and walked down the street. Hester tucked her chin against the mid-November wind and her heels snapped against the pavement. In front of us, our shadows hovered, straining to stay a step away. Was this how drag queens felt? Half in their skin, and half yearning to be in someone else's? I felt that way every day.

When Hester and I reached the club we paused for a moment by the door. It opened and closed, discharging women in pairs or amiable groups. We assessed each other's makeup. "Your cut is great," I said. "Did I tell you that already?" She smiled. Her eyeliner was smudged. I licked my finger and pulled her face to me, wiping off the excess.

Hester peeled the door open and I followed her in. When the

bouncer saw us, she got up off the stool and ushered us in free of charge. The manager, Donna, has told us that she likes to get more high femmes in the club. "You give the place class," she said last week. Hester thinks that Donna wants us to come in sometime and do a show for free. The bouncer, like most butches we know, is one of Hester's ex-lovers. Her name is Randi, and she has bristly dark hair and wears T-shirts with ripped sleeves. She complimented me on the velvet bustier I was wearing, and I gave her a wink, getting a slow kiss on my cheek in return. To me, the best flirting is with someone like her, because I'd never give her a tumble. I wouldn't go behind Hester's back. If you aren't loyal to your friends, who are you loyal to?

In bars, I usually sit in a corner, dipping my finger into a drink and scanning the crowd for a face that will seem so attractive it is almost familiar. Hester says I'm much too picky, but my little sister Melissa thinks it's good that I take my time. That night I hadn't yet found a stool and was still smarting from the cold when a woman bumped against me. Her brown eyes leaned into me and then away. She smiled, holding my arms as though I needed steadying, and our bodies slid closer as people pressed past us on both sides. Something about her reminded me of a dog that my sister and I had when we were kids. I couldn't tell you what. The woman smelled like hair gel and smoke. I could have touched her nose, a kiss so quick she wouldn't notice. I wanted to. Stunned by how much I wanted to, I stepped away, tucked my hands behind my back.

But I watched her as she shouldered her way through the crowd, with a pert salute to me before she disappeared. The wallet in her back pocket was linked to her belt with a loose chain, and, craning my head, I saw that she wore engineer boots. Her body was compact, neat. She twisted around a woman in a plaid shirt and was gone. For a few moments I stood where I was. I almost didn't have the heart to go find my drink and my seat, to watch the tide of unfriendly women eddy around me.

Later in the evening I saw her in a corner where the strobe lights weren't flashing as brightly, sipping at a tall glass of ice and lime.

She smiled, again that quick exposure of teeth, those attentive eyes. I tilted my head and she patted the seat next to her.

Above the music, mouth to ear, we talked. She told me her name. Said she was in recovery, said she was a landscaper, wanted to go back to school. As she talked she played with the thin, red-and-white-striped straw that had been in her drink. She folded it over and over, trying to make it as small as possible. I watched the straw as if I too was playing with it. Music and smoke pressed loudly against us, but I hardly noticed. Once, as she began flattening the straw against the table, talking about the classes she wanted to take, I dared a look at her face. The collar of her leather jacket was propped against her neck. Under her wild hair, her features seemed small. As I was examining her, she looked up from the straw. Her eyes dipped down, shyly. "I broke up with my lover a few weeks ago," she said.

She turned slightly away from me. Was this to tell me that she wasn't available, needed more time? I sat on my hands, looked at the straw. She had stopped playing with it. "Hey!" She said loudly next to me, and startled, I glanced at her, but she was gesturing to someone else. As her friend approached, I walked away, conscious of how I might look, my back straight in my velvet clothes.

Hester stood near the door of the club, talking to another ex-lover. On the dance floor a girl with pink hair writhed by herself, out of synch with the music. Closing time approached. I leaned against a pole, sleepy, the music thudding in my ears as though I was sick. As I waited for Hester, I peeked in the corner at the woman I had just met. At first she was still talking to her friend, but the next time I looked, she was alone, her face expectant, drumming her hands on the table. Gracie, I told myself, playing I was Hester, c'mon. Nothing ventured and all that. Pulling my eyeliner out of my bag, I picked up someone's cocktail napkin and scribbled down my number, my name. It didn't matter to me if she liked me or not. In fact, the idea that she wasn't interested made it easier. Who cared?

As I approached her, Jean smiled again, not seeming to care how it creased her face. "I didn't mean for you to go," she said.

Against me her eyes felt too bright, and I nearly stepped back—
but I already had a plan, was breathless with it. I handed her
the napkin in the sweetest way I could. "Call me when you get
a chance," I told her, and wondered what I looked like to her;
imagined how the lights were sliding across my face.

Leaving with Hester, I felt sweaty; almost savage. Stepping
into the relief of the night, the wind aggressively opening up my
coat, I wanted to play hopscotch or take a dog for a walk. I didn't
know why I'd never done something like that before. It seemed
so easy.

At work the next day, I told all the girls how assertive I'd been.
In the changing room, under the garish lights, women brushed
out their wigs, checked on their makeup. Hester said, "Shit, girl,
next time you should take her into the ladies' room for a quickie.
*That's* assertive." Everyone laughed, even the straight girls, as
they patted their faces with powder and shook their heads gently, waiting for the mascara to dry. After I pulled on my bra with
the Velcro panels, I kicked off my sneakers, stepping carefully
into my heels. You learn early, after some quick contact with
the stickiness underfoot, not to let your bare feet even brush up
against the floor or the carpet anywhere in the theater. Hester
snapped up her corset, shaking her head at me. Then she
winked. "That Jean is a cute one," she said. "That's for sure."
She jiggled her breasts to be sure they fit the cups right.

Behind Hester in line, waiting for our cue, I saw long drops
of sweat between her shoulder blades. She had worked a double shift, because lately she had it in her head that she wanted
to buy a house. Her body odor and her dull perfume mixed together strongly enough to make it seem as though there was an
extra person standing in the space she occupied. That, I thought,
was the difference between Hester and me. Except onstage.

For the first time I almost wished that I had beckoned Jean
into the bathroom for a quickie. Kneading the mothy red drapes
under my fingers, I imagined doing it: my hair hanging heavy
in my face, our tongues writhing against each other. But what
then? I couldn't picture our bodies together, only her looking

at me, exposing my breasts. I thought if she touched me I would feel like a piece of rubber, tweaked under her hands. It seemed to me that every time I'd had sex I'd felt at least a small drumbeat of fear under my skin. Didn't everyone? With someone I didn't know, I thought it would be worse. What would be the point? Though I could come to work and tell the girls, and have Hester slug me on the shoulder.

When we were cued, I had to shake my head. We climbed onstage, which is a funny word for the peepshow, really, because it's not like the rickety catwalk out front. I like it better because the guys can't touch you but the tips are just as good, wedged under the Plexiglas panel. You have to work a longer shift, but you don't have to sit out in the bar after, wearing only underwear and sequins, trying to get them to buy you drinks. Hester's favorite is the Box, especially if she's working it with another girl. In the Box, you just lounge on one side of a window, doing whatever the guy on the other side asks you to do, which is usually not all that different from what we do in the Peepshow—faked masturbation and all that. Sometimes dildos, which aren't supposed to be used, since staged penetration is illegal. Talking dirty is usually enough to get the guys off. They pay extra when there's two girls, which is why Hester likes it, especially if she's friendly with the girl. The bad side is that guys leave more irregular tips. I don't like the feeling myself, of them being able to tell you what to do. But Hester, I don't know, it doesn't beat her down.

Within the first few minutes of being onstage we flung off our clothes. There's less creativity or suspense, really, than with the catwalk—the guys pay by the minute. Even after five years at the Pink Lady, it takes me a while to get used to the dry, urine smell once I'm onstage—and in the bar, by the Box, the smell is so strong it can clog my senses. The floodlights began melting my makeup as always, and I licked my lips in a sexy way, trying to get rid of it so it wouldn't sting. It tasted bitter. Only half the booths were open, the others closed like eyes with lazy metal lids. Slow night. Hester sauntered up to one of the open booths and began rubbing herself against it, her breasts flat-

tening against the Plexiglas. That will get you a good tip, usually. In the booth closest to me, a guy looked at me blankly. I
wiggled closer to him.

The music bleated in the background. As I twisted my hips,
I saw that the guy, with bills in his hand, was beckoning me
closer. That was when I felt it—a strange spasm. I wanted to
go for him. Not just for the tip. His face, the very blankness of
it, seemed absorbing to me. He looked into my eyes, and I felt
sudden anticipation and dread churning inside me. At the same
time I was scared, scared somehow that I could fall through the
Plexiglas and into his flat hands. Though I knew it was crazy,
that fear kept me where I was, grinding my heels into the waxy
wood floor. So I squatted like it was on purpose, shutting my
eyes. His gaze on me felt as personal as a touch. I fingered my
breasts, feeling thick and awkward, unbalanced. I wasn't sure
if Hester had noticed or not. Another lid dragged itself open and
this time I danced over without looking.

At first, I thought Jean might call. Hester said she would. I
imagined the two of us on a date. Maybe out for coffee. I saw
myself picking the foam off a cappuccino, imagined her teeth
glinting in a grin. Thought that afterward we could go for a
walk. To me there's something romantic about walking on the
side of a busy street, watching the cars zoom by. Especially if
it's raining a bit and the headlights pry between the drops. People might be half-walking and half-running, that extra skipping
rain-gait, but we would be calm, unhurried.

But she didn't call. I waited for a week and then phoned my
sister. "Do you remember that dog we had when we were kids?"
I asked her.

On the other end, my sister sounded earnest. Sure, she remembered. The dog's name was Trixi. She would jump on her
hind legs, dirty paws in the air, when we came home from
school. I wondered, listening to Melissa describe the dog, if she
ever felt that funny feeling I did when the dog licked her face;
that the dog didn't care what I looked like, only how I smelled
and sounded.

I hadn't told Melissa about Jean. I didn't want to make a big deal of it. Melissa had never liked the women I dated—brash, loud women who would kiss me in front of her. Melissa and I don't get personal like that; a habit left over from when we were little. She's been dating the same guy for going on five years, and I can count the times I've seen them kiss.

Though she doesn't say so, I've known for a while Melissa doesn't exactly approve of my job. I make more money than she does working as a counselor in an abortion clinic, and if our mother was still alive, I'm not sure which of us she would be more ashamed of. But I could see Melissa getting on a talk show with the words, "My Sister Is A Stripper," in purple letters underneath her picture on TV.

"Gracie, what made you think about the dog?" Melissa asked me. The phone felt warm against my ear. I was making tea; hoping maybe the strange feelings at work were because of a cold.

"I think I'm getting sick," I said, not having an answer for her.

Melissa clucked, concerned, into the phone, and told me she'd come over to feed me chicken soup. She always says that we have to mom each other these days, and when she says that I feel myself get that leaky sensation I only have around her, like the seams in my body might not hold. So I couldn't say no, even though what I wanted to do was huddle under my electric blanket and watch *Meet Me in St. Louis* On The Movie Channel.

We had the fight in my kitchen. It was after I'd shown her how I'd organized one closet full of fabulous clothes—glittery dresses and satin mules and fuchsia boas. Melissa had glanced in for a moment and then shook her head, and I had felt anger surging up like spit in my mouth. She didn't want to try to understand that part of my life, okay, but the clothes were for me—couldn't she see that? But that wasn't what we fought about.

Melissa had given up on the chicken soup idea. Instead we ate what I used to make the two of us for breakfast before school—chocolate milk and Oreos. Sitting on the counter, swinging my legs, I said maybe I shouldn't have the chocolate, because wasn't it supposed to be an aphrodisiac? I really didn't need that right now. Melissa, staring at me with a flaky brown milk mustache, asked if I knew that Matt could easily fix me up with one of his friends.

"A lot of the guys think you're really cute, Gracie," she told me.

Like I didn't know this? This was how I made my living, for Christ's sake. I jumped down off the counter, putting my cup in the sink with a bang. "No thanks, Mel. I said I was lonely, not desperate."

Melissa, still sitting on the counter next to the sink, began swinging her legs slowly. Her hair hung down in soggy waves, tucked behind her ears. She caught a lock of it in her mouth and chewed. Melissa has always looked like she should have grown up preppy. No one in our family had an extra penny to spit at, but she has that wide, flushed face you associate with people who wear plaid, alligators, and pink and green. These days Melissa tends toward flowered skirts and beige sandals. Looking at her, I thought how she tried to dress like me when we were kids. In high school I encouraged her to wear pencil-legged jeans and gold belts; to tie a handkerchief around one thigh, to wear mismatched earrings and dotted makeup like tattoos around the eyes. Carefully we would both scrub our faces before we got home.

"Gracie, I didn't mean to offend you," Melissa said. As though she had just noticed it was there, she pulled the hair out of her her mouth. "I don't know, you've said sometimes that you might give it a chance. You know. With a guy."

Turning the sink on, I held my hand out for her cup. "I said that in high school, Mel." I pulled the sleeves of my old gray sweater up above my elbows.

Melissa kicked her foot against the air, looking away from me. "Well, I guess I don't know why you won't even try sleeping with a guy. How do you know you won't like it?"

The image of that man's blank face in the audience elbowed its way into my mind, and I pushed, pushed it back. It was true, there was something enticing about sleeping with a man, about being wanted in that way, but something repulsive, too. I couldn't put words to it—but it would be as though who I was would get washed away. Thinking about it made me feel mean. "I don't know, Mel," I said, sponging out a cup. "I guess I think the point of having sex is to actually have an orgasm or something. You know, you're supposed to enjoy it."

"I enjoy it," Mel said.

I put down the sponge and looked at her, raising my eyebrows in a casual way, though my cheeks felt pulpy with anger. I thought about Matt and his skinny face with the strident red acne, his gangly legs, his slow way of talking about the department store he managed. "Really," I said. You could tell I didn't believe her.

Vaulting off the counter, she grabbed her coat. She stood by the door for a moment and I saw that she was trembling. When she turned around to look at me her face had that sucked-in expression you get when you're trying not to cry. "You haven't got any call to say that to me, Grace Ann O'Brien. That's all I can say. You can't do it with anyone and like it for very long and you want to know why?"

I gripped the sink as if to brace myself. I did want to know why. I wanted to know more than anything.

But Melissa just dug her foot against the Barbie welcome mat on the floor. "Because you are a chicken, Gracie. You always have been. You think you're so tough, strutting your stuff onstage, but you aren't, okay?" She put her coat on and faced the door, her hand wringing the doorknob back and forth. I could barely hear her. "I know you and that's not you," she said, and then she walked out.

When I get upset I always go look in a mirror. I've always done this, ever since I was a little kid. After Melissa left, just looking at my own face in the old mirror in my bedroom calmed me down. I pulled my hair back and looked at my comforting black eyebrows and brown eyes. Still me, still me. I could remember, as a kid, sitting on top of the bathroom sink to get a look at myself, wondering if my face was the kind of face someone would want to kiss. I'd press myself up against the mirror to see how I'd look when someone did decide to kiss me.

She doesn't understand, I thought. She doesn't know me. I do feel alone up there, but it's no worse than than anywhere else. The clothes—on or off—weren't the thing at all. I dress up for myself, I wanted to tell her. I looked at myself in the mirror and didn't cry. I leaned close to the mirror and told myself I still had a face that was made to be kissed.

It was a few weeks later before Hester could convince me to go out again; and a few weeks for her to convince the manager to give us both another Saturday night off. We worked the afternoon shift and headed from the Pink Lady right to the club. Hester wore a peach shirt that showed off her stomach, and a faux fox jacket. I just wore jeans and a Lycra top. Hester made me pile my hair on top of my head. I thought it made me look more like a drag queen than ever, but I didn't argue.

Our breath puffed ahead of us like word clouds in cartoons. Christmas lights studded the small sidewalk trees, and the streets were crowded with cars and late-night shoppers. Hester hurried forward, as always, ignoring the men who looked at her with half-smiles or who made clucking noises at us. I stared at them, careful not to meet their eyes. One man, wearing a tweed hat and gray overcoat, walked into Hester's path and pressed his body against hers. He was almost as tall as she was and his breath rasped in and out against his damp mustache. He didn't say anything, but he ran his hands down the length of her body. She unwrapped herself from him and half-ran ahead, but I slowed down, looking at him. His face looked loose to me. When he noticed me, he smiled, his lips tremulous. Hester had stopped walking and had turned around to see what was keeping me. The man reached out his hand to touch my face. His lips still trembled, and he said something to me, but I didn't hear what. Hester, alarmed, stepped closer to us.

Before he touched me, I stopped his hand with my own and wrenched his fingers back. At the same time I used the sharp heel of my shoe to slam into the spiny part of his leg. He leaned toward me and his face wrinkled with pain, his mouth open, breath rushing through him noisily. He didn't cry out. I stayed where I was, wringing his fingers with my hands, my teeth shaking in my jaw; waiting for him to make some sound, even a whimper. But before he could, Hester had me by the arm. She dragged me past the people who had gathered around me and the hunched-over man. Hester kept pulling me fast enough to make my heels stutter against the pavement. It wasn't until we rounded the corner that she stopped and looked into my face.

"You okay, doll?" she asked, straightening the collar of my jacket.

"Sure," I said, as if I did that kind of thing all the time. Cold air wheezed in and out of me, painfully. I realized I was almost panting. Hester stood next to me as I leaned against the wall. She never asked me why I did it. All she said was that my lipstick needed fixing, and then, seeing how brittle my breath was still, she pulled out her own compact and fixed it for me. When we started walking again, I kept my hand in Hester's pocket, matching my strides to hers, and started to feel warm.

By the time we got to the Klit Kat, it was late. We stood in the entranceway to the club, watching the very young women careen on the dance floor. On the outskirts, a woman with a gray flattop stood watching them. Her face was absolutely still. I scanned the bar, where women sat in chrome booths or leaned, gossipy, against their stools.

Hester said, using her low tones that carried beneath the music rather than above it, "Now, don't waste your time chasing after that little butch who doesn't know a good thing when she sees it," which meant she had just seen Jean. I rubbed my hands against my legs and said to Hester, "Do you wanna drink?"

At the bar, I shook my glass of gin-and-tonic and watched the cubes shiver. There were go-go dancers in elevated cages in the center of the room. Hester and I eyed them silently for a while. We both knew we were better than those girls by a long shot, but that's why we worked full time at the Pink Lady and got the kind of tips we did, rather than taking occasional shifts

at a girls bar. Besides, both Hester and I liked to keep our working lives and our private lives separate. In the cage, a woman
strutted in a circle, then held onto the bars and tilted her pelvis
in and out. She looked tired. Just from watching her, Hester
hooked her foot against a stool and sat on it.

"Hi, Gracie." Startled, I turned to see Jean standing next to
me, her body an inch away from mine. She was smiling, that
lean, quick smile I remembered.

"Hey," I paused for a moment as though I couldn't remember her name. "Jean." But I couldn't help smiling back. Her eyes
looked wet and alive.

Jean straddled the barstool on my left. Staring straight ahead
at the go-go dancers, she somehow managed to make me feel
as though she was looking at me. We talked for a few minutes
about the music and the weather. She was still wearing her
leather jacket. Every few minutes she touched her slicked-back
hair. Then she turned to face me. "Look," she said, shrugging,
"I'm sorry I didn't call you." Her mouth stayed open and she
held her hand out, palm up. "I guess I was just sorry I didn't
ask you home that night." She flattened her palm, warm, against
my back.

I pressed my legs against the rungs of the stool, struggling to
keep still. The skin on my back itched except where her palm
was. I wanted to wrap myself around her, right there in the bar.
Sitting there, feeling my body tighten, I remembered the dreams
I would have after sex with somebody, while she slept next to
me, fitting into the slots and bends of my body. In the dreams,
there was always the sound of breathing, the movement of a
ribcage expanding and contracting into my back. Night after
night I felt as though I gained an extra pair of lungs, extra oxygen. I would feel giddy and huge—and then frightened at my
own size. The extra lungs would become attached to me, un-
wanted, and I wouldn't be able to control my own breath. I used
to feel frightened when I woke into the muddled night. But, I
remembered under Jean's light touch, recently I'd been having
that same dream. All alone under the drowsy covers, I would

wake up and have to force myself to breathe. I looked up at the go-go dancer, and then ducked my head. I had to lick my lips twice to keep myself from trembling.

"Care to start all over again?" I said, when I finally could.

I woke up when I felt Jean pulling away, her legs unlocking from mine. Air drifted over me, but before she dropped the covers down I reached for her. I didn't open my eyes, just pulled her back. She began kissing my neck, biting a little, then rested her face against my collarbone. Her breath was hot, her nose cold, and everything inside of me felt liquid, lush. I felt boneless. Her breath against my skin was like a devotion. "Shush. I have to use the bathroom," she whispered. "Go back to sleep." She tucked the covers around me as though I was a child—and childlike, I held onto one finger before I let her go. It was as though I knew that when I woke up again she'd be gone.

Oh, you're used to all that, I know. Meet a girl, lose a girl, you've heard that story before, what else is new? I woke up late and the sun was thick on my face. She hadn't left a note. My aerobics class was over. Without showering, I got dressed. I wanted to wear the smell of her, hold it on me, for a while.

After I made tea and read the comics and "Dear Abby," I packed my work bag and did my stretches. My body felt sore and open. By the time I got to work I was late, and all the girls teased me. Hester must have said something, though she denied it, examining her nails and pretending to be insulted. Everyone wanted details.

I thought about how Jean had arched herself nearly off of my bed, shivering in bursts; how she had looked at me, abashed, after; how she'd fallen asleep, curled between my breasts; thought about how I had watched her, holding my hand above her heart and marveling that it bumped on, slow, every day—and knew that I couldn't tell anyone anything. In front of the dressing table I looked in the mirror under the bald lightbulb. I stared back at myself, my eyes looking heavy and my lips looking sad. When I first started working at the Pink Lady, before

Hester began, I was the youngest of all of them. Leaning into the light, hearing the pumping music of the first set, I could see wrinkles around the hollows of my eyes.

I wondered if Melissa was getting wrinkles yet. I wondered what she thought about when she got out of bed, when she looked at herself in the mirror, when she dressed, hurrying against goosebumps, for work. Did she wake up every day and feel like she was someone important? She didn't wake up everyday and feel like a foreigner in her own skin, struggling to learn a new language, did she?

Hester, behind me, said, "C'mon, babe, hurry up, you're gonna be late!" Standing, I unzipped my pants, searching in someone else's bag for clothes. Hester watched, frowning. She was wearing her plastic boots and her peekaboo bikini. "Grace, you hung over or something? Get a grip!" She said. Her mascara had left little dots beneath her eyebrow but before I could rub it off she turned away, leaving me to pull on a velvet G-string alone.

Out on the floor we stood in our familiar spots in front of the faces, waiting for the music to begin. When it did, and the lights flicked on, I felt the familiar puckering of my makeup and the sweat gathering all over my body. For the first time I felt at home—as though there was room inside my muscles and my eyes and under my mucus membrane for only one person—no matter who might else want it. I thought maybe I would cry. But instead I smiled as I gyrated in front of the silent audience, my oldest and most consistent lover; my own salty smell rising up all around me.

# GeCo

## MONALESIA EARLE

*T*he dusky red smudge of the swirling leaves made Carolyn think of the inevitability of the coming winter. Rummaging through her pockets for warmth, she recalled with more than a little melancholy how the passion of summer had lain itself down almost meekly into the bountiful swell of the pomegranate fall. Knowing the sureness of the approaching change would trigger cycles within her, which she on the one hand relished and looked forward to, but which she at the same time wanted to hold at bay for as long as possible, she nevertheless longed for the muffled rapture of nature burrowing in on itself.

Walking through the woods on her weekend escape to the Adirondacks, she could hear the leaves rustling underfoot and the quick scurrying of small animals making their way home to nests or thick, protective underbrush. The pungent smells of nature turned into a gauzelike backdrop to her memories, causing her to slow down, then stop for a long breath of time.

Her favorite activity of all was when she could walk in the woods and be comforted by the memory of the almost imperceptible breeze of her mother's long skirts making smooth, seemingly uninterrupted passes across her young face as she lay unconcerned on the thick plush carpet watching the minutia of her life take form.

As children, my sister and I used to love the drives the family took to the Adirondacks every summer. Sally and I were two years apart in age, but got along well enough to be relatively good companions on long drives. Even though I was faster on my feet than my sister, she was the best at playing GeCo, a game our mother had made up on one of the longer, more trying trips.

GeCo was played by creating a color for a place name. The more exotic, the better. For me, Tuscany was always the color of amber, and for Sally it was green. Ceylon was burnt orange, but Sally was partial to guava. Tasmania was a brilliant purple laced with delicate traces of gold.

When I was fourteen, and Sally sixteen, our mother divorced our father and took up with a woman. Sally took it harder than anyone else, running away from home for two days and not talking to anyone for an entire month when she did return. The divorce also changed her relationship with Mother and she took to spending much of her free time in Manhattan with Dad. When she and Mother did talk, they always seemed to have a hard time making sense of each other.

Back then, me, Sally, and Mom lived in the part of Brooklyn that still had nice large houses with porches and wide, tree-lined streets. It was one of those neighborhoods where people weren't so close that we felt boxed in, but not so far away that we couldn't be neighborly if the spirit made us so inclined. In fact, until Mom took up with Maureen, Mrs. Jellit used to always let her kids come over to spend the night.

Mrs. Jellit lived across the street, but after Mom and Maureen got together, she made it a point to let us know just how studiously she was ignoring us. It wasn't any big deal, because Mom never liked her anyway, and Sally and I only liked her kids for the new toys they always brought over to show off.

The day before the accident, Sally and Mom had been having yet another battle over curfew. Sally felt she should be allowed to stay out past ten o'clock on school nights, but Mom wouldn't budge from Sally having to be in by nine. Lucky for me, it wasn't one of their usual screaming matches. In fact, for the past month or two, Mom and Sally had really started listening to each other and had gotten almost as close as they had been before the divorce. I guess Sally just needed time to get used to the idea that Mom and Dad were history and weren't going to get back together.

The senior prom was as big a deal in Brooklyn as it was everywhere else in the country. Sally had been asked to go by one of the more popular boys at school, and she was beside herself with excitement, and silly-looking at the same time trying not to show it. Even though the prom wasn't for another two months, she had narrowed down her outfit to four possibles and was bugging Mom to teach her how to slow-dance properly with a guy. Even though she had been to lots of parties, I guess there must've been some kind of unspoken rule about how people should dance at fancy gatherings.

Mom teaching Sally how to dance turned out to be one of the little things that brought them closer together, and although I was only beginning to realize that boys existed for something other than trading insults with, it was great to watch Mom and Sally pretend one of them was a boy and spin each other around on our enclosed porch. In spite of my own aversion to wearing dresses and "making nice" with the "hairy sex," I could appreciate the joy Sally seemed to find in it.

Back then, I think one of my most favorite pastimes was sneaking into my sister's room to read her diary. Indeed, if her diary entries were any indication, she was apparently enamored of muscles, french kissing, the back row of balconies at movie theaters, and cool cars. It was always a source of amazement to me how much detail about hard-ons she was able to pack into one small, tiny page of her diary. Even though she didn't seem to be having sex yet, she sure did seem to be doing most everything else leading up to it. And because she always seemed especially interested in talking to me when, after reading her diary, I had my eyes bugged out and my face scrunched up like I had just been offered a prune cake slathered in shit, I suspected that for all those years of growing up together, she knew what

I was doing and had hidden her real diary, letting me find the decoy for her own sick pleasure.

I sat in the old-fashioned swing Mom had installed on the porch a few years after she and Dad bought the house. She used to tell us stories about how she would relax in it and swing us back to sleep whenever we woke up scared about something. Sometimes she still let me act like a baby and cuddle up close to her on the swing when I needed to. Draping my arms across the back of it as I sat there pushing off gently with my feet, I watched Mom show Sally how to stand as they waited for the music to start. She was telling Sally to give a little less pelvic thrust and concentrate more on form.

Mom put on the record she said she and Dad used to dance to when they were first dating. It was one of the better songs by Anne Murray, and it suited the tender, yet somewhat comical picture of Mom and Sally gliding around the porch, giddy with laughter and renewed affection for each other.

Mom was good at showing Sally where the boys' hands were supposed to go if they were really dancing properly like they should. Holding Sally firmly around the waist, yet loose enough to let her go easy into a twirl, Mom spun Sally around a couple of times so she could get the feel for how to let a boy *think* he was in control.

Sally didn't wear dresses often, but for some reason she had put on a really soft cotton dress with those spaghetti-like shoulder straps. It hit her about mid-calf and had pastel-colored pictures of cats and dogs jumping around on it. After the fashion of the day, she wore it with a white T-shirt underneath. Watching Sally's dress balloon up like soft clouds around her knees as she and Mom went into another turn, I remembered how she used to prance around in that dress like she was Donna Reed on a picnic with the cast from *The Sound of Music*. She only stopped wearing that particular dress after one of her friends teased her about having athletic-looking legs. Back then we all knew athletic was a euphemism for muscular or manly when it was used to describe some part of a girl's anatomy. I was surprised to see Sally wearing it again.

The light from the foyer spilled out onto the porch to merge with the soft glow of the yellow bug light. The warm air bowing to the mauve curtain of dusk was just enough to make life right at that moment seem idyllic and always possible. Even the shy ribbing of the kids riding by on their bicycles added to the fun of it all. Right then, their flushed faces and high-pitched giggles framed a singularly rich moment in time.

Looking back on it, I guess because there were three women on the porch fooling around, and no man in sight, the guys in the car felt they had to do something to fix the situation. I still remember how their raucous, boozy laughter was surrealistically at odds with the peacefulness of the evening, and even their repeated screams of "fucking lesbian faggots" didn't register as being horrifying until it was joined by the almost cartoon-like crack from the gun that exploded the base of my sister's skull. All I could see through the flying red globules bathing my frozen face with the shocking wetness of death, was the athletic legs of my sister—dress swirling madly to its own sounds—propelling her forward into the arms of the woman who had given her life.

My sister never made it to the prom and Mom never took much interest in dancing again. She did take to drinking though, and also to saying over and over again with eyebrows arched in a frozen, sort of stunned position, how ironic it was that Sally died while getting herself ready for the social ritual of being appealing to men. Nothing Dad or Maureen could say would convince Mom it wasn't her fault. It was pretty sad, because I knew that when Sally had run away that time, it wasn't because Mom was queer, but simply because we were losing what we thought was a perfect family.

* * *

After the divorce, Sally and I talked a little bit about Mom's new lifestyle. I remembered how nonchalant Sally sounded about it all.

"Do you think Mom is different now that she doesn't love men anymore, Sally?" Giving me one of her rare smiles, Sally explained to me that Mom was only different in that she now had someone to help her pin up her hair right; help her paint her toenails; help her cook and do the laundry; and, best of all, she had someone who knew how to make her hot-water bottle just the right temperature when she got cramps. Other than that, Sally assured me nothing had changed.

"Look at it this way, Carolyn," Sally said as she made herself comfortable on my bed, "Mom's just done what I think every woman secretly wants to do anyway." Pushing my stuffed dog Gwendolyn's eye back into her corduroy-covered head, I asked Sally what was it that every woman wanted to do.

"Every woman wants to have her best girlfriend move in with her so she won't feel so lonely when football season starts and her husband is out with his friends drinking beer and talking about artificial turf versus the real kind."

I liked it when Sally talked to me as if I really knew what was going on. It made me feel like maybe fourteen wouldn't be as tedious an age as I had at first thought. The only thing that bothered me though was wondering which girlfriend I would want to have live with me. I didn't think it could be Peggy Baldwin because she had what Mom called a "flatulence problem." All I knew was that she laid a lot of stink bombs and it took every ounce of goodness I had inside of me not to end our friendship. But I didn't want to live with Janice either, because she stuck her tongue in my mouth once, and, at the time, I didn't think that qualified as something girlfriends did for each other. Other than that, she was a pretty good friend. Guess I needed to give this living together stuff more thought.

Since Mom's lifestyle didn't seem to be such a big deal to Sally, it wasn't a big deal to me either. I suppose that's why everytime I watched Mom agonize over Sally's death, I won-

dered if Sally would've understood just how much of a big deal
it turned out to be after all. Although Mom had never been
much of a drinker, with her enormous pain over Sally's death,
she quickly reached a point where she didn't want to come out
of her drunken fog. In her grief, I think she even forgot she had
another daughter who needed her.

In the ten years after the shooting, I grew up choosing celibacy
at first because it was easier than living up to the expectations
of men or women. It took me a very long time to reconcile
Sally's senseless death with my emerging, sometimes insistent
sexuality. There were many times when I wondered how I
would recognize my pain enough to welcome it and heal the
bitterness in my heart. I didn't know how to find my edges, bur-
nished red-brown and hard as they were by the screaming silence of my nights. The last thing I wanted to do was think
about engaging in the very ritual that had taken my sister away.

Looking around at the cool, still protectiveness of the trees, I
could feel my mother's long skirts making smooth, almost uninterrupted passes across my young face as I lay on the forest
floor drinking in the patches of sky. My sister, Sally, was Brisbane, and Brisbane was the color of all things hopeful.

# *Anhedonia*

## A. Elizabeth Mikesell

*I* tell my therapist that when I was thirteen my six-year-old brother found a hot dog under my pillow and ran down to the kitchen, laughing, waving it in the air. She asks me what happened next, and I say I can't remember exactly, only that I ran after him, yelling, "Give me that!" and he squealed, "It was under her pillow!" And that the next day, my mother asked me if I was a lesbian.

"And what did you say?"

I said, "A what?" because I had no idea what she meant.

"You really had no idea?"

None whatsoever. But I looked it up in the dictionary, and really understood about two years later, in high school, at a sleep-over at Janet Riley's house, when we tried on her older sisters' prom dresses and I couldn't stop looking at her cleavage. Janet Riley is married, I heard, and lives in California, and is expecting her third child. But I don't even think about Janet Riley at all anymore.

"What do you think about?"

My therapist is sitting in her leather chair, her feet up on the foot rest. I have told her how lonely I am, how I stay home all the time, and she gestures with empathy, her fat rock of an engagement diamond catching the light as she directs her thoughts and mine. I've told her that just because I stay home, that doesn't mean I'm idle. That I've taken up quilting, and on the weekends I bake the most incredible pies, fruit pies with woven lattice crusts that hold it all together, and how I eat the pies in one day sometimes, watching TV shows featuring nuclear families having humorous problems in their three-bedroom homes.

I look at the floor, thinking of the hundred twenty-five bucks I pay to speak to her for fifty minutes, and notice that the Oriental rug is like my last shrink's, only somehow different. I try to figure out how many visits from me it would take to buy an Oriental rug, and think about what I think about.

I think about the morning, and how it makes me think of Ann. I think of waking to the radio, the AM dial in the A.M. of the day, and of Ann Morning and her initials. Ana Mañana, Ann Matin, A. Morning. Any morning it's the same. Ana Mañana, Ann Matin, Ann Morning. I wonder what she does with her mornings.

If I were to tell my therapist about Ann Morning, she would want to know why it is I insist on torturing myself with yet another straight girl. I've heard it before. And I would tell her that, to me, Ann Morning is not a straight girl, she's just a girl, a woman if you want to quibble, which I don't. She's just a girl, same as any other.

Ann Morning works in my office, in the sales department. She has to dress up, I tell myself, because she's in sales. I don't because I'm in editorial. She sells what I make, and represents the whole company when she goes out to Barnes & Noble or one of the independents. So she has to look good. But sometimes I wish she didn't look quite so good.

"Why did the hot dog make your mother ask you that?"

I look at my therapist, whose name is Lori but who I never refer to as anything but My Therapist, nameless like all the others, mine because I'm paying, and I say, "You know. She thinks lesbians come with attachments."

She doesn't know what I mean for a moment because she has never been to a women's bookstore or one of those tacky craft festivals where at least one woman is wearing a T-shirt with a slogan that's in poor taste, like "Wellesley College: A Century of Women Coming Together."

She gets it, finally, and laughs. She wants to help me work

through my bitterness, to find its roots in Janet Riley or my brother and his laughing soprano and tiny smooth hands clutching the hot dog, which was crusty and shriveled because it had been under my pillow for about a month. I'd forgotten about it, and forgot about it again until just now.

I feel the need to justify. "I was curious." That's all I can manage to say, because I don't want to get into the mechanics of it with her. What *was* that hot dog doing under my pillow? Some other woman sitting in a leather chair once told me that what you do when you're by yourself is an indicator of what you really want to do when you're with someone else. So what did I want, at age thirteen? Oscar Mayer? And what do the pies mean?

Ann Morning is gorgeous, but I don't let myself look at her too much. Whenever she comes into the editorial department to see what we're cooking up for her to sell, I smell her perfume, see her scarf, and move my eyes to my desk. Sometimes I hear her heels clicking on the linoleum, and I think about her legs and how anyone would be a fool not to notice her. I wonder if she has linoleum in her bathroom, if she clicks about in the morning, applying her makeup, pushing the earrings through her ears.

But I can't think about her, I tell myself, because that would get me nowhere. But where is it that I want to go? my therapist would ask if I told her what I was thinking, which I won't because it would all look so easy to her, or else far too difficult for her to respond to with anything but a "Hmmmm. Interesting."

Ann Morning has chestnut hair that flips obediently up or under, and fingernails that change color weekly. I can't decide if I like Ann Morning's fingernails, or if I like her in spite of them. If I had her under my spell, would I encourage her to keep up her nails, or would I clip them in her sleep? If I clipped them, would I save them, or would I ceremoniously throw them away, or burn them, or eat them? Or put them under my pillow? Or would I learn her tricks as she'd learn mine, wink wink, and drink gelatin and use special hand lotion? Would she move into my apartment or I into hers? And if I clipped her nails, wouldn't they grow back, in time?

And what if I'm wrong about Ann Morning, Ana Mañana, Ann Matin? What if I'm over- or underestimating her mind-set? She has never presented a boyfriend named Ted with a weak jaw and five-o'clock shadow, or a six-footer named Juan who holds his briefcase against his chest as if it were bulletproof, or a nondescript Adam, or a nameless guy in leather, sporting a tiny braid at the back of his head. I've never seen her kiss any-one and feel weak and weepy. I've never heard her talk on the phone in low whispers, betraying herself as she twists her hair around her finger. She's never held both of my hands in hers and tried to explain through her tears that I really, really, was more than just a sexual-experimentation drive-through.

"Does your mother know, now?"

Know what? That I bake and quilt and probably won't re-produce, like a Shaker? Of course she knows. Do we talk about it? Of course we don't. Haven't we been over all this already? Or was that another therapist?

Ann Morning wears suits in pastels. She brought cookies from a bakery to the office party we had when my boss had a baby. She ate one cookie, holding a napkin under her mouth to collect the crumbs, and she left a print of lipstick on her coffee cup. Sometimes I think thoughts about her after I turn out the lights, and stop myself because I know that, if she knew, she would be disturbed. And then I think about her some more, for the same reason. I take my coffee black. She takes hers with milk. Nothing means anything.

"And is she comfortable with that?"

I start to ask who, Ann Morning? But she is still talking about my mother. Yes, I tell her, to close that topic.

"And your father?"

Yes, yes, they're all resigned to it.

"And your brother?"

God only knows what he knows. It's never come up. My family really doesn't talk about it, which means we really don't talk about anything.

I decide to tell my therapist a dream, to keep her mind working on something, to make her work for the money. Ann Morning was giving me acupuncture with six-foot-long needles that passed straight through my back and came out through my chest, pinning me, skewering my heart on the way. Pretty transparent. Only I tell her that it was my mother, not Ann Morning.

"And did that hurt you? What happened next?"

The rug has an intricate pattern of blue tendrils weaving through a sea of scarlet, with white accents. Another therapist's had the same pattern, with the colors switched around. It occurs to me that they all shop at the same stores, that this is somehow significant.

What happened next? I woke up, of course, almost disappointed to see that I could sit up without tearing the mattress. Or, I woke up alone, and forced myself back into sleep to find out if I'd bled.

It's just beginning, with Ann Morning. I haven't really taken off yet. Just taxiing on the runway till the lookout tower gives the all-clear.

"You control your dreams. Why do you make them happen like that?"

I am looking pensive. It buys me some time before I have to speak again. It's not "Why do I make them happen like that?" but "Why do I let them begin in the first place?" Why do I embark on a flight of fancy with Ann Morning? What kind of sickness propels me to focus on what I can't have? Or that which I can have for a short time, like a nice dinner that I will eventually finish. Or that will be taken away by some waiter before I've gotten to the good part, which I always save for last. If I were a geeky boy in love with a glamorous woman, would anyone ever tell me to realize that there are certain things I just plain can't have, or would they be more likely to congratulate me on my emerging self-confidence? What is so pathological about expecting everything I want to be mine? Why should I settle? Why did I have a hot dog under my pillow? Doesn't every girl do stuff like that, don't they all want to know what it feels like?

"If you could have a dream with your mother in it, and you could control it, what would you have happen?"

I say we would spend time at the kitchen table, talking about important things. I say she would take both of my hands in hers and say, "I love you, forever." I start to cry because it seems like the thing to do.

"This is obviously bringing up some feelings. Stay with them."

Me and Ann Morning, sitting in the kitchen, eating pie. "Ana Mañana, you like the pie?" I would ask her, and she would take my hands and say, in a fake Spanish accent, "Your pie, it pleases me, most muchly." I would feel her stockinged foot graze my ankle.

It starts to feel as funny as it sounds in my head, so I laugh. I can find things funny, which must mean I haven't completely crashed. But the laughing and crying have my therapist all tied up in knots.

"Something's funny?"

I tell her a joke an ex-girlfriend told me once, before we'd started anything. It's the one about two women at a convention, one of whom has a terrible crush on the other, but is worried that the other woman doesn't, or can't, return the feeling. But she holds on to the hope. Finally, she decides to get it all out in the open, to go for broke, and says, "Let me be frank," to which the other woman responds, "No, let *me* be Frank."

"How did that come out of what we were talking about before, about your mother?"

She wants it to be easy as that. She wants to trace my thoughts from my mother through me and into this room. An epiphany will take place, right before her eyes, and I will understand that, really, I love my mother. Or that I really hate my mother, and express it by hating myself, and eventually hating everyone I love.

I tell her I was thinking about the hot dog. A frank. This is farfetched, but she's nodding and squinting, so I know that she buys it.

"Why did your mother think what she thought based on the hot dog under your pillow?"

What else is a mother to think? That I'm hoarding phallic foods in the vicinity of my virgin child bed in case I get hungry during the night? That might be more comforting than thinking what she actually thought, which was of course the truth. But why did she make the mental leap to thinking I was a budding lesbian?

I ask my therapist if she's ever really thought about hot dogs. Really thought about the way they look. How they're so all-American, baseball and cookout food.

"It's because their casings were originally made out of intestines, which are shaped that way."

Yeah, that's true, I know. But wasn't anyone other than me embarrassed by hot dogs in their childhood? Taking a big bite out of a weenie with a bunch of boys around? It's just something we all grow up with, and accept as normal. Does anyone ever say, "Mom, this looks like a penis?" How do boys feel about hot dogs?

"But hot dogs don't really look like penises. Do they."

I ask her what she thinks the hot dog under my pillow meant.

"It's not important what I think. It's important what you think."

I ask her if she thinks lesbians come with attachments.

"As I said, it's what you think."

I tell her I've never met one who insisted on it. Maybe the side dish, but not the main course. But then again, look who I've been sleeping with. They all eventually go back to the attachment.

"But it's not about that. Why do you think they really leave you?"

Here I'm supposed to say, "Because I push them away, because I'm afraid of intimacy." Or, "Because I'm worried that they will leave me for a man and make them do it, somehow." I wish I had that kind of power! I would make Ann Morning bring me flowers and take me to lunch on the company account.

Then we would go back to her place and I would lock myself in her bathroom for an hour and look at all the bottles and tubes and stuff, and when I emerged she would be naked. She would have tiny breasts with a hint of sag, and pubic hair to match her head.

I tell my therapist that they aren't really leaving me. They weren't ever really with me, but just on a path that happened to intersect for a short time with mine.

"Do you really believe that?"

No, I don't. I don't really believe anything anymore, though. Nothing anyone ever told me about my life has turned out to be true.

"Well, you have a job. . . ."

I have a job, that's true. But where's the car, the house, the kids? Nobody ever prepared me for what I'd have to face in life.

"Is that why you're here?"

In therapy? No. I'm in therapy because I think it's easier for me to come here than for me to drag the whole rest of the world here.

"Who would you like to drag to therapy?"

Well, let's start with the parents. I would drag them retroactively into a room like this one, when they were twenty-one and considering having children. That would make it unnecessary to drag my brother in. After they left, all of my high school teachers and the cheerleading squad and football team. And as they exited, they could hold the door for Janet Riley. And after Janet Riley had figured out why she passed me endless notes that sounded like love letters, and let me unzip her sister's prom dress and unhook her bra, I would have her remember that we then took a bath together in the old footed bathtub in her parents' three-bedroom Victorian on Fluck Mill Road, and tried to shave each others legs and laughed as the water spilled over the top because two people displace more water than one and we had miscalculated. Then I'd have her remember that she stopped calling me every night and never passed me another note and became aggressive in her search for a boyfriend. I'd just want her to remember that. She wouldn't even have to think about it too much, or tell anyone.

And then I'd bring in the college girls, Nan Beekman and Sarah Chin and Roberta Joan Peavy, for a small dose of group therapy. They could compare notes and figure out what it was that caused them to drift to a sofa, a futon, a brass bed, with someone like me who would want to do it again. And then they'd be joined by Erin Mills and Erin Halloran and Erin Ryan, and everyone present could guess which one married an Irishman after knowing him for one month, after knowing me, and yes I do mean biblically, for two years and three months. And Maria Bigini and June Van Dam and Laura Nelson could hold court about their month each, serially, of sleeping and cooking and seeing movies with me, and they could remember whether I had a mole on my left or right breast, whether I was a woofer or a tweeter, whether I liked my coffee black or with milk, and could argue about it. And at the height of their dispute, Renata Farquhar and Melinda Marshall would burst into the room and demand to know why they weren't invited sooner, since they knew more about the whole thing, had slept with each other and their own string of girls before even getting to me, their final wild oat before throwing big weddings with big bouquets that they actually invited me to come hold for them. A cute waitress with short hair and a hoop in her nose would bring in a plate of hot dogs, which all present would look at for a second, claiming they weren't hungry, but then, what the heck, dig into with a vengeance. Someone would open her wallet to a picture of her husband, and then ten other wallets would fly open and display a family of boyfriends, and children, and they'd be forced, somehow, to ask themselves if they'd ever even considered giving their daughters my name, even for a minute, even if it was also both their grandmothers' names, or something. And they'd compare notes on what they did with all the stuff I'd given them, if they'd somehow incorporated it into their lives, for a laugh or an occasional twinge of guilt, or thrown it away gradually or in one spectacular heap, if rings hid in jewelry boxes as a testament, or in pawn shops or at the bottom of landfills as a denial. And what about the books? Did anyone still have a book on their shelves with my name in it? Even if they'd once loved the book did they keep it? And one brave one would say her husband knew all about me and that it turned him on, and after an ungainly pause the rest would rush to close their wallets and stuff them into purse or pocket, as silent as a lie of omission.

And then Ann Morning would come into this room, standing room only, and say what I'd told her to say:

"The topic is Revisionist History. Discuss amongst yourselves."

My therapist is smiling. "I'm glad you're opening up more and letting me see some of your fantasy life. But I think you're avoiding the point, which is why you chose to sleep with so many heterosexual women?"

I'm ready for this one. I didn't choose heterosexual women, I chose women. Or more precisely, they chose me, since I, afraid of rejection, was held back, leaving them in the driver's seat. Sure I made myself available, but for the most part, they took the initiative. I was just picking from my field of vision, or being picked from theirs. And after the preliminaries, how many of them said I'd awakened them? After the longer-term ones could bring themselves to utter the "L" word, how long did it take them to say the other "L" word, and not just during sex? And what about the third one, lust? Even if the first two were lies, how can lust, so impulsive by nature, be denied? And how much lust have I denied myself, in retrospect? If I propositioned Ann Morning, which would be truly out of the blue at this point, could I begin with anything but, "Taste me. I'm bitter"?

"But who is Ann Morning?"

In my mania of expulsion, I have slipped into revelation. And I think, who is Ann Morning?

• I look at my therapist, who is looking at her watch, and say, "Nobody special." But that's just something else that I don't feel or believe.

# Lightning Dances Over the Prairie Like Lust at a Nightclub

## ANNA LIVIA

We were Rollerblading down Lombard Street, me and Spritz, my brilliant, beloved, drop-dead gorgeous g.f., zigzagging down that one in six gradient, bent as a drag queen's hairpin, when this great dark cloud appeared in the air. It spiraled toward us across the Victorian rooftops of San Francisco, a black cone whirling in the sky, its point about twenty feet above the ground and descending rapidly. Absorbed in displaying the buff definition of our muscular quadriceps (me), or the tapering outline of our gazelle-like calves (Spritz), we failed to notice the speed of the ominous cloud and the fact that it was heading straight toward us. That is to say, I failed to notice the approach of the ominous cloud because I was too busy gazing at Spritz as she turned back toward me, and thinking how sweet her knees were—little girl knees, bare and vulnerable and likely to need a Band-Aid, a contrast to her otherwise elegant femme frame. Spritz was however staring past me, having been warned of something untoward by the sound, which seemed to double in intensity every second, of a rushing wind of unnatural force.

"Oh my God," she said, "Run, Jiffy. It's a tornado."

We don't have tornadoes in San Francisco, we have earthquakes, God's warning against smugness to a people living on the edge. Tornadoes, as every American knows, are God's punishment to the Midwest, a seasonal reminder that nowhere is isolated from the winds of change buffeting the land, and, incidentally, a third-class transportation system for adolescent faggots who need to leave the cornfields in a hurry and who have inexplicably missed the rainbow. What's more, Spritz and I were balanced on Rollerblades in the middle of Lombard Street from which the only exit is down. There is no going straight.

Well, Spritz, who is from the South (and has the accent to flaunt it) had some acquaintance with tornadoes. She jumped neatly from the road to the flowerbeds—lavender hydrangeas, if I remember right—and threw herself into the shelter of a passing doorway. It was one of those moments when you remain icily still and the whole world rushes past you.

Only vaguely can I recall what happened next, but the colors faded into black and white, the sun wrapped itself prudishly in a thick wadding of cloud, and the terpsichorean contours of the city flattened out into a thousand miles of prairie, so vast, so unchanging, that as Shade was later to remark, "You'd swear the scenery had been pasted to the car windows."

The tornado dropped me in a strange flat, stubbly land, and though my house did not fall on the Wicked Witch of the Midwest, I did tread on the toe of an accredited DMV driving examiner, armed with a clipboard, who was, incidentally, the biggest, baddest-looking bulldagger I had ever set eyes on. For, when one is tornadoed out of California and flung down in a cornfield the size of several of the smaller states, Rollerblades are no longer a totally efficient transportation system and one is drawn by some irresistible force, into secondhand car ownership.

The examiner did not wince, but stepped backward and looked at me as though she would book me for violation of personal space. You know that look. It's the one you get if ever you presume to suggest that a butch companion read the instructions before starting on the easy-to-assemble kitchen table you have just bought from Scandinavian Design. When I say "butch," I do not mean to suggest that you are not yourself butch, I mean merely "butcher-than-thou," a much more hotly debatable category. For I myself am butch, but far too hooked on the written word ever to leave the printed page unread. I'm the one carefully following the road map, announcing authoritatively, "Okay, Gold's Gym will be on the next left, at the corner of the intersection," when everyone else has already spotted the sweating, muscular bodies through the car window.

"Miss Lube?" announces the driving examiner, eyeing her clipboard severely.

"It's Dr. Lube, actually," I correct her. Since it was the achievement of this new status that caused the tornado to seek me out and abandon me here, the only job in my field in the whole of the contiguous United States, I feel I may as well insist on the correct address.

The driving examiner flicks another look in my direction and intimates that an unembellished "you" will be quite enough. We go out to the car I have just bought and set off along the road. It is nearly 7:00 P.M., the last test of the day.

"Right here."

"Left at the next intersection."

"Stop."

"Now turn into that driveway."

I obey. I've been driving for years—mostly Spritz's car—and regard this test as a mere formality necessary for the procurance of dirt-cheap car insurance.

"Okay," says the examiner. "Now pull to the side of the road." I do so. If ever woman was predestined for a role in life, the one now seated at my side was born to be a driving examiner.

"Pretend this is a hill," she continues, "and we are facing upward. Pretend the grass verge is a curb. How would you park?"

The road is completely flat. There is no hill, no hummock, no mound, no molehill for five hundred miles around. There are no curbs either, just a vista of grass verges and vast empty parking lots. Beware of towns where it's easy to park. I flash-back involuntarily to my last helter-skelter down Lombard with Spritz at my side.

"I guess I'm not in San Francisco anymore."

My examiner neither smiles nor breaks into "Somewhere, over the rainbow," but waits, eyebrows at the ready.

"I would turn the wheel to the right and let the tires coast against the sidewalk," I parrot out grudgingly.

She notes something down on her clipboard and motions me to drive on. Soon we are back at the DMV office. As she gets out of the car, she turns to me,

"You can take it again first thing in the morning if you want." I stare at her.

"Why on earth would I want to do that? This has not been an unmitigated pleasure."

"Next time you might pass."

"You mean you failed me?"

"If you park on a hill, facing upward, and there's a curb at the side of the road, you don't curb the wheels, you turn them toward the road."

"You failed me for that? There is no hill in this town, there isn't even enough dirt to prop up a children's slide. Why does it matter what you do with the wheels against a nonexistent curb on a fantasy hill?"

"We take our fantasies very seriously here in the Midwest."

For a moment I wonder whether the whole tornado-cornfield episode will turn out to be a fantasy my girlfriend has kindly masterminded for me. But it's nowhere near my birthday and I am not enjoying myself.

The tough face has finally cracked, the eyes crinkle up and the corners of the mouth stretch out to the ears. My driving examiner roars with laughter, a noise that sounds like a garbage disposal swallowing plant gravel. Any moment she will slap one of our thighs (preferably her own) and offer me a Bud™, then it's the potluck or the tailgate party. Probably the tailgate—can't see my driving examiner at a potluck somehow.

"Midwest humor!" she says, still grinning. "Now there's an oxymoron for you, Doctor."

I want to warn her that parody always contains an element of the Trojan horse, the amusing folly that turns around and bites you as soon as you allow it into the inner sanctum. And that self-parody is doubly perilous because of its propensity to backfire. But I am not sure she needs instruction and, with what little dignity I can muster, I stalk past her into the DMV office, have my photograph taken, lie about my weight, and leave ten minutes later the proud owner of a new Midwestern driver's license in the name of "Jiffy Loob," a map of the state coming out of my left ear.

I have a car. I have a local license. I even have comprehensive automobile insurance. But there is no one to tell and nowhere to drive. I am tempted to go straight back to the ugly, semi-windowless apartment I have rented for a year and call Spritz, since she was spared by the tornado and remains in San Francisco living a normal life in our house in the Castro. I reflect, however, that she is, right at this moment, undoubtedly watching a rerun of that ER show in which the junkies chop off one of their arms to claim on automobile insurance. She might not be gracious about interruption.

Gothic is making a comeback, I don't know if you've noticed that. I myself am rather pleased by this development. I had feared that with the advent of therapy and scientific explanations for neurotic personal problems that gothic—with its championing of the gruesome, the hidden, and the grotesque—would go to the wall, that the pent-up imaginations of overwrought, repressed, incestuous nobodies with quaint tongues and even quainter folkways would be smoothed flat by the ultramodern glare of psychiatric understanding. I am relieved that ghoulish interest in blood and body parts is not altogether a thing of the past, though mostly contained and hygenicized in popular television and queer theory. The severed, twitching feet of the Wicked Witch of the West still beshadow our postmodern floodlights.

You must forgive me if I bore you. I am accustomed to saying these things to Spritz as we choose between blood sausage, pig's liver, or lamb kidneys at the twenty-four-hour Safeway on Market Street. Now that I have lost my constant companion I must make do with you, dear reader. As you with me.

What is there to do in small-town America but shoot BB pellets at the Yield sign or drink Bud™ at the local bar? (I guess the local lesbians lie down on the nearest train tracks in deathless embrace.) Since the line in front of the nearest Yield sign is already six people deep, I pick the bar. As I drive past, six faces turn to stare at my buzzed, one-inch red hair. The young man at the head of the line makes as if to shoot me with his index finger. I roll down the window—two taps of a button, my car is as automated as you can get without turning into Commander Data.

"Don't get out much, do you?" I yell. I think I look like a cross between Annie Lennox and Laurie Anderson and I would like a little recognition.

"What do you mean? I'm from Romeoville, up by Chicago!"

"That's more than a hundred miles away," someone else offers.

"Romeoville, imagine that. Why, I bet you have a Dairy King and a Burger Queen and everything."

There is only one decent bar in this town and that's the Five Legged Prairie Dog. I park my car right outside the front door. My plates say "Lube 3." Can you believe there are two other Jiffy Lubes in the I-states? When the plates arrived in the mail I felt usurped.

Once inside the bar I go up to the counter and do what I have to do.

"I'll have a Bud.™"

The bartender is a small, good-looking woman with a cheerfulness that seems to have infused even her short curly hair. She bends down, gets the beer, flicks it open, and slides it over to me. I take out my wallet.

"It's paid for," she says cheerfully, nodding in the direction of a tableful of women seated at the back of the bar.

When did that happen? I'd only just walked in and I hadn't seen any meaningful looks pass between the back table and the bartender. I pick up the beer, raise it toward the women, and park myself at a table in a corner.

"Whassa matter?" someone yells, "Think we're a bunch of Typhoid Marys? Come on and join us."

I approach the back table. Someone kicks out a chair and I see someone I recognize.

"Well hello, Doctor Lube," says the now familiar voice of my megabutch driving examiner.

"Hi," I mumble. "Never did catch your name."

"Shade," she says. "That's Inspector Shade to you."

The others laugh and the bartender moves down to our end of the bar.

"That's Dancy," says Shade, raising her right eyebrow toward the bartender.

"Pronounced 'Dancy,'" someone else explains helpfully. "And I'm Jo-Allen Jones. And this is Jo-Allen Smith. And this is Tender Buttons."

Shade looks on as the rest of the introductions are made, eyebrows furrowed watchfully. I shake hands, sit down, and gulp my Bud™. I have penetrated the inner sanctum of I-state dykedom only to find it guarded by a DMV driving examiner who confines all emotional display to her eyebrows, which are, admittedly, possessed of fierce powers of expression.

Right now Shade's eyebrows are forming pointed arcs over her battleship gray eyes.

"Two nil to me," she pronounces. "Just keeping you on your toes. You thought you'd sail through your driving test on account of we don't got no traffic out here in the Midwest."

I glance at her eyebrows but they have fallen silent.

"And you assumed us big-boned prairie gals would just flock around your San Francisco charm."

"You trying to tell me there's an initiation ceremony? I have to poach a salmon in the dishwasher? Carve salt and pepper shakers out of corncobs?"

Shade grins. "Just letting you know there's a gatekeeper. And I'm keeping score."

I buy a pitcher and we begin to get comfortable.

"Don't like the Midwest much, huh?"

"I miss the ocean."

"California has ocean," Dancy agrees cheerfully.

"But we got sky," says Tender Buttons. "You lie out in the cornfields with your Bud™ by your side one of these late summer afternoons when the breeze makes the cornstalks sway above you and the shadows walk across your cheek, and you look up at the sky and see white clouds dotted about like girls in summer dresses."

"And then the air grows colder and the temperature drops and a noise rushes through the cornstalks, making the husks rattle, and the sky turns gray as slate and the clouds are dark green and lightning dances over the prairie like lust at a nightclub," says Jo-Allen Jones.

"And then the rain comes," says Jo-Allen Smith. "First just a few drops wetting your cheeks and forehead like a damp sponge passed over your face by a friend as you drive in the heat in a beat-up old truck with no air-conditioning, then a torrent like sheet iron, and you're pinned to the ground with sweet fresh water in your mouth, your hair, your ears, and in between your fingers."

"And you're wet, and the ground is wet, and the cornstalks are wet, and the rain has already passed over," says Dancy, "And in the sky there's a . . ."

"Giant rainbow?" I say. "I think I know that song."

"And now you're looking for a man with a hot-air balloon to send you back home again."

"That or a yellow brick road." I nod.

"What does that make us?" asks Shade with a dangerous tilt to her eyebrows. "The Munchkins?"

"Unless you turn out to be Glenda the Good Witch," I say brightly.

"Close your eyes, kick the heels of those bright red Rollerblades three times, and make a wish," orders Shade in a tone I recognize.

I look down. It's true. I'm still wearing my Rollerblades. No wonder it's been so easy for me to look down on the people here.

Dutifully, I close my eyes, kick my heels (difficult to do in Rollerblades) and wish I was home. When I open my eyes again I am still in the bar, but the black-and-white tinge has gone, the colors are back and as I look at the faces of Shade and Dancy, Jo-Allen Smith, Jo-Allen Jones, and Tender Buttons they begin to look like the friends I left behind in San Francisco, though my beloved Spritz is still nowhere to be seen.

"I know," says Shade, her face impassive as usual but her eyebrows rounded with concern, "it's the ache that tells you that you love her."

# Notes on Contributors

**Donna Allegra** has been anthologized in *SportsDykes, Out of the Class Closet: Lesbians Speak, Lesbian Erotics, All the Ways Home: Short Stories about Children and the Lesbian and Gay Community, Queer View Mirror, Dyke Life: From Growing Up to Growing Old,* and *My Lover is a Woman: Contemporary Lesbian Love Poems.*

**Gwendolyn Bikis** lives, teaches, writes, and plays the alto saxophone in Oakland, California. "Me and Cleo" is a selection from her novel *Soldiers*. Other chapters have been published in *Catalyst, Conditions, The Persistent Desire, Sleeping with Dionysis,* and *Sister/Stranger.*

**Karen Cook** is a journalist who lives in New York City with her dog Molly, whom she adores.

**Monalesia Earle** is a native New Yorker, poet, and dyke. Her poetry has appeared in *Backbone, Plexus, Off Our Backs, The Optimist,* and *New Horizons.*

**Rhomylly B. Forbes** grew up in Berea, Kentucky, where she enjoyed many summer afternoons hiking and swimming at nearby Sinks and Rises (sans snakes). She now lives near Washington, D.C., where she writes, sings with the lesbian and gay chorus of Washington, and is copriestess of a Wiccan training coven. Her stories have appeared in *Tomboys! Tales of Dyke*

*Derring-Do* and various erotic publications. This one is for her best friend, Kent, who puts up with an awful lot.

**Emily Fox** practices law in New York City. This is her first published story. She is writing under a pseudonym.

**Kathryn Kingsbury** has had fiction and nonfiction appear in several publications, including *Vegetarian Journal* and *GW,* and her writing has received awards from *Seventeen* and *Sassy* magazines. She studies linguistics, with an emphasis on signed languages, at Bryn Mawr College.

**Rebecca Lavine** has been published in a variety of literary journals, including *Footwork, The Paterson Literary Review, the literary hot girl review, The Glacial Erratic,* and *The Virginia Review.* She has an MFA from Emerson College.

**Sharon Lim-Hing** is the editor of *The Very Inside: Writings by Asian and Pacific Islander Lesbian and Bisexual Women* and her work has been published in several journals and anthologies. Born in Kingston, Jamaica, she grew up there and in Miami, Florida. She now lives in Boston.

**Anna Livia** is the author of four novels and two collections of short stories, including *Minimax* and *Incidents Involving Mirth.* She has also translated a novel by Lucie Delarue-Mardrus and a collection of writings by Natalie Barney, both lesbians who lived in Paris in the 1920s. By day she is assistant professor of French linguistics at the University of Illinois, Champaign-Urbana. The Spritz and Jiffy Lube stories are turning into an episodic novel. For this story she gives thanks to the girls of C-U: Cris and Liza, Natasha and Diane, Maria and Lissy. And in memory of the girls of SF: Jennifer and Nona, Roxxie, Mo and Veronica—oh, and Adam (he's a boy, but hey).

**A. Elizabeth Mikesell** received an Emerging Writers Grant from the Astraea Foundation in 1994. She has taught creative writing at NYU and at the 53rd Street YWCA, and was a resident at the Millay Colony in Austerlitz, New York. She lives in New York City, where she works as an editor at Farrar, Straus & Giroux.

**Sue Pierce.** After an exciting and fulfilling career as Miss Toro Tractor at the Osaka Expo Golf Course Equipment Show and a Heineken Beer Girl at the Happy Beer Garden, as well as a two-and-a-half-year stint as the coproducer of a lesbian radio show, Sue Pierce has settled down to write stories. She lives in Philadelphia with her partner, Christine. Sue's new dream is to make a movie that combines two of the most popular Hollywood trends—kung fu action pictures and Jane Austen—and call it *Sense and Senseless.*

**Zélie Pollon** translated from the French the *Essential Teachings* of His Holiness the Dalai Lama. She works as an editor in San Francisco.

**Shelly Rafferty** is a lesbian poet, writer, editor, and parent. Her recent work has appeared in numerous gay and lesbian anthologies, including *Queer View Mirror* and *Contemporary Lesbian Love Poetry.* A frequent contributor to *The Lesbian Review of Books,* she writes about medical research in Upstate New York.

**Ruthann Robson** is the author of the novel *Another Mother* and two collections of short stories, *Cecile* and *Eye of the Hurricane,* the latter of which received a Ferro-Grumley Award for lesbian fiction.

**Linda Smukler** is the author of *Normal Sex,* which was a finalist for a Lambda Literary Award, and *Home in Three Days. Don't Wash,* with accompanying CD-ROM. She has received fellowships in poetry from the New York Foundation for the Arts and the Astraea Foundation.

**Wickie Stamps** is a writer whose published works have appeared in *For Shelter and Beyond—Ending Violence Against Women, Sister and Brother, Looking for Mr. Preston, Dykescapes, Doing It for Daddy,* and many others. She is the editor of *Drummer* magazine.

**JoNelle Toriseva** is the literary director of a performing arts/gallery space called Build, collectively run by five women. She teaches an on-going writing class entitled "Urban Scrawl" and teaches writing to Hispanic youth in San Francisco. Her work has been published in several 'zines, including *Planet Girl* and *Fat Girl.*

**Barbara Wilson** is the author of two novels, a collection of short stories, and five mysteries. She is cofounder of Seal Press. "Still Life" is a chapter in her forthcoming novel *If You Had a Family* (Seal Press).

**Jeanne Winer** is a writer and an attorney living in Boulder, Colorado. She was one of the two lead trial attorneys in the Amendment Two lawsuit in Colorado. She has had stories published in *The Evergreen Chronicles, Paper Radio,* and *The Crescent Review.* Besides those, she has received numerous, handwritten rejections from some of the best literary magazines in the world. Currently, she is working on a novel entitled *Aiding and Abetting* about a female public defender. This story is for Molly.

**Lynne Yamaguchi** is the author of *The First Gay Pope* (under the name Fletcher) and, with Adrien Saks, *Lavender Lists.* With Karen Barber she edited the collection *Tomboys! Tales of Dyke Derring-Do.*